Where the Sea had an Ending

A Caribbean Travel Miscellany

BRIAN DYDE

MACMILLAN
CARIBBEAN

Macmillan Education
Between Towns Road, Oxford OX4 3PP
A division of Macmillan Publishers Limited
Companies and representatives throughout the world

www.macmillan-caribbean.com

ISBN 0 333 75200 7

Designed by Bob Elliott
Illustrated by Lorna Barnard and Trevor Parkin/Linda Rogers Associates
Cover design by Gary Fielder, AC Design
Cover photographs:
Front cover is of Harbour Island, The Bahamas by Nick Gillard
Back cover is of the author by Veronica Dyde

Author's acknowledgements
For providing help and information, and many of the books I needed, I wish
to thank the following: Terry Barringer of Cambridge University Library;
David Butler of the Institute of Commonwealth Studies; Timothy Duke,
Chester Herald at the College of Arms; Jane Grell of the Anguilla Library
Service; Charles Kidd of Debrett's Peerage Ltd; Captain P.H.D. Marr of the
Northumberland Fusiliers Museum; Alastair Massie of the National Army
Museum Library; and Veronica Valarino of the Venezuelan Embassy in
London. I also received valuable help from the staff of Haverford West
Public Library, the Library of the Institut Français, and the National
Geographic Society Library.
The extracts from the article by Robert Schomburgk in *The Journal of the
Royal Geographical Society* 2, 1832, are reproduced by kind permission of the
Royal Geographical Society (with IBG)*.

* Institute of British Geographers.

Printed and bound in Malaysia

2005 2004 2003 2002 2001
10 9 8 7 6 5 4 3 2 1

FOR MY SISTER

MARGARET SHRIGLEY

MY SISTERS-IN-LAW

SONIA SINGHAM AND KATHLEEN ROBERTS

AND MY BROTHER-IN-LAW

CONRAD JOSEPH

Columbus had none of the Western Islands set foorth unto him, either in globe or card, [and] himself had neither seene America nor any of the Islands about it … but only comforted himselfe with this hope, that the land had a beginning where the sea had an ending.

Sir Humphrey Gilbert
Discourse of a Discovery for a New Passage to Cataia (1576)

Contents

Preface

I had heard and read much, from boyhood, about these 'Lesser Antilles'. I had pictured them to myself a thousand times: but I was altogether unprepared for their beauty and grandeur ... Ahead of us, one after another, rose high on the southern horizon banks of gray cloud, under each of which, as we neared it, descended the shoulder of a mighty mountain, dim and gray. Nearer still the gray changed to purple; lowlands rose out of the sea, sloping upwards with those grand and simple concave curves which betoken, almost always, volcanic land. Nearer still, the purple changed to green. Tall palm trees and engine-houses stood out against the sky; the surf gleamed white around the base of isolated rocks. A little nearer and we were under the lee, or western side, of the island. The sea grew smooth as glass; we entered the shade of the island-cloud, and slid along in still unfathomable blue water, close under the shore of what should have been one of the Islands of the Blest ...

(CHARLES KINGSLEY, 1871)

Where the Sea had an Ending is an attempt to produce a different kind of travel book about the West Indies. It results from a long love affair with the region (given an extra dimension by a not quite as long love affair with one of its inhabitants), and is distilled from my experiences of living and working in, as well as reading and writing about, the Caribbean over nearly half a century.

My introduction to the West Indies began in January 1954 when, as the greenest of greenhorns, I arrived off St Lucia with 212 other would-be naval officers in the vessel which then served as the Royal Navy's cadet training ship. (HMS *Triumph* was of such a size, and had such a large complement, that she provided a ratio of one officer, nine naval ratings, one Royal Marine, and no less than 340 of her many displacement tons for every four cadets. She belonged to a class of warship, the Light Fleet Aircraft Carrier, for which – like such extravagance in tonnage and manpower devoted to officer training, as well as the designation (hardly a rank) of naval cadet – there was little future.)

Unlike the author Charles Kingsley who 'had heard and read much, from boyhood, about these Lesser Antilles' before he first saw them in 1870, I had heard very little and read nothing of any consequence, and so was quite unprepared for the unforgettable experience of an early morning landfall on a mountainous West Indian island. Nor had anything in my education and upbringing prepared me to be anything but surprised and delighted by all I was to see and experience on St Lucia and various other islands during the next three months, as our colossal flat-topped yacht, immaculate and gleaming from the daily attention of 213 pairs of hands (the use of deck mop, squeegee and brass polish then being considered a major element in officer training), cruised between Trinidad and the Virgin Islands.

As the cruise progressed, our seagoing education, solidly based on the training methods, tactics and technology which had brought the navy through the Second World War – with the very occasional nod towards innovations which had resulted from the participation of some of its units (including *Triumph* herself) in the recently concluded Korean War – became increasingly desultory. For our instructors, time spent in lecturing or demonstrating meant less time to spend on more pleasurable activities. It was bad enough trying to enthuse about such subjects as the firing rate of the quadruple-barrelled pom-pom, the Marcq St Hilaire method of finding one's position at sea, or the contents of a sadly outdated *Admiralty Manual of Seamanship* to a semi-comatose audience in some stuffy compartment (air-conditioning, as far as any of us then knew, had not yet been invented) while the ship was underway. How much worse when she lay at anchor within earshot of a colonial capital such as Castries or Bridgetown, with its promise of sailing, riding, golf, tennis and swimming parties, gubernatorial receptions and yacht club dances; or even off some deserted beach in the Grenadines. As for their torpid pupils – complete with peeling noses, 'Bluebell' brass-polish-stained fingers, and regulation-issue white shorts flapping around their as yet far from brown knees – what arcane bit of naval lore could compete with the prospect of a day on a sugar plantation in St Lucia, of seeing the likes of Len Hutton, Dennis Compton, Clyde Walcott and Sonny Ramadhin in action during a test match in Barbados, of assisting in the restoration of the old dockyard at English Harbour in Antigua, or of watching preparations being made for Carnival in Trinidad?

Although *Triumph* returned to England at the beginning of April, and I was not to enter the Caribbean again for another five years, part of me remained behind. Nor even nearly fifty years later, while I write these words looking out over a Pembrokeshire landscape, has it ever come back. I had had the chance to see something of a part of the world of almost unbelievable natural beauty, and enjoyed a whole range of experiences not then available to too many young men of my age. Even more importantly, I had been introduced to West Indians: to open, friendly people of many shades of skin colour and all social classes, who possessed, regardless of the widely varying conditions under which they lived, a great ability to enjoy themselves and a remarkable propensity for showing kindness to strangers. The West Indian way of life I had briefly sampled was as different from that of someone of my background and upbringing in a lower middle class family from the English Midlands as it was possible to imagine.

The rest of my naval service, most of which was spent as a hydrographic surveyor, lasted almost exactly twenty-five years. In that time I had the great good fortune to return to the West Indies in three survey ships and to spend, in total, several years working in the waters of places as far apart as British Guiana (as it then was) the Bahamas, Barbados and Belize. The perhaps almost inevitable outcome of the attraction I felt towards the region and its people came in 1973, when, to the detriment of an existing marriage, I met and fell in love with one particular West Indian on one particular island. We were married two years later. Four years after that, having been made well aware that an inter-racial marriage had ended whatever hopes I may have entertained of further promotion, I resigned my commission.

This only strengthened my connection with the Caribbean, as from 1979 my wife and I lived there; at first in Antigua and then in Montserrat. Our idyll came to an abrupt end after sixteen years when the latter island's highest mountain, the long-dormant Chance's Peak, burst into violent volcanic activity. From being among the select few thousand living peacefully on the 'Caribbean's best-kept secret' (or on one at least of the several such which have now been discovered by West Indian tourism directors), we then found ourselves rendered homeless on an island receiving worldwide media attention. Hence, dear Reader, why this is being written some thousands of miles away in west Wales.

The contents of this book have no purpose other than to entertain. I have taken the opportunity to give a fresh airing to the words of, for the most part, long-forgotten writers who once visited the Caribbean, and whose work, considerably fresher then, I began to seek out soon after my first visit to the West Indies all those years ago. If nothing else, their views, I hope, will provide an unusual and diverting insight into some of the lands and islands found by me, in just the same way of Columbus, where the sea had an ending.

Pembroke
August 2000

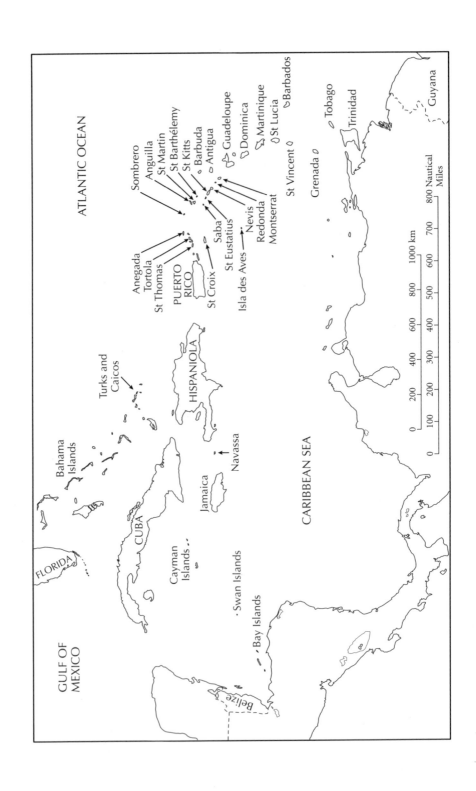

GULF OF
MEXICO

FLORIDA

Bahama
Islands

Turks and
Caicos

CUBA

Cayman
Islands

Jamaica

HISPANIOLA

Navassa

Swan Islands

Bay Islands

Belize

CARIBBEAN SEA

ATLANTIC OCEAN

Sombrero
Anguilla
St Martin
St Barthélemy
St Kitts
Barbuda
Antigua

Anegada
Tortola
St Thomas
PUERTO
RICO
St Croix
Isla des Aves

Saba
St Eustatius
Nevis
Redonda
Montserrat

Guadeloupe
Dominica
Martinique
St Lucia
Barbados

St Vincent

Grenada

Tobago
Trinidad

Guyana

0		100	200	300	400	500	600	700	800 Nautical Miles

0	200	400	600	800	1000 km

Introduction

The amount of travel literature about the Caribbean, considering the length of time which has elapsed since the recorded history of the region began, is not that great; something all too evident from even a cursory glance at the shelves of any bookshop, whatever the age of its stock. Such as is available however has been added to steadily for well over 400 years, and West Indian travel books now range from works such as the multi-volume *Nouveau Voyage aux Îles de l'Amérique* published by Jean Baptiste Labat in 1722 as a record of his twelve years in the Caribbean, to slender present-day tomes by authors who sometimes appear to have spent little more than the same number of days in the region.

The genre became properly established during the nineteenth century, with a spate of weighty volumes being turned out by historians, missionaries, successful novelists and other men of letters, along with a trickle of well-heeled yachtsmen and world travellers. Books of a similar type and degree of seriousness, added to by those from the odd natural scientist or retired colonial official, continued to be written during the first half of the following century; the last probably being Patrick Leigh Fermor's *The Traveller's Tree*, published in 1950. Since then the scope of West Indian travel literature has been greatly extended, with the inclusion of books written about journeys through the region undertaken by a wide variety of men and women for an equally diverse number of reasons. As well as those from not so successful novelists, rather less professional travellers and now not so well-heeled yachtsmen, more recent additions include those from authors who double as jazz musicians, journalists, blues singers or restaurateurs.

In this book I have drawn exclusively on the work of the earlier authors, particularly those of the nineteenth century, all of whose books are long out of print and not easy to find. In nearly all the books from which extracts have been taken, the amount of text devoted to each island the author visited is roughly in proportion to the size and importance of the island. This is not the case here, where I have made no attempt to let the content of any section reflect in its length anything but the degree of my own interest in the island or territory it deals with. Neither, following the pattern established in the great majority of the books from which I quote, have I included anything about Cuba, Hispaniola or Puerto Rico; all in any case being much too large to find a comfortable place in this particular miscellany. Full details of each book from which I have taken an extract, giving the author's name and a date only, will be found in the Bibliography. Brief information about the majority of the people whose works I have used appears in the Biographical Notes which follow the Bibliography.

Regardless of the era in which their visit took place, or of the lasting worth of what he or she wrote about it afterwards, nearly every author of a West Indian travel book moved around the Caribbean, following the arc of the Lesser, and occasionally the Greater, Antilles, in either a clockwise or anticlockwise direction. Following the pattern of the majority, those whose travels started in the south and progressed to the north and west, this book begins – no doubt as its inhabitants would consider only right and proper – in Barbados.

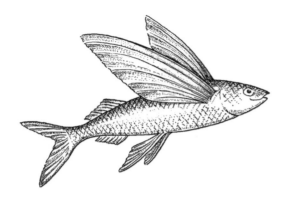

1 Barbados

'That prosperous and civilised little cane-garden'

This Island is one of the Riches Spotes of ground in the wordell and fully inhabited. But ware the pepell sutabell to the Illand it ware not to be compared: it is a most rich soile, all wayes Grone and baring frut, and the Chefest commoditie is sugar, and some Indieco, and Cotaine, and tobacoe, but the chefest commoditie they now plant is Shuger and Cottaine . . . This Island is inhabited with all sortes: with English, french, Duch, Scotes, Irish, Spaniards thay being Iues [Jews]: with Ingones and miserabell Negors borne to perpetuall slauery thay and thayer seed . . . This Illand is the Dunghill wharone England doth cast forth its rubidg: Rodgs and hors and such peopel are those which are gennerally Broght heare. A rodge in England will hardly make a cheater heare: a Baud brought ouer puts on a demuor comportment, a whore if hansume makes a wife for sume rich planter. But in plaine the Illand of it selfe is very delightful and plesant . . .

HENRY WHISTLER, 1654

Barbados is the Crown and Front of all the Caribbee Islands towards the rising sun, being the most east of any and lies more conveniently than any of the rest for a seat of war, being most healthful, fruitful and stored with all things necessary of its own innate growth which are necessary for life. The greatest mart of trade, not only of the Caribbees, but of any island in the West Indies, being inhabited with many wealthy planters and merchants, and hath very great conveniency for a hole where ships might hide among the houses as in Amsterdam and Venice, of great conveniency for trade and in time of war free from the danger of any enemy, except so powerful as to invade the island, which well managed would be too great a task for any Prince in Europe.

MAJOR JOHN SCOTT, c. 1667

During the time we lay in Barbados Harbour the black people supplied us with country fruit and roots, cocoanuts, guavas, plantains, bananas and yam and tarro and the best Cayenne pepper I ever saw and the worst rum I ever tasted.

JAMES AYTOUN, 1788 (see AYTOUN, 1984)

The characteristic beauty of Barbados is its finished cultivation and the air of life and domestic comfort which the entire face of the country presents. For this particular it is, without competition, the most delightful island of the Antilles . . .

HENRY NELSON COLERIDGE, 1826

Of many of his sister colonies a Barbadian can speak with temper. When Jamaica is mentioned philanthropic compassion lights up his face, and he tells you how much he feels for the poor wretches there who call themselves planters. St Lucia also he pities, and Grenada; and of St Vincent he has some hope. Their little efforts he says are praiseworthy; only, alas! they are so little! He does not think much of Antigua; and turns up his nose at Nevis and St Kitts, which in a small way are doing a fair stroke of business. The French islands he does not love, but that is probably patriotism: as the French islands are successful sugar growers such patriotism is natural. But do not speak to him of Trinidad; that subject is very sore. And as for Guiana – ! One knows what to expect if one holds a red rag to a bull. Praise Guiana sugar-making in Bridgetown, and you will be holding up a red rag to a dozen bulls, no one of which will refuse the challenge. And thus you may always know a Bim.

ANTHONY TROLLOPE, 1859

More wistfully still did we look to windward when we thought of Barbados, and of the kind people who were ready to welcome us into that prosperous and civilised little cane-garden, which deserves – and has deserved for now two hundred years, far more than poor old Ireland – the name of 'The Emerald Gem of the Western World'.

CHARLES KINGSLEY, 1871

. . . the island of Barbadoes lay before us shining in the haze of a hot summer morning. It is about the size of the Isle of Wight, cultivated so far as eye could see with the completeness of a garden; no mountains in it, scarcely even high hills, but a surface pleasantly undulating, the prevailing colour a vivid green from the cane fields; houses in town and country white from the coral rock of which they are built, but the glare from them relieved by heavy clumps of trees . . . You could see at a glance that the island was as thickly peopled as an ant-hill, not an inch of soil seemed to be allowed to run to waste. Two hundred thousand is, I believe, the present number of Barbadians, of whom nine-tenths are blacks. They refuse to emigrate. They cling to their home with innocent vanity as though it was the finest country in the world, and multiply at a rate so rapid that no one likes to think about it. Labour at any rate is abundant and cheap. In Barbadoes the negro is willing to work, for he has no other means of living. Little land is here allowed him to grow his yams upon. Almost the whole of it is still held by the whites in large estates, cultivated by labourers on the old system, and, it is to be admitted, cultivated most admirably. If the West Indies are going to ruin, Barbadoes, at any rate, is being ruined with a smiling face.

JAMES ANTHONY FROUDE, 1888

Barbados is almost perfect; there is no place in the world where I would rather live.

THE MOST REVEREND WILLIAM SWABY, Archbishop of the West Indies, 1900

A serious Bim

Let us thank now each polypite
Who laboured with all his tiny might
Through countless aeons till he made us
This little island home, Barbados.

FRANK COLLYMORE, *The Coral Polyp*

Frank Appleton Collymore, from whose Rhymed Ruminations on the Fauna of Barbados, *written in 1968, the above verse is taken, was for several decades of the twentieth century a prominent figure in the cultural life of Barbados. He was born in Bridgetown in 1893 and died there eighty-seven years later. Although he rarely left the island and, like a Caribbean Mr Chips, spent his entire working life as a schoolmaster, by the time of his death he was just as well known outside Barbados, and had influenced the work of a whole generation of West Indian writers from as far apart as Guyana and Jamaica.*

His professional life was spent at Combermere School in Bridgetown, the establishment in which he received his own education, and from where he eventually retired in 1963 after a sixty year-long connection, and after having served on the staff since 1910. As well as being a highly respected teacher, a poet and a more than competent painter, he was also a remarkably good actor who did much to promote local drama. In 1942 he helped found the literary magazine Bim, *in which for over thirty years as its editor he did much to foster the talent of writers from all over the English-speaking Caribbean, for whose creative abilities up until then there had been very few outlets.*

Although of less importance than his editorship of Bim *or his overall contribution to Barbadian culture in the twentieth century, a small book he published in 1955 with the unprepossessing title of* Notes for a Glossary of Words and Phrases of Barbadian Dialect *may well turn out to be his most enduring memorial. In this Collymore wryly provides not only the definitions of such expressive Barbadianisms as* **crab-mash** ('to iron clothes badly'), **downalong** ('an adjective applied to any person from another island'), **piss-to-windward** ('someone of 'lubberly ineptitude''), and **rest-off** ('The Barbadian rests, or rather rests himself, at night, but by day he rests off from his work'), *but also examples of the Barbadian's use of what, among other English speakers, might be thought to be quite ordinary litle words:* **keep** ('No Barbadian makes a noise, he keeps it. Stop keeping that noise, will you? is to be heard at any time, any day, in any school'), **leave** ('A Badian seldom if ever misses a bus: the bus always leaves him. I was so busy shopping that the bus left me'), **man** ('The favourite nominative of address of the Barbadian. The sex of the person addressed is immaterial, as, Let's go to the pictures, Mary, man'), **swing** ('Motorists always swing, not turn to the right or left as the case may be. The Englishman might think that such an operation involves some risk, since, properly speaking, swinging would imply a sharp, even violent turn: but when he notes that pedestrians also swing a corner, and this without resort to acrobatics, his fears vanish'), and **tot** ('The Barbadian tot is a mug made of tin. The capacity of the tot varies; some tots may hold as much as a pint. "A tot of rum" thus conveys quite a different connotation to the Barbadian').

The Glossary *remains in print today and is a particularly apt and pleasing reminder of a much esteemed, self-effacing man – one who deserves to be recalled as a truly* **serious** ('remarkable, worthy of notice') **Bim** ('a native of Barbados').

Stories of an extraordinary nature?

About the latter End of Queen *Anne's* Wars, Captain *John Beams* Commander of the *York Merchant,* arrived at *Barbados* from *England.* Having disembark'd the last Part of his Loading, which was Coals, the Sailors, who had been employ'd in that dirty Work, ventured into the Sea to wash themselves; there they had not been long, before a Person on Board 'spyed a large *Shark* making towards them, and gave them Notice of their Danger; upon which they swam back and reach'd the Boat, all but one; him the Monster overtook almost within Reach of the Oars, and griping him by the Small of the Back, his devouring Jaws soon cut asunder, and as soon swallow'd the lower Part of his Body; the remaining Part was taken up and carried on Board, where his Comrade was. His Friendship with the deceased had been long distinguished by a reciprocal Discharge of such endearing Offices, as imply'd an Union and Sympathy of Souls. When he saw the sever'd Trunk of his Friend, it was with an Horror and Emotion too great for Words to paint. During this affecting Scene, the insatiable *Shark* was seen traversing the bloody Surface in Search after the Remainder of his Prey; the rest of the Crew thought themselves happy in being on Board; he – alone unhappy, that he was not within Reach of the Destroyer. Fired at the Sight, and vowing that he would make the Devourer disgorge, or be swallowed himself into the same Grave, He plunges into the Deep, arm'd with a large sharp-pointed Knife. The *Shark* no sooner saw him, but he made furiously towards him, both equally eager, the one of his Prey, the other of Revenge. The moment the *Shark* open'd his rapacious Jaws, his Adversary dextrously diving, and grasping him with his left Hand somewhat below the upper Fins, successfully employs his Knife in his right Hand, giving him repeating Stabs in the Belly: the enraged *Shark,* after many unavailing Efforts, finding himself overmatch'd in his own Element, endeavours to disengage himself, sometimes plunging to the Bottom, then mad with Pain, rearing his uncouth Form (now stain'd with his own streaming Blood) above the foaming Waves. The crews of the surrounding Vessels saw the unequal

Combat, uncertain from which of the Combatants the Streams of Blood issued; till at length, the *Shark*, much weaken'd by the Loss of Blood, made towards the Shore, and with him his Conqueror; who, flush'd with an Assurance of Victory, pushes his Foe with redoubled Ardour, and, by the Help of an ebbing Tide, dragging him on Shore, rips up his Bowels; and unites and buries the sever'd carcase of his Friend in one hospitable Grave.

The Story, I confess, is of so extraordinary a Nature, that I would not have dared to give it my Reader, had I not been authorized thereto by the Testimony of a very credible Gentleman (. . . who was not far from the Place when this happened), who is ready to confirm by Oath, the Truth of what is here related. This action, intrepid as it is, will unquestionably fall under the Censure of those, who are accustomed to judge by the Rules of moral of political Fitness; it not being prudent in any Man to expose himself to Danger, from which he must owe his Escape as much to Chance as to Valour . . .

GRIFFITH HUGHES, 1750

Bridge Town lies round the bay, is nearly two miles in length, scarcely half a mile in breadth, and contains upwards of 20,000 inhabitants . . .

His Majesty's council, the general assembly, the judges, the juries, the debtors and the felons, all live together in the same house. It is a large one, with an open space around it, and inclosed by a wall. With whom the mere right to the tenement is, I could not learn; whether the legislature lends it to the judicature, or whether both are only tenants at will to the worshipful company of debtors and rogues, is a point not clearly ascertained. I am inclined however to think that the latter gentlemen have the title-deeds, from observing that they invariably do the honours of the house to all the rest. Their civility is unbounded; they help you out of your carriage and hold your horse and your stirrup, they line the staircase on either side in token of respect to you, show you through their apartments, and are forward to give you every piece of information which the most expert cicerone can furnish. Their loyalty is without suspicion; in sign whereof, they turn out of their best bedroom to make way for a session of the council, and their civic patriotism is as clear, from the interest they display in the public debates – the men, the women and the children crowding inquisitively round the open door of the council, and lounging in the gallery, or leaning familiarly over the rails in the hall of assembly. These are their virtues; a few failings they have, such as the habit of not returning any thing left in their house, an appetency after the contents of a stranger's coat pocket, and a somewhat too profuse employment of the imprecatory part of the Barbadian dialect . . .

HENRY NELSON COLERIDGE, 1826

During the few days which we passed at anchor in Carlisle Bay, parties of our officers went ashore at Bridgetown, where we were hospitably entertained at the mess of the 64th regiment. Between the noise of lizards, musquitoes, and other tormenting devils, which sing and bite throughout the night, and unite all their efforts to destroy one's slumbers, I got but a small allowance of sleep, in spite of the liberal potation of old Madeira imbibed at the 64th mess. I may here remark, that during the whole of my stay in the West Indies, I suffered less than the generality of my brother-officers from the bites of musquitoes, although their eternal singing has tired my patience many a night.

LIEUTENANT-COLONEL J. LEACH, 1831

Glorious self-congratulation

. . . West Indians make jokes about Barbados in much the same way as do Americans about Boston and Englishmen about Wigan Pier. A famous West Indian joke, in which England is supposed to have carried on in 1914 only because of a cablegram of Barbadian support against the enemy, sums up the attitude. Probably apocryphal – for Trollope repeated the joke, in a different context, as going back to the period of the Napoleonic Wars – it nonetheless testifies to a temper of glorious self-congratulation most outsiders find amusing, sometimes intolerable.

GORDON K. LEWIS, 1968

Frank Collymore may well have been the epitomy of a Bim or Bajan, a man quite content with his place in an island no more than 430 square kilometres in extent, but he surely would have appreciated and been quietly amused by the way in which, both during and after his lifetime, the story of the fabulous telegram has been transmogrified. Long before his death in 1980 the joke was no longer on the Barbadians, but on all those writers from outside the region who had taken up the tale and, regardless of which war they were writing about, turned it into part of the accepted wisdom about the West Indies.

The story runs, that when Europe was convulsed by revolutions and wars – when continental sovereigns were flying hither and thither, and there was so strong a rumour that Napoleon was going to eat us – the great Napoleon I mean – that then, I say, the Barbadians sent word over to poor King George the Third, bidding him fear nothing. If England could not protect him, Barbados would. Let him come to them, if things looked really blue on his side of the channel. It was a fine, spirited message, but perhaps a little self-glorious. That, I should say, is the character of the island in general.

ANTHONY TROLLOPE, 1859

It is related that at the outbreak of the Great War in 1914 the Barbados Legislative Council cabled direct to King George V: 'Carry on – Barbados is with you.' This yarn has never been corroborated, but, in fact, I believe it is true of the South African War and that King Edward VII did receive such a cable when he came to the Throne after Queen Victoria's death.

RAYMOND SAVAGE, 1936

The other islands take the keenest delight in defeating Barbados in anything they can, which I must say does not happen very often. The Barbadians, on their side, have a reputation for always thinking they are the salt of the earth; which perhaps is not such a bad trait after all . . . In consequence of this there are innumerable and piquant legends in the other islands about the BIMS, as they are called, after a Commission said to have been issued by an old-time Sovereign, referring to Barbados Island Men. One of the best of these is that when the War started Barbados sent home a telegram, 'England, 'tan' 'tiff. Barbados behin' you.' But this may have been the Boer War. It is immaterial . . .

SIR REGINALD ST JOHNSTON, 1936

The crew of the Harbour Master's boat were dressed in uniforms that took us back to the time of Nelson, and as soon as we were taken ashore we stepped into a 100 per cent British atmosphere, which pervades the entire island. No wonder that Barbados is proud of its nickname, 'Little England'. There is a story told that at the outbreak of the First World War a cable was sent to London saying: 'Go ahead England, Barbados is behind you.'

EVERILD YOUNG and K. HELWEG-LARSEN, 1955

The Barbadians have had a reputation of being more loyal to Britain than the inhabitants of almost any other colony and the story goes that when the

British Government declared war against Germany in 1914 the Barbados legislature sent the following cable: 'Go ahead England. Barbados is with you.'

JOHN CROCKER, 1968

Hitler went to war, wrote King George VI of England in his diary in September 1939, 'with the knowledge that the whole might of the British Empire would be against him . . . A cherished cable from the Caribbean was received in Whitehall that same summer. 'Carry on Britain!' it said. 'Barbados is behind you!'

JAMES MORRIS, 1978

On 3 September 1939, when Britain declared war on Nazi Germany, the first message of support came from the tiny West Indian island of Barbados . . .

ROBIN NEILLANDS, 1996

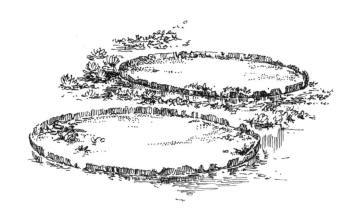

2 Guyana

'The Transatlantic Eden'

. . . Guiana is a country that hath yet her maidenhead, never sacked, turned, nor wrought; the face of the earth hath not been torn, nor the virtue and salt of the soil spent by manurance; the graves have not been opened for gold, the mines not broken with sledges, nor their images pulled down out of their temples. It hath never been entered by any army of strength, and never conquered or possessed by any Christian prince.

SIR WALTER RALEIGH, 1595

Guiana, whose rich feete are mines of golde,
Whose forehead knockes against the roofs of Starres,
Stands on her tip-toes at faire England looking
Kissing her hand, bowing her mightie breast,
And every sign of all submission making,
To be her sister, and the daughter both
Of our most sacred Maide: whose barrennesse
Is the true fruite of vertue, that may get,
Beare and bring forth anew in all perfection,

Whate heretofore savage corruption held
In barbarous Chaos; and in this affaire
Become her father, mother, and her heire.

De Guiana Carmen Epicum   GEORGE CHAPMAN, 1596

The first thing generally done by a European on his arrival in this country is to provide himself with a mistress from among the blacks, mulattoes, or mestees, for here they are to be found of all the different shades of colour . . . The price varies from £100 to £150. Many of these girls read and write; and most of them are free. Some of them are tasteful and extravagant in their dress, but inviolable in their attachment, and scarcely a particle of inconstancy can ever be established against them. They perform all the duties of a wife except presiding at table, and their utility in domestic affairs, their cleanliness, and politeness, are acknowledged by all . . .

One of the officers whom I found here, Lieutenant Dudgeon, 4th West India Regiment, used to turn out for morning parade as drunk as when he tumbled into a soldier's hammock in which he slept at night. At the end of six months he killed himself by drinking rum; and I have often heard him, when he could say nothing else, stammer out: 'Drunkenness is a bewitching devil, a pleasant poison, and a sweet sin.'

LIEUTENANT THOMAS STAUNTON ST CLAIR, 1808
(*see* STAUNTON ST CLAIR, 1834)

When I settle out of England, and take to the colonies for good and all, British Guiana shall be the land of my adoption. If I call it Demerara perhaps I shall be better understood. At home there is prejudice against it I know. They say it is a low, swampy, muddy strip of alluvial soil, infested with rattlesnakes, gallinippers, and musquitoes as big as turkey-cocks; that yellow fever rages there perennially; that the heat is unendurable; that society there is as stagnant as its waters; that men always die as soon as they reach it; and when they live are such wretched creatures that life is a misfortune. Calumny reports it to have been ruined by the abolition of slavery; milk of human kindness would forbid the further exportation of Europeans to this white man's grave; and philanthropy, for the good of mankind, would wish to have it drowned beneath its own rivers. There never was a land so ill spoken of – and never one that deserved it so little. All the above calumnies I contradict; and as I lived there for a fortnight – would it could have been a month! – I expect to be believed.

If there were but a snug secretaryship vacant there – and these things in Demerara are very snug – how I would invoke the goddess of patronage; how I would nibble round the officials of the Colonial Office; how I would stir up my friends' friends to write little notes to their friends! For Demerara is the Elysium of the tropics – the West Indian happy valley of Rasselas – the one true and actual Utopia of the Caribbean Sea – the Transatlantic Eden.

ANTHONY TROLLOPE, 1859

The steamer arrives in the Demerara River, and a thin coast-line is perceived, behind which is a flat expanse variegated with tall chimneys and cocoa-nut palms. Behind the sea wall the barracks are visible, spacious buildings with deep verandahs. A quantity of shipping is in the river. Large warehouses line the bank. The steamer comes alongside, and the visitor finds himself in Georgetown, one of the most promising and prosperous places in or rather contiguous to the West Indies. It is a handsome, well-built town, lively and full of activity notwithstanding the heat . . .

The Government building is a large, fine-looking ediface; the many churches are pleasant and picturesque, and there is an appearance of prosperity associated with cleanliness (if such a juxtaposition of ideas may be pardoned) which makes this town one of the very nicest in the West Indies . . . The hospitality afforded to visitors shows the kind spirit which success does so much to encourage. The 'swizzle' is ideally perfect . . .

C. WASHINGTON EVES, 1889

There is great truth in the soldier's remark that Demerara was a 'rare place where there's lots of drink, and you're always a dry'. The perpetual state of perspiration in which one lives in the colony creates a perpetual thirst, and I know no place where drinking is carried out on more scientific principles. The drink, *sui generis*, of the country is the swizzle. This subtle and delicious compound is sometimes ignominiously confounded with the cocktail, but though related, they are not identical. The cocktail is a stronger, shorter, and less sophisticated drink than the swizzle; there is no disguise about it; you know you are drinking something hot and strong, thinly disguised by the ice which cools without quenching its potency. But in the swizzle the potency is so skilfully veiled that the unsuspecting imbiber never discovers he is taking anything stronger than milk, until he finds that his head is going round, and that the road seems to be rising up and trying to slap him in the face.

The ingredients of a swizzle are simple enough; a small glass of hollands, ditto of water, half a teaspoonful of Angostura bitters, a small quantity of syrup or powdered white sugar, with crushed ice *ad libitum*; this concoction is whipped up by a swizzle-stick twirled rapidly between the palms of the hands until the ice is melted, and the liquid is like foaming pink cream, to be swallowed at one draught and repeated quantum suff . . . In Georgetown the sound of the swizzle-stick is heard all day . . .

HENRY KIRKE, 1898

Altogether British Guiana presents a rich field of possibilities and probabilities, and not a few certainties to the enterprising capitalist. Unlike most of the West Indian islands, it is as yet undeveloped save on the coastal belt, the source of the famous Demerara Sugar. There is vast scope in its mineral wealth, in tropical agriculture of various kinds – Sugar, coffee, coconut, rubber and other plantations – in domestic industries, as yet almost non-existent, and in the task of improving its means of communication. There is room for millions of new population. When the people come in their numbers, as they must come sooner or later as the other empty spaces of the world fill up, British Guiana will quickly establish a just claim to the title that is at present little more than a pious aspiration – the 'Magnificent Province'.

British Guiana Handbook, British Empire Exhibition at Wembley, 1924

An expedition to the interior

Between November 1959 and the following February the Royal Naval hydro-graphic vessel Vidal, *in which I was then serving as the most junior surveyor, was engaged in recharting the coastal waters of British Guiana. Every two weeks, in order to provide the ship's company with a change from the endless routine of ploughing up and down through muddy waters normally well out of sight of what, on the odd occasion when it was in view, was seen to be an extremely low and to-tally uninteresting coastline, the ship spent a weekend alongside in Georgetown. This was still the 'handsome, well-built town, lively and full of activity' noted by Eves seventy years or so earlier, and even if it no longer echoed to the sound of swiz-zle-sticks it still had more than enough attractions on which time and money could be most enjoyably wasted.*

However, for the more frugal, timid, innocent or priggish (and I fell uncom-promisingly into all four categories while admitting to nothing but high-mind-

edness) a little rum, a short burst of steelband music, and a brief sampling of
Georgetown nightlife went an exceedingly long way, and more exalted, 'serious'
leisure pursuits were required. As a result one Sunday in January 1960 I found
myself, together with twenty or so of the less hung-over among my shipmates,
boarding an aircraft for a flight over the Kaieteur Falls and a visit to the Rupu-
nuni savannas in the south of the country.

A steel bench in a Douglas DC-3 cargo carrier of British Guiana Airways was
not the ideal vantage point from which to view the famous waterfall, nor on
which to endure the two hours or more it took to reach a landing strip in the
Rupununi, and it was some time after we had all left the aircraft before any of
us could again move comfortably or hear properly. We had landed about 400
kilometres south of Georgetown at a small settlement close to the Ireng, the river
that formed the colony's boundary with Brazil. As such, it was the river rather
than the settlement which drew our attention, and it was on its bank or in its
water that we remained until it was time to board the aircraft for the return
flight.

This was a pity, as the name of the settlement which none of us could be both-
ered with was Pirara: a place which I was to discover many years later had once
been at the centre of a lengthy border dispute between Britain and Brazil. It also
had been – something I found of even greater interest – the scene of a weird con-
frontation between troops belonging to both countries, as was recorded forty-
odd years after it had taken place by the then commanding officer of the British
regiment involved:

On the 11th of January, 1842, a detachment of the [1st West India] regiment,
consisting of two lieutenants (Bingham and Wieburg), two sergeants and
twenty-seven rank and file, left Georgetown, Demerara, by direction of the
Under-Secretary of State for the Colonies (Lord John Russell), to proceed to
Pirara, on the south-western frontier of British Guiana, and expel a party of
Brazilians who had for some time encroached on British territory. The
country through which the party had to pass was unexplored and almost
unknown, and the duties were most arduous. It was intended to reach Pirara
by ascending the Essequibo and Rypumani [Rupununi] Rivers, and, to
effect this, a particular description of boat, locally called *corials*, had to be
built, each capable of holding eight men, including the Indians who
paddled. During the journey seventy-three rapids or falls were crossed, in
most instances the *corials* being unladen and the stores carried above the
falls; and it was not until February 12th that Lieutenant Bingham's party
reached a point on the Rypumani, eleven miles from Pirara. Next day they
took possession of the village of Pirara, which they found occupied by a

detachment of Brazilian troops who had been quietly sent over the border. Having selected and fortified a position, and raised temporary shelter for his men, Lieutenant Bingham – as the Brazilian commander declined to withdraw – dispatched Lieutenant Bush, 1st West India Regiment, who had accompanied the party as a volunteer, to Georgetown for further instructions. That officer arrived there on March 11th, and on April 19th he again started with a small reinforcement under Ensign Stewart. This second party reached Pirara on May 21st, and found the detachment all well, but half-starved, as the Brazilians refused to sell them anything, and the stores had been some time exhausted. However, on the arrival of the reinforcement the Brazilian troops considered it advisable to withdraw across the frontier; and, with the exception of a few occasional night forays made by half-breeds and Indians in the pay of the Brazilians, the detachment met with no further opposition.

LIEUTENANT-COLONEL A.B. ELLIS, 1885

A true Boys' Own *tale if ever there was one, complete with stiff upper lips, half rations, voluntary efforts well beyond the call of duty, and even dastardly half-breeds. Had I been aware of the story in 1960 it would have been interesting to have gone to see just what it was about Pirara that had aroused the ire of Lord John Russell, and to find out what if anything remained of Fort New Guinea, the name given to the position selected and fortified by Lieutenant Bingham. From what I remember of the place, as seen from the air just after we had taken off, it certainly did not look as if it had changed very much since the previous century.*

As for those in the ship's company for whom such things as the Kaieteur Falls and trips into the hinterland held no attraction there were pleasures and excitements enough in and around Georgetown; some no doubt on a par with those experienced by two of their predecessors many, many years earlier:

The Governor [of Demerara] has a large electric eel, which he has kept for several years in a tub, made for that purpose, placed under a small shed near to the house. This fish possesses strong electric powers, and often causes scenes of diversion among the soldiers and sailors, who are struck with astonishment at its qualities, and believe it to be in league with some evil spirit. Two sailors wholly unacquainted with the properties of the fish, were one day told to fetch an eel, which was lying in the tub in the yard, and give it to the cook to dress for dinner. It is a strong fish of seven or eight pounds weight, and gives a severe shock on being touched, particularly if at all irritated or enraged. The sailors had no sooner reached the shed, than one of them plunged his hand to the bottom of the tub to seize the eel, when he received a blow which benumbed his whole arm; and without knowing what it was, he started from the tub shaking his fingers, and holding his elbow with his other hand, crying out 'Damme, Jack, what a thump he fetched me with his tail.' His messmate laughing at 'such a foolish notion', next put down his hand to reach out for the eel, but receiving a similar shock, he snapped his fingers likewise, and ran off crying out 'Damme, he did give you a thump! He's a fighting fellow: he has fetched me a broadside too! – Damme, let's both have a hawl at him together, Jack, then we shall board his d——d slipper carcase spite of his rudder.' Accordingly they both plunged their hands into the tub, and seized the fish, by a full grasp round the body. This was rougher treatment than he commonly experienced, and he returned with a most violent shock, which soon caused them to quit their hold. For a moment they stood aghast, then rubbing their arms, holding their elbows, and shaking their fingers, they capered about with pain and amazement, swearing that their arms were broke, and that it was the devil in the tub in the shape of an eel. They now perceived that it was not a simple blow of the tail, which they had felt before; nor could they be prevailed upon to try again to take out the fish, but stole away rubbing their elbows, swearing the devil was in the tub, and cursing 'the trick about the cook and the eel'.

GEORGE PINCKARD, 1806

Among those in the nineteenth century who did manage to get hold of one of the rare 'snug secretaryships' craved by Anthony Trollope was a man who spent twenty-five years in the colony's judiciary, ending up as the Attorney-General. His long residence, and equally long connection with West Indian legal proceedings, gave him a somewhat jaundiced view of his fellow lawyers:

The Bar in British Guiana, like most colonies, was composed of a very mixed lot of men . . . Several of the barristers were men who had failed in other pursuits, and, having the gift of the gab, had been called to the Bar in England, and returned to make what they could in the land of their adoption. One of the best and most amusing of these was Dick Whitfield, who had formerly been a dry-goods merchant; but failing in that interesting occupation, and being a voluble Irishman, he turned his thoughts to the law, and after an absence in England of a couple of years, returned a full-fledged barrister . . .

On one occasion I was presiding over a trial in Georgetown where the prisoner was accused of murder, and, as the custom was, Dick Whitfield had been assigned as his counsel. The case was a clear and simple one, and I was rather curious to hear what the learned counsel could say in defence. He called no witnesses, but proceeded to address the jury . . . 'when God planted Adam and Eve in the Garden of Eden, they lived a life of blissful innocence and happiness. Joy was theirs, the fruits of the earth were their food, the limpid streams their only drink; they knew neither care nor sorrow. But, alas! the devil entered in, the tempter was there' – and so on, for some ten minutes. I interposed, 'Really, Mr Whitfield, I cannot see what this has to do with the case. You must come to the point.' 'I am coming to the point, your honour.' However, he still went on with his biblical narrative; but when he had got as far as Noah's Ark, I again interrupted him . . . But it was no use, he went on rambling over all kinds of subjects, sacred and profane, until he wound up abruptly by an impassioned appeal to the jury not to send the unfortunate man in the dock to a violent death, drew an affecting picture of the man's weeping widow and wailing children (there was no evidence that the prisoner had any children, and he was being tried for murdering his wife), and ended by a commonplace peroration, imploring the jury to remember the sanctity of their oaths and not condemn an innocent man. All his eloquence was of no avail. The man was convicted, sentenced by me to death, and was hanged in due course of law.

HENRY KIRKE, 1898

3 Trinidad

'Only one Mother'

I love to recollect the days which I spent in Trinidad, and would fain record some of their events whilst the impressions which they made are still fresh upon my mind. Gentle reader, whilst thou pokest thy coal fire, and cleavest to the grate as if Satan were at thy back, think, O! think of the mercury at 94° of Fahrenheit!

HENRY NELSON COLERIDGE, 1826

In the vast colonial empire of Great Britain there does not exist an Island so valuable for its extent as Trinidad. The fertility of its soils equals, if it does not excel, that of the most productive parts of St Domingo. There are not on its surface ten acres of land which might not be easily brought under cultivation. It possesses a greater number of navigable rivers, and rivers that might with little labour be rendered navigable, than any Island of its extent on the face of the Globe. Through some inexplicable cause, Trinidad has hitherto been exempt from hurricanes, these awful visitations of the West Indies, while Islands which lay almost in sight of it are from time to time exposed to the ravages of those frantic convulsions of the elements . . .

No one in Trinidad should lay in bed after the sun makes its appearance, as he loses the most pleasant time of the day: the climate then is agreeable . . . I can form no better idea of the climate of Paradise than by imagining it to resemble that of Trinidad during the night: there is a blandness in the air that even the inhabitants of the Caribbean Islands who have not visited us can form no conception of . . .

During the nights here, the English inhabitants seem to enjoy the delicious climate gravely, silently, and inactively; the French promenade and serenade each other; the few Spaniards we have here, often in the country spend half the night in playing the guitar, while their dames enjoy the luxury of a nocturnal bath . . .

And here it may not be out of place to remark, that of all European nations which have colonized in this part of the world, the Spaniards seem to have adopted habits the best suited to the climate, while the customs of the English West Indians are the least wise of any . . .

The Englishman in this part of the world generally grumbles that he cannot get Leadenhall beef; he endeavours to have on his board the repast he has been accustomed to at home . . . and were he to approach a dinner-table without a long coat made of broad cloth, he would, in this Island, be thought a barbarian by his countrymen.

A medical friend of mine has often expressed his pity for the English ladies, who often pay visits of ceremony during the heat of the day, dressed, laced, and braced in a manner most unsuitable to the climate. This system of wearing whalebone cuirasses, the Doctor tells me, is injurious in Europe, but most pernicious within ten degrees of the Equator . . .

E.L. JOSEPH, 1838

In a colony like Trinidad, diversity of races will probably continue to exist for many years, a contingency which some may deplore but which should not disturb their equanimity. In fact it would be a most suicidal policy on the part of the Government to allow, much less encourage, any one class of colonist to arrogate to itself a superiority over the rest. Mere differences of origin, or religion, or of social habits should not be permitted to raise barriers between different sections of the community; still less should they form an excuse for hedging in a few as a superior caste.

SIR LOUIS DE VERTEUIL, 1856

We are now speaking more especially of Trinidad. It is a large island, great portions of which are but very imperfectly known; of which but comparatively a very small part has been cultivated. During the last eight or ten years, ten or twelve thousand immigrants, chiefly Coolies from Madras and Calcutta, have been brought into Trinidad, forming now above an eighth part of its entire population . . .

. . . the Anti-Slavery Society is as anxious to prevent this immigration on behalf of the Coolies, who in their own country can hardly earn twopence a day, as it is on the part of the negroes, who would with ease, though they won't, earn two shillings a day . . . The present system of indenturing the immigrant on his first arrival is the only one to which we can safely trust for the good usage of the labourer. For the present this is clearly the case. When the Coolies are as numerous in these islands as the negroes – and that time will come – such rules and restrictions will no doubt be withdrawn. And when these different people have learned to mix their blood – which in time will also come – then mankind will hear no more of a lack of labour, and the fertility of these islands will cease to be their greatest curse.

ANTHONY TROLLOPE, 1859

The first thing notable, on landing in Port of Spain . . . is the multitude of people who are doing nothing. It is not that they have taken an hour's holiday to see the packet come in. You will find them, or their brown duplicates, in the same places to-morrow and next day. They stand idle in the market-place, not because they have not been hired, but because they do not want to be hired . . . You are told that there are 8000 human beings in Port of Spain without visible means of subsistence, and you congratulate Port of Spain on being such an Elysium that people can live there – not without eating, for every child and most women you pass are eating something or other all day long – but without working . . . Every one, plainly, can live and thrive if they choose; and very pleasant it is to know that.

CHARLES KINGSLEY, 1871

Trinidad is the largest, after Jamaica, of the British West Indian Islands, and the hottest absolutely after none of them . . . To walk is difficult in a damp steamy temperature hotter during daylight than the hottest forcing house in Kew. I was warned not to exert myself and to take cocktail freely. In the evening I might venture out with the bats and take a drive if I wished in the twilight. Languidly charming as it all was, I could not help asking myself of what use such a possession could be either to England or the English nation. We could not colonise it, could not cultivate it, could not draw a revenue from it. If it prospered commercially the prosperity would be of French and

Spaniards, mulattoes and blacks, but scarcely, if at all, of my own countrymen. For here too, as elsewhere, they were growing fewer daily, and those who remained were looking forward to the day when they could be released. If it were not for the honour of the thing, as the Irishman said after being carried in a sedan chair which had no bottom, we might have spared ourselves so unnecessary a conquest.

JAMES ANTHONY FROUDE, 1888

Trinidad is not only a very beautiful island, but it is typical of the tropics and of the West Indies generally. It is a place, therefore, for a prolonged sojourn ... There is just one drawback to the island, which even the generous hospitality and ready kindness of the inhabitants cannot make quite imperceptible, and that is the climate. It is hot, damp, and enervating, while the insects of the colony are rather overwhelming in their attentions to newcomers.

... Trinidad is an island of a thousand hills, of incessant peaks and ridges, and a maze of winding valleys. From the sea margin to the sky line it is one blaze of green, the green not of grass but of trees. Trees cover it from the deepest gorge to the broken-glass edge of the highest peak ... Viewed from a long way off it would seem to be covered uniformly with green astrachan. Seen nearer one wonders if there can be a level road in the place, or indeed any road at all, and if the inhabitants can ever find their way out of the woods, so as to get a glimpse of the sky.

SIR FREDERICK TREVES, 1908

... the traveler cannot but realize that at last he has come to the end of the West Indies and is encroaching upon the South American continent. The 'Trinity' of fuzzy hills ... for which Columbus named the island have quite another aspect than the precipitous volcanic peaks of the Lesser Antilles. Plump, placid, their vegetation tanned a light brown by the now truly tropical sun, they have a strong family resemblance to the mountains of Venezuela hazily looming into the sky back across the Bocas. Fog, unknown among the stepping-stones to the north, hangs like wet wool over all the lowlands, along the edge of the bay. The trade wind that has never failed on the long journey south has given place to an enervating breathlessness; by seven in the morning the sun is already cruelly beating down; instead of the clear blue waters of the Caribbean, the vast expanse of harbor has the drab, lifeless color of a faded brown carpet.

HARRY A. FRANCK, 1920

Trinidad is a lovely island with an unlovely capital. As the ship enters the Dragon's Mouth the far-away crinkled line of jungle-covered mountains proclaims the tropics. Once you are ashore there is no doubt . . . Never have I seen such profusion of vegetation, even in the tropics of the Far East. The whole island is a riot of green. The trees, particularly the saman trees, are giants. And there are flowers everywhere . . .

OWEN RUTTER, 1933

Trinidad and Tobago is . . . the most distinctive of the Caribbean countries.

It is, in the first place, the most European of all the Caribbean territories – Trinidad being a Spanish colony with profoundly French influences later annexed by Britain; Tobago, with its alternating Dutch and French influence, until it was annexed by Britain.

Trinidad and Tobago, in the second place, is the most cosmopolitan of all the West Indian territories – its African stock having been supplemented in the last century by large numbers of immigrants from India and lesser numbers from China and Syria, all superimposed on its diverse European base.

In the third place, Trinidad and Tobago is the most truly West Indian of all the Caribbean countries. The French immigrants in the Spanish period with their African slaves came from Grenada and Haiti, and Martinique, and throughout the nineteenth and twentieth centuries, culminating in the large-scale importation of West Indian labour for the construction of the large American bases in 1941, Trinidad and Tobago has received large numbers of immigrants from all the smaller countries of the British Caribbean and from British Guiana.

ERIC WILLIAMS, 1964

There can be no Mother India for those whose ancestors come from India . . . there can be no Mother Africa for those of African origin . . . there can be no Mother England and no dual loyalties . . . there can be no Mother China even if one could agree as to which China is the mother; and there can be no Mother Syria and no Mother Lebanon. A nation, like an individual, can have only one mother. The only mother we recognize is Mother Trinidad and Tobago, and Mother cannot discriminate between her children.

ERIC WILLIAMS, 1972

Eric Williams, a hint of whose love of his native island and no-nonsense ap-proach to the way its cosmopolitan society needed to develop can be gathered from the above extracts from his speeches, became the Chief Minister of the then colony in 1956 when he was forty-five years old. Four years later, having earlier paraphrased Winston Churchill by declaring 'I did not have the honour of becoming the Queen's first Chief Minister of Trinidad and Tobago to preside over the perpetuation of colonialism', he became the first Prime Minister of the Republic of Trinidad and Tobago, a position he held until his death in 1981. He was a consumate politician, dominating the domestic scene from the moment he entered politics in 1955, who quickly developed into an astute statesman more than able to hold his own among older and more experienced West Indian leaders, with British Government ministers, and on the world stage.

He was also a remarkable scholar and historian, being the first known West Indian to gain a PhD in history (an academic qualification which few other national leaders can ever have held or even aspired to). The thesis for which this was awarded, after it became the first of his many publications was, in the words of a modern historian, 'to remain the centrepiece of West Indian historiography until the end of the twentieth century'. His other books, some written while he was Prime Minister, include a History of the People of Trinidad and Tobago, *a history of the Caribbean entitled* From Columbus to Castro, *and an autobiography with the expressive title* Inward Hunger. *The opening words of an early chapter of the last are characteristically candid, and could well serve as an epitaph for a man of a stature not found among too many national leaders at the beginning of the twenty-first century:*

Some are born great, some achieve greatness, some have greatness thrust upon them. Greatness, Trinidad style, was thrust upon me from the cradle.

Among the very few predecessors of Williams as an author of a history of Trinidad was the otherwise unknown E.L. Joseph who not only in 1838 produced the first history of Trinidad to be written in English, but in it he provided his readers with descriptive and entertaining details of events in a way quite alien to the style of his more austere and academically-minded twentieth-century counterpart:

In 1808 the Colonial Office appointed Judge Smith over all the Tribunals of this island. He was empowered to hear appeals from his own Court; hence the monstrous absurdity was practised in Trinidad of a Judge deciding a cause in one Court, changing his dress, hearing the case, and reversing his own sentence in another Court, and condemning the party who lost the suit, in the Court of Appeal, to all costs. The commission of Judge Smith is a masterpiece of wisdom, even considering that it came from Downing-street to this island of experiment; when mentioned in the House of Commons, it created shouts of laughter.

This legal farce could not last very long; but after it had amused and plagued the colony for two years, the Governor, with the advice of the Council and Cabildo, superseded Judge Smith, notwithstanding that he wore a wig in one Court, and a cocked hat in the other.

The greatest calamity

1808. March 24th, the greatest calamity that ever befel this island occurred, namely the destruction of Port of Spain by fire.

The town had been regularly built according to South American mode: the streets were all of equal length and breadth, running east and west, and north and south, and consequently intersecting each other at right angles; but although the hills immediately in the neighbourhood of the town abounded in the finest building and lime stone, yet all the houses were allowed to be built of wood; the best were covered with what are called shingles; many were thatched, and many had galleries which projected far into the streets. During the dry season, in the West Indies, a wooden house become inflamable to a degree scarcely conceivable to an inhabitant of a more temperate region. There was little excuse for the houses of Port of Spain being formed of wood: the impropriety was admitted, but, with the thoughtlessness of colonial communities, the custom of enlarging the town with wooden houses was persisted in, although at this period, in consequence of the clandestine trade with the Main, the amount of merchandise in Port of Spain was enormous.

About ten o'clock, a certain Dr Schaw, who kept an apothecary's shop . . . went into a small out-house in which there was some wood shavings; the Doctor, it is said, was not quite sober, and carried a brand of fire with him; this dropping among the shavings, soon set the apothecary's shop in a blaze, the inflamable materials of which were peculiarly calculated to cause a conflagration: the shop blew up, and wherever the sparks fell the houses ignited more like gunpowder than wood. Before the fire commenced, the night was perfectly calm; too soon a brisk but unsteady breeze sprang up, which spread the flames on all sides. In an incredibly-short space the whole town was in a state of conflagration . . .

The bells were set ringing, the drums beat, and the troops hurried to the conflagration; these sounds were mingled with the shrieks of women and children; all was in a frantic haste, but nothing was done in concert, save breaking open and robbing grog-shops on the part of the soldiers of the garrison, who in general behaved disgracefully. The conduct of the slaves in general was also bad – robbing rather than aiding the distressed.

Sir Thomas Hislop, the governor, hurried to the spot, and was advised by some engineer officers to blow up a few houses with gunpowder, in order to stop the ravages of the flames. This he refused to do, lest human life might be lost, and he was blamed by some for not doing it.

The sight and sounds of woe continued; none expected to save any thing, although most endeavoured, by throwing their property in streets and yards, to preserve it; often there it fell prey to the infernal element, or the scarcely-less infernal rapacity of thieves who, to the disgrace of human nature, gave way to their selfish passion, amid scenes of distress that might have brought tears of commiseration from the eyes of the coldest stoic that ever bore the prostituted title of philosopher. Thousands were ruined, hundreds were doomed to beggary, until broken hearts consigned them to welcome graves. A few made their miserable fortunes by the general calamity.

With such violence did the devouring element spread that some threw their goods into wells; it being the height of the dry season, little water was in them, yet they went on piling bales of goods in those wells until they caught fire from the top, and absolutely burnt until nearly to the bottom . . .

The destruction by fire of a West India town is a calamity of an awful nature. Few of these colonies grew enough of provisions to supply the wants of its inhabitants, because they find it more advantageous to purchase provisions from the United States of America; hence the fire of Port of Spain, by consuming the American supplies in store, threatened nothing less than famine to the people of Trinidad . . .

On the 25th of March the sun shone on a scene of supreme wretchedness: a cheerful town stood on the plains of Port of Spain the previous day – a set of smoking ruins were in its place. A few goods that had escaped the cruel conflagration and the more cruel thief, were collected in its square, guarded by soldiers. Women and children were weeping, and men in deeper but less vociferous agony were walking to and fro, not knowing where to procure the means of breaking their fast.

Three-fourths of the town was burnt. It is said, property to the amount of half a million sterling was destroyed by this calamity. Most of the merchants and storekeepers were insured; the principal loss fell on the humble industrious order of society.

E.L. JOSEPH, 1838

Port of Spain was destroyed by fire in 1808 as the result of an accident, whether the wretched quack who started it was drunk or not. This was something which cannot be said about the conflagration which gutted the centre of the city 182 years later, causing equal consternation if not actually reducing quite so many people to total destitution.

The fire which burned over the last weekend of July 1990 was brought about by the actions of an ex-policeman, masquerading as a Black Muslim champion of the city's poor and dispossessed who, at the head of a small gang of armed sansculottes, attempted a coup d'état. *Such is the normally relaxed way in which the affairs of state are conducted in the West Indies – as much in Port of Spain with its over half a million inhabitants as, say, in Roseau in Dominica with only 20,000 – that the raggle-taggle revolutionaries were able not only to enter the Parliament Building without too much trouble, but to take the Prime Minister and several of his ministerial colleagues hostage. They subsequently attacked and set alight the police headquarters, from where the fire quickly spread to the surrounding buildings. Although the attempted* coup *came to nothing, by the time all the insurgents had surrendered after three days of negotiations the entire centre of Port of Spain – just as in the great fire of 1808 – had been razed and looted. It was a very heavy price to pay for the actions of a deluded fanatic with not even, as in the case of the hapless Doctor Schaw, the possibility of alcohol being held partly to blame.*

Phosphoric and other scintillations

No man can conceive from dry description alone the magical beauty of these glorious creatures [fireflies]; so far from their effects having been exaggerated by travellers, I can say that I never read an account in prose or verse which in the least prepared me for the reality.

There are two sorts, the small fly which flits in and out in the air, the body of which I have never examined; and a kind of beetle, which keeps more to the woods, and is somewhat more stationary, like our glowworm. This last has two broad eyes on the back of its head which, when the phosphorescent energy is not exerted, are of a dull parchment hue, but, upon the animal's being touched, shoot forth two streams of green light as intense as the prest gas. But the chief source of splendour is a cleft in the belly, through which the whole interior of the beetle appears like a red hot furnace. I put one of these natural lamps under a wine glass in my bedroom in Trinidad, and, in order to verify some accounts, which I have heard doubted, I ascertained the hour on my watch by its light alone with the utmost facility.

HENRY NELSON COLERIDGE, 1826

We have three beautiful varieties of the Fire Fly; the first is the Cicindela, which displays luminous matter in the abdomen as it respires . . . After rain in the evenings, our savannas seem covered with transitory scintillations as far as the eye can reach. These luminous appearances are caused by the Cicindela.

The Great Fire Fly . . . is beyond comparison the most beautiful of the Phosphoric insects. It has two round azure lights above his eyes when he walks; when he leaps or flies, he discovers a large lambent ruby-coloured light in the abdomen; the contrast of his pair of blue lights in the thorax, and the more brilliant flame in his abdomen, is most beautiful. They possess the power of rendering those Phosphoric spots dull or brilliant at pleasure . . . It belongs to the order Hemiptera. We have also the Elater Noctilucus, order Coleoptero.

Some years since a Spanish lady of this town had a Carnival dress composed thus: it was of the finest gauze, puckered (I believe I use the right phrase); between these puckers small and great fire flies were introduced: the effect of this costume was splendid beyond description; the phosphoric scintillations were tri-coloured – the Cicindela, as it respires, emits a pale blue light, while the greater insect displayed its deep azure and dark red sparks. This dress was worn at a masquerade; but it put an end, for that night, to all masking, as on its appearance every one in the room removed his or her mask through astonishment.

A lady informed me, that she saw the dress dissected the next day, when all the insects were allowed their liberty; none of them died during their imprisonment.

I have a great friendship for these flies, as eight or ten of them served me for a lamp by which I for some months read and wrote, when I was an overseer of an estate, and not allowed the use of candle in my chamber. I fed them with pieces of sugar-cane.

E.L. JOSEPH, 1838

The particular room assigned to myself would have been . . . delightful but that my possession of it was disputed even in daylight by mosquitoes, who for bloodthirsty ferocity had a bad pre-eminence over the worst I had ever met elsewhere. I killed one who was at work upon me, and examined him through a glass. Bewick, with the inspiration of genius, had drawn his exact likeness as the devil – a long black stroke for a body, a nick for neck, horns on the head, and a beak for a mouth, spindle arms, and long spindle legs, two pointed wings, and a tail. Line for line there the figure was before me which in the unforgetable tailpiece is driving the thief under the gallows, and I had a melancholy satisfaction in identifying him. I had been warned to be on the look-out for scorpions, centipedes, jiggers, and land crabs, who would bite me if I walked slipperless over the floor in the dark. Of these I met with none, either there or anywhere, but the mosquito of Trinidad is enough by himself. For malice, mockery, and venom of tooth and trumpet, he is without a match in the world.

JAMES ANTHONY FROUDE, 1888

Coming to the Asphaltum

Wee came to Ancor at Terra de Bri short of the Spanish port some 10 leagues. This Terra de Bri is a piece of land of some 2 leagues longe and a league brode, all of stone pich or bitumen which riseth out of the ground in little springs or fountaynes and so running a little way, it hardneth in the aire, and covereth all the playne; ther are also many springs of water and in and among them fresh water fishe.

SIR WALTER RALEIGH, 1596

I now come to the Asphaltum or Pitch Lake. On approaching the point called La Brea from the sea, a strong bituminous odour is smelt at the distance of two leagues or more, and large black masses are perceived towards the shore; these appear like rocks at a distance, but are in fact bodies of asphaltum ... This lake is about half a geographical league in circumference; it is surrounded on all sides by dark woods, save towards the sea; the surface seems perfectly black during the rainy season, but in dry weather it has a partial greyish hue; it appears as though billions of tons of pitch had boiled up from the earth from the effects of an immense subterraneous fire which has been extinguished, and left the asphaltum to cool in enormous bubbles.

Chasms between these black masses or bubbles extend in different directions all over the surface of the lake; you can scarcely walk thirty yards without having to cross one of them. These chasms are not abrupt, but gradually shelve off in an elliptical manner, the masses of asphaltum meet at the bottom; these appertures vary from three to thirty feet in width, and are from two to six feet in depth. They are filled with water, which, although it has a slight bituminous taste, is wholesome. Small fresh-water mullets and little caymans (alligators) are caught therein.

Nearly all over the lake arise at intervals little islets (if I may be allowed the expression) of stunted trees; these taking advantage of the slightest layers of soil, dart their hardy roots into the asphaltum and enjoy a precarious vegetable life, supporting myriads of wild pines, aloes, and parasites. These clumps of dwarf trees are by no means stationary; the imperceptible yet incessant movement of the asphaltum perpetually transports these vegetable islets from one part of the lake to another; sometimes one of them sinks into the lower regions of asphaltum, and is again thrown up at some distance, its dark verdant hue changed to the blacker dye of the Lagoon; it is encrusted with bitumen, and its vegetable juice changed to petroleum.

E.L. JOSEPH, 1838

At last we surmounted the last rise, and before us lay the famous lake – not at the bottom of a depression, as we expected, but at the top of a rise, whence the ground slopes away from it on two sides, and rises from it very slightly on the two others. The black pool glared and glittered in the sun. A group of islands, some twenty yards wide were scattered about the middle of it . . .

We walked, with some misgivings, on to the asphalt, and found it perfectly hard. In a few yards we were stopped by a channel of clear water, with tiny fish, and water-beetles in it; and, looking round, saw that the whole lake was intersected with channels, so unlike anything which can be seen elsewhere, that it is not easy to describe them . . .

In one of the star-shaped pools of water, some five feet deep, a column of pitch had been forced perpendicularly up from the bottom. On reaching the surface of the water it had formed a sort of centre table, about four feet in diameter, but without touching the sides of the pool. The stem was about a foot in diameter. I leaped out on this table, and found that it not only sustained my weight, but that the elasticity of the stem enabled me to rock it from side to side. Pieces torn from the edges of this table sank readily, showing that it had been raised by pressure, and not by its buoyancy.

True, though strange: but stranger still did it seem to us, when we did at last what the Negroes asked us, and dipped our hands into the liquid pitch, to find that it did not soil the fingers. The old proverb, that one cannot touch pitch without being defiled, happily does not stand true here, or the place would be intolerably loathsome. It can be scraped up, moulded into any shape you will; wound in a string . . . round a stick, and carried off: but nothing is left on the hand save clean gray mud and water . . .

CHARLES KINGSLEY, 1871

Trinidad has one wonder in it, a lake of bitumen some ninety acres in extent, which all travellers are expected to visit, and which few residents care to visit. A black lake is not so beautiful as an ordinary lake. I had no doubt that it existed, for the testimony was unimpeachable. Indeed I was shown an actual specimen of the crystallised pitch itself. I could believe without seeing and without undertaking a tedious journey. I rather sympathised with a noble lord who came to Port of Spain in his yacht, and like myself had the lake impressed upon him. As a middle course between going thither and appearing to slight his friends' recommendations, he said that he would send his steward . . .

JAMES ANTHONY FROUDE, 1888

There are some things the traveller finds it hard to avoid. Among them is the Pitch Lake at Trinidad . . .

The visitor to La Brea will see neither flames nor smoke, nor anything boiling, nor will he be helped in other ways to realise the awfulness of the stream by Charon's ferry. The place is by no means terrible or awe-inspiring. It is as bare of the poetic afflatus as is a coal-merchant's yard . . . people can only sink in the lake with difficulty and with infinite patience. A man who attempted suicide by this process would die of starvation and boredom before he had sunk much above his knees, and to get even so far he would have to be pertinacious.

When I saw the lake there was but a solitary man upon it, near about its centre. He was . . . squatting on the pitch on his hams, washing clothes in one of the many little puddles on the lake's surface.

If a Londoner would realise the Pitch Lake, he must imagine the pond in St James's Park emptied of water, its bottom filled with asphalt, pools left in places, and some tropical vegetation disposed about the margin of the depression. Such a landscape would only inspire in the susceptible conceptions of the scenery of Hell.

SIR FREDERICK TREVES, 1908

The lake consists of a vast deposit of bituminous matter with a surface 114 acres in extent. For years after its first discovery by Sir Walter Raleigh no uses were found for its apparently inexhaustible supplies of pitch . . .

The resourceful Sir Ralph Woodford caused [it] to be laid down in the square in Port of Spain that now bears his name, in the hope that it might check the growth of grass there. Far from achieving this result, it actually encouraged the weeds. Indeed, it appeared to contribute so greatly to the richness of the soil that it was seriously suggested that it might be used as a fertilizer. The enterprising Governor then suggested that the pitch might make an illuminant. He accordingly had carburetted hydrogen distilled from it, and burned in a beacon on the tower of Holy Trinity Cathedral. The gas burned splendidly, but the stench was so appalling that the experiment had to be abandoned.

SIR ALGERNON ASPINALL, 1927

. . . although millions of tons of its substance have been removed, the surface has sunk no more than twenty feet in all those years. As a view, it is not impressive . . . It is though someone had spread over the ground a vast and rather dusty tarpaulin, not quite flat, but caught up into ridges and crinkles and small hollows where the rainwater had collected . . .

In the pools left by the rain the gas comes bubbling up with a queer humming sound and in these pools are the pitch fish noticed by Raleigh. They are tiny creatures and when one pool dries up they wriggle their way at night, when the asphalt is moist with dew, into the next. If these fish are placed in a jar they will be gone by morning, for however high the sides of the jar above the water-line they attach themselves to the glass by suction and wriggle their way upwards until they escape . . .

The asphalt is always moving, with incalculable undercurrents, though the movement is imperceptible . . . a pipe 160 feet long, which had been driven down to find the bottom of the lake, had vanished overnight and reappeared some years later eight hundred feet away, battered and twisted as though it had been through fire.

In February 1928 the stump of a tree suddenly made its appearance above the surface of the lake in a perfectly upright position. It went on slowly rising from the lake until ten feet showed above the surface. For some days it remained stationary; then it began to tilt over to one side. When it had reached an angle of thirty degrees it started to sink once more into those uncanny depths, and within a few days it had completely disappeared. I was shown a section of this tree, which scientists estimate to be four or five thousand years old.

OWEN RUTTER, 1933

4 Tobago

'A mere Apanage?'

Thou art here presented with The Present Prospect of the Island of Tobago, about forty Leagues distant from Barbadoes; but far excelling that Island, and indeed any other of the Caribee-Islands, in the Fertility and Richness of the Soil, and in the Commodiousness of its Bays and Harbors: and it is no paradox to affirm, That though it lies more south, the Air is as Cool and Refreshing as that of Barbadoes: and yet Exempted from those affrighting and destructive Hurricanes that have been often Fatal to the rest of the Caribee-Islands . . . And I am perswaded that there is no Island in America, that can afford us more ample Subjects to contemplate the Bounty and Goodness of our Great Creator in, than this of Tobago; And this, I speak not by hearsay, or as one that had liv'd always at home; but as one that has had Experience of the World, and been in the greatest part of the Caribee-Islands, and most parts of the Continent of America, and almost all His Majesties Forreign Plantations; and after having view'd them all, have chosen this Island of Tobago to take up my *quietus est* in.

CAPTAIN JOHN POYNTZ, 1683

Military men generally dislike being ordered to Tobago, and are always anxious to quit, but this proceeds from the very limited society and want of public amusement, whilst the unprepossessing appearance of the northern coast, when passing at sea or on a short stay in the principal town may lead the traveller to pass from it with distaste. Throughout the whole island there is but little social intercourse, as the habitations are scattered, and the roads the greater part of the year, are in such a state as precludes visiting. But most of the estates are advantageously situated, and the scenery around them picturesque and attractive. The variety of its trees, shrubs, flowers and vegetables must render it interesting to the botanist, whilst the naturalist may there find birds not to be met with in other colonies. Of the former I am acquainted with one hundred and twenty-three different kinds, and doubtless there are many others.

LIEUTENANT-COLONEL HENRY CAPADOSE, 1845

Tobago has had a chequered and turbulent history. It has changed hands more often than any other West Indian island, and has belonged in turn to Barbadians, Courlanders, Zeelanders – to whom it was New Walcheren – Dutch, French, and English . . . in 1899 it was reduced to the ranks and became a mere apanage of Trinidad . . .

Apart from its salubrious climate and varied scenery, Tobago has another claim on the notice of wayfarers by reason of the reputation it enjoys of having been the island on which Defoe, inspired, no doubt, by the adventures of Alexander Selkirk on Juan Fernandez, marooned his mythical hero . . . Robinson Crusoe . . .

SIR ALGERNON ASPINALL, 1927

Tobago is an island of exciting names: Man of War Bay, Englishman's Bay, Columbus Point and Bloody Bay still appear upon the maps. Sluggard's Bay has given place to the more prosaic Hillsborough, and Kill Devil Bay to King's Bay; while I have looked in vain for Flying-Fish Point, shown on an old chart . . .

Tobago is quite unspoilt by the tourist, and I, for one, hope it may long remain so. For those who look to find in the West Indies counterparts of Brighton, Deauville or Monte Carlo, it has little to offer. There is 'nothing to do'. There are no casinos, no picture palaces, no cabarets, no expensive restaurants, no Grand Hotels . . . Tobago is remote from modern improvements . . . It is the one island in the Caribbean I should like, above all others, to see again.

OWEN RUTTER, 1933

Courlanders at bay

In April 1960 I had the great good fortune to live for several weeks in the small town of Plymouth in Tobago. Together with a motor survey boat and a small team of naval ratings I had been detached from HMS Vidal, *then the Royal Navy's newest survey ship, to carry out the work needed for a new chart of the bays on the south-west coast of the island. For a novice surveyor (I had joined the Surveying Service less than a year earlier) no better job could have been envisaged. The waters to be surveyed were calm and sheltered, the people of Plymouth were welcoming and helpful, everything I needed in the way of stores and equipment had been landed, and once our base had been established the ship disappeared over the horizon.*

Except in minor ways Tobago was then very little different from how Rutter had described it in the early 1930s – there were still no casinos, nightclubs, grand hotels or fancy restaurants – and was the ideal of the West Indian island I had carried in my mind's eye ever since I had left the Caribbean in HMS Triumph *six years earlier. In 1960 Tobago still slumbered in its pre-mass tourism dawn, and in Plymouth that April one young man at least needed no one to remind him that it was indeed bliss to be alive.*

The area to be surveyed, extending from the high water line to two to three miles offshore, was along the coast between Plymouth and the south-western tip of the island. Among the geographical features within this area was a huge stretch of very shallow water, the then completely unspoilt and totally deserted Buccoo coral reef, and two large indentations in the coast called Great Courland Bay and Little Courland Bay. At first I thought that the name Courland, as so often with the naming of natural features throughout the West Indies, was that of an early settler – some English or Scottish planter perhaps. I was only partly right, the name was connected with the original European settlement but had nothing to do with any part of the British Isles.

I knew enough about West Indian history by this time to know that the Danes and Swedes, as well as the Spanish, English, Scots, French and Dutch had all had interests in the Caribbean. What I now discovered was that so had people from a part of northern Europe once known as Courland.

With a history even more chequered than that of Tobago, being at various times under Lithuanian, Polish, Swedish, Prussian and Russian rule, today this forms the western province of Latvia and is called Kurzeme. It was all very interesting, but why and how had the inhabitants of such a place developed any interest in the West Indies, let alone an island like Tobago?

The Duchy of Courland had been created by the King of Poland out of a diocese of the Teutonic Order when the Order was secularized in 1562. Its association with Tobago stemmed from the action taken by the British monarch James I when he became godfather to Frederick Kettler, the elder son of the first duke. As a christening gift James presented his godson with the island; a place about which he, the king, could have known next to nothing and in complete disregard of the fact that at the time the British had no more claim to it than any other nation. It remained very much a symbolic gift until 1634 when, long after he had succeeded to the dukedom, and spurred on by the early English attempts at Caribbean colonization, Frederick dispatched 200 settlers to take up his inheritance. It was an attempt doomed to failure. The island already had a well-established Amerindian population and the duke, stuck in his Baltic backwater, had none of the enterprise or resources needed to maintain such a remote colony. Nothing remained of it by the time the first English expedition arrived five year later.

Frederick was succeeded in 1641 by his nephew Jacob, a man whom his later enemy King Charles X of Sweden was to characterize as being 'too rich to be a duke and too poor to be a king', but who was determined to transform his obscure duchy into a major maritime power. This was something he managed to do during his forty years as ruler, by building an impressive fleet of warships and supporting a huge increase in the number of the duchy's merchant vessels. His first attempt to regain Tobago, an island which he now viewed as a legitimate Courland possession, took place within a year or so of his succession, but well before his marine initiative had had any effect. Although more than 300 settlers were sent out in 1642, apart from naming their landing place Great Courland Bay they achieved nothing of any permanence. They were too few in number to withstand constant harassment by the Amerindians, and the duchy still lacked the wherewithal and dynamism to maintain and nurture a colony. In 1650 the last few dozen surviving settlers gave up and abandoned the island in order to take their chances on the South American mainland.

Four years later Jacob tried again, sending out eighty families under the protection of a body of troops. This time, with all the resources needed, with financial support of the bankers of Danzig, and under proper leadership, the settlement was more successful. A fort was constructed at Great Courland Bay and, as the land around it was cleared, the planting of tobacco, sugar, indigo and cotton began. Another 400 families arrived during the next four years, and by 1658 the settlement covered around 500 hectares of the hinterland of both Great Courland and Little Courland Bay. Shortly after the arrival of the first group a party of Dutch settlers had landed on the opposite coast at what later became Rockly Bay. This was an event that created tension on the island for a while, and began a long dispute in Europe about the ownership of Tobago, which had not even begun to be resolved before the Duchy of Courland became caught up in the war between Sweden and Poland which began in 1655. The war greatly reduced home support for the settlers, and after the duke was taken prisoner in 1658 communication with them ceased altogether.

The Dutch settlers were then in a position to dominate, and by the time Jacob had been released from captivity in 1660 and was able to send ships to the Caribbean once more the Courland settlement had been all but abandoned. In spite of the duke persuading the English monarch, Charles II, to renew his title to Tobago four years later in return for Courland's support in the Second Anglo-Dutch War, and of his sending a number of ships to the island, the settlement never recovered. Numbers of his subjects continued to be sent out to try to turn the duke's colonial dream into reality until his death in 1682, but such were the perils of war, piracy and navigation throughout this period that only half the ships that were dispatched ever reached their destination. In 1668 a Dutch decree laying claim to sovereignty of the whole island hardly filled those Courlanders who had made the transatlantic crossing safely with any confidence about their future and fifteen years later, shortly after the duke's death, those who had stuck it out left for the Danish settlement on St Thomas.

A final attempt to refound the colony was made by the fifth duke, Jacob's son Frederick, in the late 1680s, but by this time the English (led by Captain Poyntz with his sales pitch for the 'Famous and Fertile Island') and French were just as interested in claiming the island as the Dutch and the attempt came to nothing. In 1688 the majority of the eighty or so harassed and despondent Courlanders who remained departed for a better life in New England, and two years later the remainder returned to Europe.

There remains very little evidence of the time these dour Northern Europeans spent in Tobago except on maps of the island. Until well into the eighteenth century the administrative name for the area they had once occupied was the Courland Bay division, but this disappeared when the island was divided into parishes. Today, in addition to the names of the two bays which had first attracted my attention in 1960, the name Courland remains attached to the low bluff on which Plymouth is situated at the northern end of the larger bay, to the river which flows into the same bay, and to an estate a little to the south of the river mouth: not bad going for a presence of only a little over fifty years which ended more than three centuries ago.

The history of Tobago became a little less turbulent after 1763 when the dispute over to which colonial power the island belonged settled into one between Britain and France only. The inhabitants were British subjects until 1781, French until 1793, British until 1802, and finally French again for just over one more year before becoming irrevocably British for the remainder of the colonial period. During the island's last brief period under French rule Napoleon Bonaparte became the dictator of France by making himself First Consul for life, an action which the members of the Legislative Council of Tobago felt warranted their approval.

In November 1802, resolutely backing the wrong horse, they unctuously begged the First Consul for

leave to express these sentiments of loyalty and fidelity to the French Republic and of gratitude to you for the many marks of paternal solicitude you have condescended to show for the welfare of this colony, and that at a time when your thoughts must have been employed in deciding the fate of Europe and arranging the weighty concerns of nations.

On this occasion, words fail us to convey an adequate idea of our sentiments. To no man recorded in ancient or modern history is the character of being an accomplished Hero and consummate Statesman so appropriate and so justly applicable as to you; we therefore see with joy and satisfaction that you have justified the wish of the French Nation in consenting to be First Consul for life . . .

First Consul, we entreat you to believe that the minds of the inhabitants of this Colony are . . . impressed with sentiments of gratitude for the intentions you have shown to their known interests and means of promoting the prosperity of the Colony by granting to them the enjoyment of their laws and internal legislation, for which the inhabitants of Tobago may, from education and habit, be pardoned for having a partiality and which may, on that account, be better suited to their character and circumstances.

And we do humbly hope that our loyalty and fidelity to the Republic and our obedient and respectful attachment to you may induce you to continue to these people whom you have reunited to the Empire . . . an institution which they feel essential to their happiness.

Could anything add to the sentiments which we have faintly expressed, it would be the proof you have lately afforded of the interest you have in our gratification by extending the benefits of your protection and patronage to our posterity, in the way in which you have honoured our children in the National Printannee where they will be taught to realise the virtues of the regeneration of France, to comprehend the value of such a Benefactor, and to perpetuate the sentiments of their Fathers by their gratitude and by their emulation to render themselves worthy of such a Protector.

We salute you with respect.

It was probably just as well that the proto-Uriah Heeps who composed and signed this letter received no reply, as less than seven months after it had been sent they were once again British subjects. But, as Eric Williams commented very succinctly in his History of the People of Trinidad and Tobago:

The whole history of the West Indies reveals the curious ability of the West Indian planter to accommodate himself to another flag and to switch loyalties as well . . .

Thus in 1802, as Bonaparte stood poised, ready to launch his attack for world domination which was to plunge the whole world into a further twelve years of war that ended only with the Battle of Waterloo, Bonaparte could proceed with absolute confidence. Tobago had advised him, if we may parody a famous West Indian joke at the expense of Barbados, 'go ahead, Bonaparte, Tobago is behind you'.

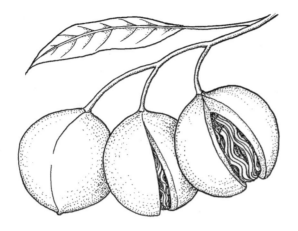

5 Grenada

'The headquarters of the world for fruit'

If Grenada belonged to the English, who knew how to turn to profit natural advantages, it would be a rich and powerful colony. In itself it was all that man could desire. To live there was to live in paradise.

JEAN BAPTISTE LABAT, 1722

Grenada, the only place I ever left, after no matter how short a residence without a particle of regret.

WILLIAM HICKEY, *Memoirs*, Comment of 1775

If Trinidad is sublime, Grenada is lovely . . . The harbour is one of the finest in the West Indies, and the hurricanes have not ranged so far to the south yet . . . The rest of the prospect is delightful; in every direction the eye wanders over richly cultivated valleys with streams of water running through them, orchards of shaddocks and oranges, houses with gardens, negro huts embowered in plantain leaves, mountains and little hills romantically mixed and variegated with verdant coppices of shrubs and trees. The view from

Government House, which is situated on a ridge at the end of Hospital Hill, is the Bay of Naples on one side, and a poet's Arcadia on the other . . .

. . . Grenada is perhaps the most *beautiful* of the Antilles, meaning by this that her features are soft and noble without being great and awful. There is an Italian look in the country which is very distinct from the usual character of the intertropical regions, and is peculiar to this colony.

HENRY NELSON COLERIDGE, 1826

Grenada is . . . very lovely, and is, I think, the headquarters of the world for fruit. The finest mangoes I ever ate I found there; and I think the finest oranges and pineapples.

The town of St Georges, the capital, must at one time have been a place of considerable importance. It is more like a goodly English town than any other that I saw in any of the smaller British islands. It is well built, though built up and down steep hills, and contains large and comfortable houses . . .

Indeed, Grenada was once a prince among these smaller islands, having other islands under it, with a Governor supreme, instead of tributary. It was fertile also, and productive – in every way of importance.

But now here, as in so many other spots among the West Indies, we are driven to exclaim, Ichabod! The glory of our Grenada has departed, as has the glory of its great namesake in the old world. The houses, though so goodly, are but as so many Alhambras, whose tenants now are by no means great in the world's esteem.

ANTHONY TROLLOPE, 1859

But if Grenada must yield the palm for beauty to some of its neighbours, St Georges, the capital, unquestionably presents the loveliest picture from the sea of any port in the Lesser Antilles, if not of the West Indies. Nestled among and piled up the green hills that terminate in a jagged series of peaks above, its often three-storey houses pitched in stages one above the other, larger buildings crowning here and there a loftier eminence, the whole delightfully irregular and individualistic, it rouses even the jaded traveler to exclamations of pleasure.

HARRY A. FRANCK, 1920

Grenada is a singularly pleasant island for many reasons, spiritual as well as climatic and geographical. It is a friendly place where politics, incessantly interesting to anybody with brains and a voice, have the complexion of rational culture. Grenada is rich – on cocoa and nutmeg, both extremely valuable crops – so she can afford to be sane. She has no efficient agitators to trouble her conscience, destroy her substance and embitter her workers . . . the island has everything to commend it. The views are rich in design and colouring. They are not always over-clothed. Generally there are just enough hills around the exquisite bays. The coconuts are sufficiently lavish without being overwhelming. The forest trees break into flowers wherever these are necessary to relieve the greens.

ROSITA FORBES, 1949

Grenada is a thing of beauty and a joy forever. This reminds me of the old saying: 'See Naples and die.' But . . . I say: 'You may see Naples and die, but see Grenada and LIVE!'

F.M. COARD, 1970

By itself, Grenada's distance from the USSR, and its small size, would mean that we would figure in a very minute way in the USSR's global relationships. Our revolution has to be viewed as a worldwide process with its original roots in the Great October Revolution. For Grenada to assume a position of increasingly greater importance, we have to be seen as influencing at least regional events. We have to establish ourselves as the authority on events in at least the English-speaking Caribbean, and be the sponsor of revolutionary activity and progressive developments in this region at least . . . meeting with the progressive and revolutionary parties in the region is therefore critical to the development of closer relations with the USSR . . . We must ensure though that we become the principal point of access to the USSR for all these groups even to the point of having our Embassy serve as their representative while in USSR . . . To the extent that we can take credit for bringing any other country into the progressive fold, our prestige and influence would be greatly enhanced.

W. RICHARD JACOBS, A report from the
Grenadian Ambassador to the USSR, 1983

In that same harbour of Grenada

In 1869 the ship in which the vicar of an English village church, a past professor of modern history at Cambridge, a celebrated novelist and the recently appointed Canon of Chester (all one and the same man) were travelling to spend a long-anticipated vacation in Trinidad called briefly at St George's:

. . . We did not enter the harbour: but lay close off its gateway in safe deep water; fired our gun, and waited for the swarm of negro boats, which began to splash out to us through the darkness, the jabbering of their crews heard long before the flash of their oars was seen.

Most weird and fantastic are these nightly visits to West Indian harbours. Above, the black mountain-depths, with their canopy of cloud, bright white against the purple night, hung with keen stars . . . Below, a line of bright mist over a swamp, with coco-palms standing up through it, dark, and yet glistering in the moon. A light here and there in a house: another here and there in a vessel unseen in the dark. The echo of the gun from hill to hill. Wild voices from shore and sea. The snorting of the steamer, the rattling of the chain through the hawse-hole; and on deck, and under the quarter, strange gleams of red light amid pitchy darkness, from engines, galley fires, lanthorns; and black folk and white folk flitting restlessly across them.

The strangest show: 'like a thing in a play', says every one when they see it for the first time. And when at the gun-fire one tumbles out of one's berth, and up on deck, to see the new island, one has need to rub one's eyes, and pinch oneself . . . It is always worth the trouble, meanwhile, to tumble up on deck, not merely for the show, but for the episodes of West Indian life and manners . . . One such I witnessed in that same harbour of Grenada, not easily to be forgotten.

A tall and very handsome middle-aged brown woman, in a limp print gown and a gorgeous turban, stood at the gangway in a glare of light, which made her look like some splendid witch by a Walpurgis night-fire. 'Tell your boatman to go round to the other side', quoth the officer in charge.

'Fanqua! (François) You go round oder side of de ship!'

Fanqua, who seemed to be her son, being sleepy, tipsy, stupid, or lazy, did not stir.

'Fanqua! You hear what de officer say? You go round.'

No move.

'Fanqua! You not ashamed of yourself? You not hear de officer say he turn a steam-pipe over you?'

No move.

'Fanqua!' (authoritative).

'Fanqua!' (indignant).

'Fanqua!' (argumentative).

'Fanqua!' (astonished).

'Fanqua!' (majestic).

'Fanqua!' (confidentially alluring).

'Fanqua!' (regretful).

And so on, through every conceivable tone of expression.

But Fanqua did not move; and the officer and bystanders laughed.

She summoned all her talents, and uttered one last 'Fanqua!' which was a triumph of art.

Shame and surprise were blended in her voice with tenderness and pity, and they again with meek despair.

To have been betrayed, disgraced, and so unexpectedly, by one she loved, and must love still, in spite of this, his fearful fall! – it was more than heart could bear. Breathing his name but that once more, she stood a moment, like a queen of tragedy, one long arm drawing her garments round her, the other out-stretched as if to cast off – had she the heart to do it – the rebel; and then stalked away into the darkness of the paddle-boxes – for ever and a day to brood speechless over her great sorrow? Not in the least. To begin chattering away to her acquaintances, as if no Fanqua existed in the world.

It was a piece of admirable play-acting; and was meant to be. She had been conscious all the while that she was an object of attention – possibly of admiration – to a group of men; and she knew what was right to be done and said under the circumstances, and did it perfectly, even to the smallest change of voice. She was doubtless quite sincere the whole time, and felt everything which her voice expressed; but she felt it, because it was proper to feel it; and deceived herself probably more than she deceived any one about her.

CHARLES KINGSLEY, 1871

Not too many Englishmen ever looked back on their stay in Grenada with such aversion as did the young attorney William Hickey, following the visit he made while looking for a position in the West Indies in 1775. One who undoubtedly did, however, was Lieutenant-General Edward Mathew, who left the island in 1789 after six years as governor.

As the son and grandson of men who, as well as having been generals, had both served as Governor-General of the Leeward Islands, Mathew had excellent credentials for such a post, something which had been recognized when he was offered the appointment by King George III. Prior to this he had enjoyed a distinguished military career, beginning with his being made first equerry to the king while serving as a captain in the Coldstream Guards, and ending with his part in the British successes in the early stages of the American

War of Independence. Unfortunately the king had no interest in anything but the power and prestige which Mathew would enjoy as his representative in Grenada, and omitted to make any arrangement for payment of an appropriate salary. This was something unknown to the new governor, who once he had taken up the post drew freely for his pay and expenses on the local treasury.

In 1792, after his return to England and when three years into what he must have considered his well-earned retirement, he was presented by the British Treasury with a bill for the entire amount he had drawn – a sum which came in the terms of the day to the enormous figure of over £11,000. An appeal was made to the man who had sent him to Grenada, but periodic bouts of insanity (brought on by the then undiagnosed kidney disorder called porphyria) also seem to have affected the king's memory, and the retired governor's protestations proved totally unavailing.

As Mathew refused to pay for the remainder of his life, the bill accrued compounded interest and his heirs inherited a debt of some £24,000. When paid just after his death in 1805 this ruined his estate. From then on, for an entire family, mention of the name Grenada – no doubt like that of George – could have been little but anathema.

6 St Vincent

'A peaceful, soothing retreat'

The view of the town and surrounding country is thought by many to be the most beautiful thing in the Antilles; it is indeed a delightful prospect . . . Kingstown lies in a long and narrow line upon the edge of the water; on the eastern end is a substantial and somewhat handsome edifice containing two spacious apartments, wherein the council and Assembly debate in the morning, and the ladies and gentlemen dance in the evening . . . In the background a grand amphitheatre of mountains embraces the town, and there was a verdancy and freshness in the general aspect of the country which certainly exceeded any thing I saw in the West Indies.

. . . The botanical garden is much fallen off from the state in which it once was, but there are still some very fine specimens of the valuable exotics of the East, such as nutmegs, cinnamon and cloves . . . It is a great pity that any establishment of this sort should be allowed to decay; for trees and fruits and flowers are humanizing things, soothing the passions, calling forth only the peaceful energies of the intellect, and attaching mankind to the soil on which they have both grown together; a virtue much wanted in the colonies of America.

HENRY NELSON COLERIDGE, 1826

At waking we were at anchor off St Vincent, an island of volcanic mountains robed in forest from shore to crest ... When I saw it, Kingstown, the principal town, looked pretty well to do, reminding me, strange to say, of towns in Norway, the houses stretching along the shore painted in the same tints of blue or yellow or pink, with the same red-tiled roofs, the trees coming down the hill sides to the water's edge, villas of modest pretensions shining through the foliage, with the patches of cane fields, the equivalent in the landscape of the brilliant Norwegian grass.

JAMES ANTHONY FROUDE, 1888

After a night in a stuffy cabin, it is a sheer delight to step out on to the deck at daybreak, when the cool spice-laden land breeze is still gently ruffling the surface of the deep-blue water. Before you is extended an enchanting panorama. Nestling snugly at the foot of lofty mountains lies Kingstown, its neat and brightly painted houses fringing the symmetrical curve of the bay, with pretty villas beyond, peeping out of luxuriant foliage on the hillside. To the south is Cane Garden Point with its one formidable battery, and opposite to it, a conspicuous rocky hill upon which is perched Fort Charlotte ... These two promontories combine to make Kingstown Bay a sheltered and safe anchorage, where ships may lie in perfect safety except on those rare occasions when the island is visited by a hurricane ...

The Botanic Garden is historic. It is the oldest in the West Indies, and in its groves were nurtured the breadfruit and other plants which Captain Bligh succeeded in carrying from the South Seas in 1793. It is a curious fact that almost every economic plant of importance in the West Indies should have been introduced from outside: the sugar-cane from the East Indies, cocoa from South America, nutmegs from the Moluccas, ginger from tropical Asia, limes from India – the list is a long one.

SIR ALGERNON ASPINALL, 1927

Then there is St Vincent, a mountain mass with forested peaks rising towards the centre. The volcano is often hidden in clouds and from the air the whole island looks mysterious. It is dark and splendid under a storm, with palm trees along the shore and the small capital of Kingstown at the head of the bay.

St Vincent is only eighteen miles by eleven. It grows arrowroot, too homely a product for its tempestuous appearance, but profitable ...

There are few roads in this land of magnificent tropical growth. In the mountains mules take the place of American cars. There is much undeveloped land and for anybody who likes a pioneer flavour to settlement and farming, St Vincent should be ideal.

ROSITA FORBES, 1949

Much to feast the eyes on

The Botanic Garden in Kingstown which Coleridge noted as 'much fallen off' during his visit in 1825 had been laid out sixty years earlier by Doctor George Young, an Army surgeon who was also an expert horticulturist. It was established in order to promote the cultivation and propagation of plants 'of a medicinal and commercial value' in the West Indies. While Young can claim most of the credit for the 'enviable reputation' and 'wide acclaim' the Garden had achieved by 1783, when his curatorship ended, the support he received from the three men who were responsible for governing St Vincent during this period was vital to his success.

In 1765 the British Governor-in-Chief of St Vincent and a number of other islands, General Robert Melville, not only appointed Young in the first place, but also had the land on which the Garden was to be established cleared at his own expense. Between 1773 and 1779, the year in which St Vincent was captured by the French, the curator received a great deal of advice and encouragement from the island's governor, Valentine Morris, who with estates both in England and Antigua was 'a very keen advocate of horticulture and agriculture'. The four years during which the island remained in French hands were perhaps even better for the Garden. The French Commander-in-Chief, General the Marquis de Bouillé, proved to be just as interested in horticulture as Morris had been and in addition was a keen botanist. He and Young developed a friendship and the Garden benefited accordingly from the Marquis's importation of a whole range of new plants.

Doctor Alexander Anderson, who took over from Young some time after the island had been recaptured, was an equally capable curator and it was he who, among many other activities which enhanced the reputation of the Garden, tended the breadfruit and other plants brought there by Captain Bligh in 1793. Unfortunately, after Anderson's death in 1811, the next two curators proved to be far less capable and eight years later the Garden, which up until then had been the responsibility of the British War Department, was handed over on a care and maintenance basis to the local government. This spelt disaster, as Coleridge recognized in 1825, and within another twenty years the Garden was little more than 'a jungle of weeds'.

Efforts to resuscitate it began in 1884, following a general move among the British West Indies to encourage a new interest in agricultural development. A committed, professional agriculturist was appointed as curator in 1890, and fourteen years later the island's first Superintendent of Agriculture took over the running of the Garden as part of his duties.

Today it remains very much as a vistor recorded in the middle of the twentieth century: 'an attractive, alluring, peaceful, soothing retreat where one can retire to admire the many beautiful trees, flowers, lush lawns and colourful plants, or just relax in a tranquil shady atmosphere'. At the same time, as doctors Young and Anderson would undoubtedly have approved, 'for those with deeper botanical interests there is much to feast the eyes on and exercise the intellect'.

Valentine Morris, one of the three men who assisted in establishing the Garden, was another governor – like Edward Mathew in Grenada – who had cause to curse the name of the island he had administered once he had left it, and to execrate the parsimony and bloody-mindedness of the British Treasury for the rest of his life.

He took up the post of Lieutenant-Governor of St Vincent in 1773, under a Governor-in-Chief – based in Grenada – of what were then termed the Southern Caribbee Islands. His troubles began three years later when, because the colonists had asked for an administration independent of Grenada, he was appointed Governor, Captain-General, Commander-in-Chief and Vice-Admiral of the island. From then on his salary, doubled from that he had received as a mere Lieutenant-Governor, together with his contingent account, became charges on the St Vincent treasury, but to his chagrin he found the legislature unwilling to pay the former or to contribute to the latter. To decide to waive his salary was an action which, as a man with substantial private means, he could well afford to take; but to leave himself with no proper means of recovering legitimate expenses incurred in his administration of the colony, in order not to offend the legislature, was a gross mistake he would live long to regret.

Over the next three years, in trying to govern an island inhabited by disgruntled planters who objected to his plans to encourage new settlers by disposing of Crown lands, to deal fairly with a large and resentful Carib population, to cope with the problems posed by large numbers of runaway slaves, and to prepare some sort of defence against a prospective French invasion, he was obliged to incur considerable debts covered by bills on the British Treasury. All might have been well had the French not been able to capture the island without a fight in June 1779, or if the Treasury had been willing to honour the bills. As it was, when Morris left for Antigua in February 1780 an application had already been made by one of his creditors for his committal to gaol for the non-payment of one such bill, and further claims pursued him when he returned to England later in the year.

In April 1782, unable to extract from the Treasury any of the money owed to him as salary or any recompense for debts incurred in his administration of St Vincent, he was sent to King's Bench Prison, a debtors' gaol, for a debt of over £4500 owed to a woman on the island 'on accounts of several bills, drawn officially on the Lords of the Treasury'. Eighteen months afterwards his wife, driven insane by his treatment, was sent to a mental asylum, where she spent the rest of her life. Morris himself was kept in prison until 1787, and released only after his debts had been cleared through the sale of his English properties at a knock-down price, and through the sequestration of his estates in Antigua. He died a poor and broken man less than two years later at the age of 62, and five years before the Treasury eventually reimbursed his estate with £5000.

As the English historian and divine William Coxe wrote in a book he published a few years after Morris had died, 'from his life we at least may draw this salutary instruction; that there is no error more fatal to human happiness than to be confident that, in the hour of misfortune, we shall receive protection from the justice, or relief from the gratitude of the world'.

7 St Lucia

'The Helen of the West Indies'

This morning att 9 wee saw land, and about 10 we came up with it, it beeing the Illand of St Lucca; this Illand wose inhabited by our Inglish, but they ware cut ofe by the Indgons and sume ffrench, soe that now thare is noe inhabitant, att this plas wee came to anckor and watered: att this plas our Gennerall and Gennerall Venables went ashore, and wee that war with them had fouling peces with us: heare wee found very braue game of pelicans and other large foules: heare is many Wild cattell and much foule: upon this Illand are many great snakes: heare are many parates: . . . hear is and are many braue harbors and rods about this Illand: in the south side neare the midell of this Illand is a very braue road whare many sayle of shipes may ride in 50 fatham water, or les as you goe nearer the shore . . .

HENRY WHISTLER, 1654

The first approach to this island from the south offers the most striking combination of various kinds of scenery that I have ever seen. Two rocks, which the Gods call Pitons and men Sugar-loaves, rise perpendicularly out of the sea and shoot to a great height in parallel cones, which taper away towards the summit like the famous spires of Coventry. These rocks, which are feathered from the clouds to the waves with evergreen foliage, stand like pillars of Hercules on either side of the entrance into a small but deep and beautiful bay. A pretty little village or plantation appears at the bottom of the cove; the sandy beach stretches like a line of silver round the blue water, and the cane fields form a broad belt of vivid green in the back ground. Behind this the mountains, which run north and south throughout the island, rise in the most fantastic shapes, here cloven into steep-down chasms, there darting into arrowy points, and every where shrouded or swathed, as it were, in wood, which the hand of man will probably never lay low. The clouds, which within the tropics are infallibly attracted by any woody eminences, contribute greatly to the wildness of the scene; sometimes they are so dense as to bury the mountains in darkness; at other times they float transparently like a silken veil; frequently the flaws from the gulleys perforate the vapors and make windows in the smoky mass, and then again the wind and the sun will cause the whole to be drawn upwards majestically like the curtain of a gorgeous theatre.

HENRY NELSON COLERIDGE, 1826

Among all these beautiful islands, St Lucia is, I think, the most beautiful; not indeed on account of the size or form of its central mass, which is surpassed by that of several others, but on account of those two extraordinary mountains at its south-western end, which, while all conical hills in the French islands are called Pitons, bear the name of The Pitons *par excellence*. From most elevated points in the island their twin peaks may be seen jutting up over the other hills, like, according to irreverent English sailors, the tips of a donkey's ears. But, as the steamer runs southward along the shore, these two peaks open out, and you find yourself in deep water close to the base of two obelisks, rather than mountains, which rise sheer out of the sea . . . about a mile from each other. Between them is the loveliest little bay; and behind them green wooded slopes rise toward the rearward mountain of the Souffrière. The whole glitters clear and keen in blazing sunshine: but behind, black depths of cloud and gray sheets of rain shroud all the central highlands in mystery and sadness. Beyond them, without a shore, spreads open sea. But the fantastic grandeur of the place cannot be described in words . . .

CHARLES KINGSLEY, 1871

As to St Lucia itself, if I had not seen Grenada, if I had not known what I was about to see in Dominica, I should have thought it the most exquisite place which nature had ever made, so perfect were the forms of the forest-clothed hills, the glens dividing them and the high mountain ranges in the interior still draped in the white mist of morning. Here and there along the shore there were bright green spots which meant cane fields.

JAMES ANTHONY FROUDE, 1888

A beautiful fantastic shape floats to us through the morning light; first cloudy gold like the horizon, then pearly gray, then varying blue, with growing green lights – Saint Lucia. Most strangely formed of all this volcanic family – everywhere mountainings sharp as broken crystals. Far off the Pitons – twin peaks of the high coast – show softer contours, like two black breasts pointing against the sky . . .

. . . As we enter the harbor of Castries, the lines of the land seem no less exquisitely odd, in spite of their rich verdure, than when viewed afar off: they have a particular pitch of angle . . . Other of these islands show more or less family resemblance: you might readily mistake one silhouette for another as seen at a distance, even after several West Indian journeys. But Saint Lucia at once impresses you by its eccentricity.

LAFCADIO HEARN, 1890

No island in these waters will be approached with greater interest and expectancy than the island of St Lucia. This is not on account of its winsome beauty, although there are many who hold it to be the loveliest spot in this gorgeous crescent. It is not by reason of its size, for it covers an area less than that of the county of Middlesex. It has no natural features to make it remarkable, unless they be certain sulphur springs and the towering rocks known as the Pitons. Yet for centuries little St Lucia was the most important island in the West Indies. As such it looms majestically in the history of these troubled seas . . .

There can hardly be a spot that, for its size, has played a more stirring part in the history of arms or in the chronicles of the British navy and army. There is no dot of land that has been so desperately fought over, so savagely wrangled for, as this too fair island. St Lucia is the Helen of the West Indies, and has been the cause of more blood-letting than was ever provoked by Helen of Troy.

SIR FREDERICK TREVES, 1908

St Lucia . . . is an engaging mixture of France, Britain and America, but she is not actively volcanic in any sense of the word. She has been called the

Helen of the West Indies because of her position in the recurrent wars between France and England, and as Helen she is beautiful, although less superbly mountained than St Vincent. During three centuries she changed hands fourteen times and caused more bloodshed than any other island of her size in the world. Within sight of Martinique and still closely related by religion, fashion, speech and smuggling, she is more Latin than Anglo-West-Indian.

ROSITA FORBES, 1949

The plume hackle of St Lucia

The possession of St Lucia was something over which Britain and France fought repeatedly from the middle of the seventeenth century until 1814, when the status of the island as a British colony was finally established. A great deal of its attraction lay in Castries Harbour, the deep and sheltered bay on the north-west coast which was the largest and best of Henry Whistler's 'manie braue harbors'. Protected by batteries situated on the Vigie peninsula to the north, and a fortress on Morne Fortune to the south, it was perhaps the finest and most secure harbour anywhere in the eastern Caribbean.

In December 1778, as part of the conflict between Britain and France brought about by the latter's support of the American colonists in the War of Independence, the third successful British invasion of the island took place. Landing in a smaller bay to the south of Morne Fortune the fortress was taken without too much trouble, but the invading force then had to prepare to repel a massive French counter-attack from the north by occupying and defending the Vigie peninsula. A reserve brigade of about 1500 men of the Fifth Regiment of Foot was all that could be spared to take up this forward position, and it was the men of this regiment who on 18 December fought an action which is still recalled in the headgear worn by one unit of the British Army today.

Early that morning over 3000 freshly-landed French troops were sent into action, advancing on to the peninsula in columns screened by a line of infantrymen, expecting to encounter and overwhelm the traditional 'thin red line' of British defenders. Instead they came under fire from several directions from men who had been positioned in such a way, using the contours of a low hill to provide them with cover, that they dominated the battleground. Assisted by a few well-placed guns which quickly managed to silence a bombardment begun by the enemy artillery, the defenders eventually brought the French advance to a halt just as their own ammunition was about to run out. During the lull which followed the men of the Fifth were ordered to fix bayonets in preparation for a last-ditch stand, and once the French had re-organized themselves their advance continued.

That this was with considerably less resolve than earlier was immediately apparent, and when the British guns fired off their last remaining rounds the leading troops were seen to waver. The order was then given for the defending infantrymen to fire off their last shots before making a bayonet charge. This fusilade was superbly timed and so effective that the French stopped, turned, and began to retreat. No bayonet work was needed, the battle was over, and the enemy was allowed to withdraw in an orderly fashion. Once the field was clear the men of the Fifth came down from their positions, plucked the white feather plumes from the caps of the enemy dead and injured left behind, and stuck them in their own caps in triumph. From among the 400 dead and over 1000 wounded found lying on the peninsula, enough of these plumes were obtained to provide one for every man in the regiment, which had lost no more than ten killed and 130 wounded.

The white plume was then worn by the Fifth, or Northumberland, Regiment of Foot, instead of the red and white tuft worn by the other regiments of the line, for the next fifty years until new regulations in 1829 authorized it to be worn by all infantry regiments other than the Rifles and Light Infantry. This caused so much dismay to the Fifth that their Colonel complained to the Commander-in-Chief and obtained sanction for the regiment to wear a feather plume, half red, half white, red uppermost 'as a peculiar honour whereby its former services will still be commemorated'. The plume, instead of being a swan's feather, was to be a hackle, 'due to the difficulty of dyeing a swan's feather'. This distinction was retained by the Fifth – which became the Northumberland Fusiliers in 1881 and the Royal Northumberland Fusiliers in 1935 – until 1968 when the regiment was amalgamated with three others to form the Royal Regiment of Fusiliers, by whose officers and men it is still worn today.

As is only to be expected, one of the many battle honours emblazoned on the colours of the Royal Regiment of Fusiliers is 'St Lucia 1778'.

Parsimonious habits in private life

The book that Henry Nelson Coleridge, a nephew of the poet Samuel Taylor Coleridge, wrote about his six-month sojourn in the West Indies in 1825 has provided other writers (as will be all too apparent in this work) with a *valuable source of information and a ready supply of apt quotations ever since it was published in the following year. The author's purpose in visiting the Caribbean was to act as the private secretary to another of the poet's nephews, William Hart Coleridge, recently consecrated as the first Bishop of Barbados, during the initial tour of a diocese which covered the whole of the eastern Caribbean from Trinidad to the Virgin Islands.*

Although after this first tour the bishop based himself in Barbados, the size of his diocese was such that he could never remain there for very long. Given the prevailing type and condition of the transport and accommodation facilities available throughout the region in the first half of the nineteenth century, constant travelling eventually ruined his health and he was forced to resign in 1841. The sort of treatment he received in St Lucia, during a visit he made there in the middle of his period as head of the Anglican Church in the eastern half of the Caribbean, can have done little to aid his general well-being, or to have reinforced any views he may have held about the charitableness of his fellow men, and probably speeded the date of his resignation:

In 1832 the Bishop of the diocese, being on a tour among the islands, arrived at Castries, and immediately received a polite invitation from General Farquharson (the Governor in question). The General was remarkable for his parsimonious habits in private life, and having left his family in England, the establishment at Government House was conducted on quasi-bachelor principles. He had made no preparation for the reception of the Bishop, except in the eating line; and indeed, had he been disposed to do so, he must have had recourse to the officers of the garrison; for, his accommodation, especially in the way of bedding, was very scanty. Perceiving after dinner that the Bishop and his suite showed no inclination to encounter the fatigue of a ride to Castries during a dark night, the wily General, being resolved to dislodge them from their snug position, had recourse to a *ruse de guerre.* 'My Lord', said he, 'perhaps this is the first time you have visited Government House: come with me and I'll show you the apartments. I suppose your Lordship has heard of the insalubrity of the place: every room in the house has already witnessed the death of some Governor; but none of them has had the honour of killing a Bishop: so, My Lord, you have only to make your selection: I leave you to the *embarras de choix.*' The good Bishop was so mightily shocked that he thereupon ordered his horse to be brought round and descended to Castries.

HENRY H. BREEN, 1844

Achilles attacks Castries

The harbour of Castries, which had witnessed so much toing and froing of warships and been fought over so many times up until 1814, remained a safe and peaceful place thereafter right up until the middle of the Second World War. Then, on the night of 10 March 1942, two ships berthed in the harbour – the Canadian passenger vessel Lady Nelson *and the British freighter* Umtata – *were each hit and sunk by a torpedo.*

These were fired from within the harbour by the U161, a German submarine under the command of Kapitanleutnant Albrecht Achilles, a resourceful captain, a skilful navigator and a man who, as an ex-Merchant Marine officer, knew the Caribbean well. Having left her base at Lorient in January the U161 had already sunk two ships off Port of Spain, another close to Martinique, and a fourth to the west of St Vincent.

Having arrived off Castries Harbour before nightfall and studied the entrance through his periscope, Achilles decided an attack on the ships he could see inside was feasible and surfaced at ten o'clock in order to carry it out. The entrance is narrow, and as no one ashore considered that vessels inside could be in any danger all the dockside and inner navigation lights had been left on. Together with the light of a waning moon this made the U-boat's passage into the harbour relatively easy, and shortly before midnight Achilles was in a position to begin his attack.

The U161 had been sighted on the way in by the solitary look-out posted at the harbour entrance but, because of a faulty telephone connection, he had been unable to raise the alarm. His period of desperation and running around in circles ended when the first torpedo struck the stern of the Lady Nelson *and exploded. A few minutes later his useless vigil ended with a second shattering explosion as the* Umtata *was hit.*

Almost before the colossal reverberations from the surrounding hills had died away the U-boat had been turned around in its own length, and Achilles was on his way out of the harbour. He left behind two ships on fire and rapidly settling on to the seabed, most of the buildings in Castries devoid of windows, and a dazed and deafened populace in a state of panic. Some desultory machine-gun fire opened up from the Vigie peninsula as the submarine, now at full speed, made for the harbour mouth, but stopped soon after it had begun. No damage was sustained, and well before one o'clock in the morning the U161 was well clear of the land and out of sight, racing into the Caribbean to avoid the search by anti-submarine aircraft which was bound to begin at daylight.

Three days later Achilles torpedoed another Canadian vessel about 200 nautical miles west of Guadeloupe, and the day after, having now expended all his torpedoes, sank by gunfire a US lighthouse tender he came across in the Caribbean entrance to the Mona Passage between Hispaniola and Puerto Rico. The U161 then returned to her base in France, having completed what was later recognized as having been the most successful Caribbean U-boat patrol of the war. Achilles took her out on five more such patrols but never with the same sweeping success. The end came in September 1943 when, after being found on the surface off the coast of Brazil, the U161 was depth-charged by a US aircraft. It is not known what damage was inflicted, but having dived nothing of Achilles, his crew or the submarine was ever seen again.

The Lady Nelson and the Umtata were more fortunate, as both were quickly patched and refloated. The former, before being towed to Nova Scotia for proper repairs and conversion into a hospital ship, off-loaded the four-inch gun with which she had been fitted only a few weeks earlier. Given to the St Lucia Police Force to act as the bolt in the stable door by being mounted at the harbour mouth, it remainded there for the rest of the war without ever firing a shot in anger or otherwise.

The economist and the poet

St Lucia has the unique distinction among all the Caribbean islands, large or small, of having produced two Nobel laureates. This is made all the more remarkable by the fact that the two men concerned at birth formed part of a population which probably numbered less than 100,000, both received their secondary education at the same small school in Castries, both spent many years of their manhood as colonial subjects, and neither was the recipient of the somewhat devalued prize for peace.

William Arthur Lewis, who preferred to be known by his middle name, was born in 1915. After winning one of the very few and highly prized island scholarships in 1933 he left for England to obtain a degree in business management, economics and accountancy at the London School of Economics. His subsequent university education culminated with the award of a PhD in industrial economics in 1940, after which he worked as a civil servant in London for the next seven years. This was followed by a year as Reader in Colonial Economics at the University of London before, in 1948 at the age of 33, he became Professor of Political Economy at Manchester University. During the eleven years he held this chair he became a highly respected and much sought-after consultant on the economic affairs of developing countries, and wrote the book for which today he is best remembered, The Theory of Economic Growth. This was probably the most important of the twelve books he wrote in all and, when published in 1955, was soon hailed as worthy of being classified along with the works of Adam Smith and John Stuart Mill.

In 1959 he was caught up in the euphoria felt throughout the Caribbean and among many West Indian expatriates concerning the Federation of the West Indies, which had been created a year earlier, and accepted the position of Principal of the University College of the West Indies in Jamaica, with the primary task of transforming it into a fully-fledged university.

This he achieved in 1962 when he became the first Vice-Chancellor of the University of the West Indies, but only at considerable cost to his health and equilibrium. His intellectual standing, metropolitan outlook, and lofty approach towards such matters as local politics, race and class issues, and inter-island rivalries led to opposition from among the student body and faculty alike. In 1963 he was knighted for his efforts, but at much the same time he resigned in order to accept a chair in Economic and Political Affairs at Princeton University.

Lewis remained at Princeton for the rest of his academic career, becoming Professor of Political Economy from 1968 until he retired in 1983. In the early 1970s he obtained a three-year leave of absence in order to set up the Caribbean Development Bank in Barbados. In 1978 he was awarded the Nobel Prize for Economics jointly with Professor Theodore Schultz of the University of Chicago, becoming the first black recipient of any Nobel Prize other than that for peace. After his retirement he lived in Barbados where, at the age of 76, he died a year before it was announced that a fellow-Saint Lucian had also won a Nobel Prize.

Derek Alton Walcott was born in 1930. After schooling in St Lucia he went on to the University College of the West Indies in Jamaica where later, having established a reputation as a poet, he taught for several years. In 1959 he moved to Trinidad and, having founded what was soon to become the highly respected Trinidad Theatre Workshop, launched into a career as a poet, playwright and theatre director. His work achieved considerable recognition both within the Caribbean and outside the region during the next decade and a half, but in 1976 he ended his connection with the Theatre Workshop in order to pursue an academic career in the United States. From 1981 he taught at Boston University, eventually filling the chair of Professor of Poetry. His achievements as a poet with an international reputation were recognized by the award of the Nobel Prize for Literature in 1992.

As the first English-speaking West Indian to be given this prize (the French poet Alexis Saint-Léger Léger, who was born in Guadeloupe and wrote under *the name Saint-John Perse, won it in 1960) Walcott was understandably de-lighted when informed of the award. It is not known how Sir Arthur Lewis felt or what he said on hearing of his prize in 1978, but one may be sure that he would have been more than delighted with such a succinct expression of an eco-nomic truth as that expressed by his fellow countryman in 1992: 'I'm very happy and I'm rich!'*

8 Martinique

'Le Pays des Revenants'

... we came faier in sight of Martaineneco, and att 6 att night we came clos abord the shore, it is very high Land and full of mountains. This Illand is inhabited with Ingons and french: they liue very comfortably together, and doue mary the one the other very often.

HENRY WHISTLER, 1655

He who first gave to Martinique its poetical name, Le Pays des Revenants, thought of his wonderful island only as 'The Country of Comers-back', where Nature's unspeakable spell bewitches wandering souls like the caress of a Circe – never as the Land of Ghosts. Yet either translation of the name holds equal truth: a land of ghosts it is, this marvellous Martinique! Almost every plantation has its familiar spirits – its phantoms: some may be unknown beyond the particular district in which fancy first gave them being; but some belong to popular song and story – to the imaginative life of the whole people. Almost every promontory and peak, every village and valley along the coast, has its special folk-lore, its particular tradition.

LAFCADIO HEARN, 1890

67

Perhaps the most interesting island in the most attractive archipelago of all this world is that in which the French ardour of soul is comingled in the highest degree with the native blood of the tropics. Martinique is about thirty miles due south across the blue Caribbean waters from Dominica. Columbus made its discovery on his last voyage in 1502, but if he tried to fix a saint's name upon it, it did not stick. The native Caribs called it Madiana, or, some say, Matinina, and whichever it was the present name is a French corruption of it.

AMOS KIDDER FISKE, 1899

. . . Fort de France has been termed a 'ville des fonctionnaires'. In it reside the Governor, the Government officials, garrison, consuls, and merchants. It contains a cathedral, which though quite modern and not very interesting, presents a striking spectacle on Sundays, when the people, arrayed in the most brilliant costumes, attend high mass. The native women of Martinique are of a type quite distinct from the natives of other West Indian Islands, and many, with their mixture of Latin, Negro, and Carib blood, of quite extraordinary beauty. From the mountain-side at the back of the town the Rivière Madame is conducted . . . through the principal streets, by means of wide ditches, which 'irrigate' the roadways, and no doubt materially help to maintain the reputation for healthiness which the place possesses . . .

W.B.F., *In the West Indies*, 1905

. . . Fort de France on Martinique is sadly in need of an efficient street-cleaning department. The towns on the islands under British administration may be drab and dreary looking without being uncleanly or unsanitary, but the condition in Fort de France creates apprehension. No stranger wants to eat in its hotels, or drink the city water, or even sit on the park benches. He is continually washing his hands, blowing his nose, and holding a handkerchief before his mouth . . .

JOHN C. VAN DYKE, 1932

Une vraie femme

Although today Lafcadio Hearn's remarks about the ghosts of Martinique seem just as innocent and fey as John Van Dyke's comments about Fort-de-France appear gratuitously offensive, if there is one place on the island which it seems ought to harbour a familiar spirit it is the derelict remains of an old plantation house at Les Trois Ilets, on the southern side of Fort-de-France bay.

Marie-Joseph-Rose Tascher de la Pagerie, who was born there in 1763, was the eldest of the three daughters of the dissolute and incompetent owner of the plantation, a Frenchman whose father – an equally shiftless character – had acquired Les Trois Ilets through marriage. At the age of sixteen Rose (the name by which she was known for over half her life) was taken to Paris by her father, and given away in marriage to Alexandre de Beauharnais, a young man who had also been born in Martinique when his father, the self-styled Marquis de Beauharnais, had lived there as the governor of the French West Indian possessions. As the union had been arranged between the Marquis and one of the girl's aunts who was his mistress, and the groom – calling himself the Vicompte de Beauharnais – was already a confirmed libertine and about to become the father of a daughter by one of his conquests, the marriage was hardly one which could be said to have been made in heaven.

And so it turned out for Rose who, although she gave birth to a son, Eugene, in 1781 and a daughter, Hortense, two years later, saw very little of a husband who preferred to divide his time between his duties as an army officer and the company of other women. They separated amid great animosity after six years and in 1788, after entering into a number of illicit liaisons of her own, Rose returned to Martinique. During the two years she remained with her family at Les Trois Ilets the fall of the Bastille in Paris, and the euphoria which accompanied the beginning of the French Revolution, particularly concerning the 'Rights of Man' and proposals about the abolition of slavery, brought about radical changes in the island's society. Towards the end of 1790, no longer able to enjoy the pleasant, slightly scandalous and indulgent position she had created for herself in Martiniquoise society, and under the threat of an imminent uprising among the slave population, she returned to France. She was never to see Martinique again.

Rose arrived in Paris to find her errant husband a celebrity, an elected member of the National Assembly who was about to become its president. In spite of being separated from him, bearing his name gave her an entry into the new Parisian society, and Citoyenne Beauharnais lost no time in assimilating its revolutionary ideology and jargon.

All was well until towards the end of 1793, when the period now known as the Great Terror began, and anyone connected to the nobility found themselves under suspicion of disloyalty to the Revolution. Beauharnais, whether a genuine aristocrat or not, failed to make the grade as an Army commander in the war which was then being waged with other European countries and was arrested in April of the following year. Rose, to her credit, attempted to intercede with the Committee of Public Safety on his behalf, and ended up by being arrested herself.

The thirty-one-year-old Citizeness Beauharnais remained in prison until after the Great Terror ended in July, a week too late to save her estranged husband from the guillotine. Once released the far from grieving widow had little trouble in arousing pity as an innocent victim of the Revolution, and in less than a year she had become the mistress of Paul Barras, one of the new Revolutionary leaders who had acted to end the Terror. It was Barras who, in October 1795, was responsible for having the almost unknown Corsican officer, Napoleon Bonaparte, appointed as commander-in-chief of the Army of the Interior and, within the same month, introducing Rose to Napoleon.

As well as being an inspired military leader, the twenty-six-year-old Bonaparte was also, as he later recorded, 'not insensible to women's charms'. Within a few days of making the introduction Barras had lost his mistress and Napoleon had, in a letter he sent to Rose after their first night together, given her the name she was to bear for the rest of her life: 'Sweet and incomparable Josephine, I draw from your lips, from your heart, a flame which consumes me . . . A thousand kisses, but do not give me any for they burn my blood.'

Less than six months later they were married in a civil ceremony at which both falsified their ages, Josephine reducing hers by four years and Napoleon increasing his by two. Two days later the groom departed to take command of the army in Italy, and to begin the long series of military victories which in 1799 led to his becoming – as the first of three consuls – the virtual ruler of France. Five years later the First Republic came to an end when he and Josephine, in an impressive ceremony performed by the Pope in Notre Dame Cathedral, were crowned as the French Emperor and Empress. In her youthful-looking and still bewitchingly attractive early middle age, and twenty-five years after her first arrival in the city, the failed sugar-planter's daughter from Martinique was at the summit of Parisian society.

As with all such fairy tales it was all too good to last. In order to satisfy his pride and to ensure the foundation of a Napoleonic dynasty, the Emperor needed a son, and this was something which his Empress – possibly because of complications arising from an abortion carried out during the time she spent in Martinique after separating from her first husband – was unable to provide. In 1809, under pressure from the Bonaparte family and for 'reasons of state', they were divorced in order that Napoleon might marry Marie Louise, the daughter of the Emperor of Austria.

Josephine retired to the Château de Malmaison about six miles from Paris, where she then spent the remainder of her life as the Empress Dowager. In the grounds she built up and maintained a private zoo which contained animals and birds from as far away as Australia, and cultivated extensive nurseries with a huge variety of plants, including over two hundred which had never been grown before in France. It was as if amid outlandish foliage, exotic blooms, powerful scents, alien animal cries and weird bird calls she was attempting to recapture her childhood, and re-create something of the lovely island – rendered magical by time – which she had left so many years earlier.

After having caught a severe chill while out riding she died in May 1814, the same month in which Napoleon was forced into his brief exile on Elba. There is evidence, both in his own writings and in those of others who knew him well, that he always regretted his divorce and, although he was fond of Marie Louise, he had always loved Josephine more. To him, as he recorded much later while in exile on St Helena, she was une vraie femme – a real woman – and one he would never have left had she been able to bear his child.

Noxious reptiles

In 1809 Martinique was invaded and captured by a British force composed of a number of regiments, including the 23rd Foot, better known as the Royal Welch Fusiliers. During the fighting one of this regiment's officers was wounded in the arm – receiving an injury which led to his being not only hospitalized but subjected to an unusual ordeal:

. . . Preparations were now made to convert the sugar plantation, into which I had been carried when first wounded, into a regular military hospital, and I was borne out on some Indian corn straw, and laid in a small hut, near the house. The French Lady, to whom the plantation belonged, treated me with great kindness, and used frequently to send or bring me broths and fruit. She sent one of her Negroes to attend me in the little hut, where I had been deposited. It was exceedingly low, and thatched with the bruised stalk of the sugar-cane, after the juice had been extracted. My removal into this place, had caused me a good deal of pain, and of nervous irritability. My black attendant had left me to go to his dinner. I was lying on my back quite incapable of moving, when I saw just above me, hanging by one or two of its claws, a large Tarantula. In any other situation this creature would have been an object of interest & curiosity, but under the influence of severe pain, my imagination passed quickly in review, all I had ever read of its venom, and the deadly effects of its bite, and that I was quite at its mercy, should it let go its hold, and drop upon me. I watched the creature, with a degree of intensity that worked my whole frame into a state of fever, and my fancy had magnified it into ten times more than its reality. This state of things lasted perhaps a quarter of an hour, and I really began to believe that my senses were giving way, when in came my sable servant. I had just strength left, to shew him what had produced upon me an effect, which had evidently caused his surprise, when he displayed his white teeth in a most extensive grin, and taking off his head, a little blue cloth cap that he wore, with a bamboo that lay on the floor he poked the Tarantula into it, and bore it away. I afterwards had it preserved very carefully in a wide mouthed phial, filled with white rum and hermetically sealed. It had not been in the least injured, and when I grew stronger and the remembrance of its effects upon me had subsided, I used frequently to look at it, in the sun and admire it exceedingly. The hair with which its claws were covered exhibited, purple, green and red in their brightest hues, and never was a noxious reptile clad in such dazzling apparel. I took it with me when we returned to America, and made a present of it, to a Medical Gentleman who was forming a cabinet of natural History in Halifax, where it was considered one of the best specimens that had ever been seen.

CAPTAIN THOMAS HENRY BROWNE, 1809
(*see* BUCKLEY, 1987)

A visitor to the island some eighty years after this encounter seems to have been even more disturbed by the mere prospect of coming across another, albeit this time genuinely reptilian, sample of Martinique's less pleasant wildlife:

... the fer-de-lance reigns absolute king over the mountains and the ravines; he is lord of the forest and the solitudes by day, and by night be extends his dominion over the public roads, the familiar paths, the parks, and pleasure resorts. People must remain at home after dark, unless they dwell in the city itself: if you happen to be out visiting after sunset, only a mile from town, your friends will caution you anxiously not to follow the boulevard as you go back, and to keep as closely as possible to the very centre of the path. Even in the brightest noon you cannot venture to enter the woods without an experienced escort; you cannot trust your eyes to detect danger: at any moment a seeming branch, a knot of lianas, a pink or gray root, a clump of pendant yellow fruit, may suddenly take life, writhe, stretch, spring, strike ... Then you will need aid indeed, and most quickly; for within the span of a few heart-beats the wounded flesh chills, tumefies, softens. Soon it changes color, and begins to spot violaceously; while an icy coldness creeps through all the blood. If the panseur or physician arrives in time, and no vein has been pierced, there is hope; but it more often happens that the blow is received directly on a vein of the foot or ankle, in which case nothing can save the victim. Even when life is saved the danger is not over. Necrosis of the tissues is likely to set in: the flesh corrupts, falls from the bone sometimes in tatters; and the colors of its putrefaction simulate the hues of vegetable decay – the ghastly grays and pinks and yellows of trunks rotting down into the dark soil which gave them birth. The human victim moulders as the trees moulder – crumbles and dissolves as crumbles the substance of the dead palms and balatas: the Death-of-the-Woods is upon him . . .

LAFCADIO HEARN, 1890

9 Dominica

'This romantic spot of earth'

... this Iland ... is ... so Mountainous (certaine in the places where we came neere the Sea-coasts) that the Vallies may better be called Pits than Plaines, and withall so unpassably wooddie, that it is marvailous how those naked souls can be able to pull themselves through them, without renting their naturall cloathes. Some speake of more easie passages in the Inland of the Iland, which make it probable that they leave those skirts and edges of their Countrie thus of purpose for a wall of defence. These Hils are apparelled with very goodly greene Trees, of many sorts ...

GEORGE CLIFFORD,
*A Briefe Relation of the Severall Voyages
of George, the Earl of Cumberland,* 1598

In the evening in Dominica, is the most amazingly glorious scenery that can possibly be imagined; the heavens bespangled with innumerable stars, which the dense climate of Europe hides from mortal sight, or which are but barely to be distinguished, are in this island open to full view; and the lovers of astronomy have there an opportunity to make new discoveries in that science.

In the evenings, although the air is cool, yet it is not accompanied by those noxious vapours, so remarkable for their dangerous effects in some parts of the West Indies; so that it is not uncommon for people in this Island to sit whole evenings in the open air, without any detriment to their healths.

THOMAS ATWOOD, 1791

Dominica is watered by a vast number of little streams which flow (as we were told) from a fathomless lake embosomed in the mountains, at a high level above the sea. It is in consequence a moist island, and of luxuriant fertility; and nine-tenths of the soil, productive as it is by nature, are wholly unoccupied – in a state of absolute wildness . . . One cannot approach this romantic spot of earth, without feeling a kind of fascination. A late writer describes it as a land of 'mists and torrents and rainbows', and such it truly is. The mountains, peaked and picturesque as they are, and some of them very lofty – the highest five thousand six hundred feet above the level of the sea – are mantled to their very tops with luxuriant vegetation; and through the deep ravines and luxuriant dells which divide them, many a sudden gust of wind assails the mariner, and many a mountain stream finds its way into the ocean.

JOSEPH JOHN GURNEY, 1840

To my mind, Dominica, as seen from the sea, is by far the most picturesque of all these islands. Indeed, it would be difficult to beat it either in colour or grouping. It fills one with an ardent desire to be off and rambling among those green mountains – as if one could ramble through such wild, bush country, or ramble at all with the thermometer at 85. But when one has only to think of such things without any idea of doing them, neither the bushes nor the thermometer are considered.

One is landed at Dominica on a beach. If the water be quiet, one gets out dry shod by means of a strong jump; if the surf be high, one wades through it; if it be very high, one is of course upset . . .

And then, the perils of the surf being passed, one walks into the town of Roseau. It is impossible to conceive a more distressing sight. Every house is in a state of decadence. There are no shops that can properly be so called; the people wander about chattering, idle and listless; the streets are covered with thick, rank grass; there is no sign either of money made or of money making. Everything seems to speak of desolation, apathy, and ruin. There is nothing, even in Jamaica, so sad to look at as the town of Roseau.

ANTHONY TROLLOPE, 1859

We are steaming on Dominica, the loftiest of the Lesser Antilles. While the silhouette is yet all violet in distance, nothing more solemnly beautiful can well be imagined: a vast cathedral shape, whose spires are mountain peaks, towering in the horizon, sheer up from the sea.

We stay at Roseau only long enough to land the mails, and wonder at the loveliness of the island. A beautifully wrinkled mass of green and blue and gray; a strangely abrupt peaking and heaping of the land. Behind the green heights loom the blues; behind these the grays – all pinnacled against the sky-glow – thrusting up through gaps or behind promontories. Indescribably exquisite the foldings and hollowings of the emerald coast. In glen and vale the color of canefields shines like a pooling of fluid bronze, as if the luminous essence of the hill tints had been dripping down and clarifying there. Far to our left, a bright green spur pierces into the now turquoise sea; and beyond it, a beautiful mountain form, blue and curved like a hip, slopes seaward, showing lighted wrinkles here and there, of green. And from the foreground, against the blue of the softly outlined shape, cocoapalms are curving, all sharp and shining in the sun.

LAFCADIO HEARN, 1890

There is a special fascination about islands, and I doubt that there are, anywhere in the world, more lovely ones than those which, like a necklace of gigantic jewels, are strung across the throat of the Caribbean Sea.

Dominica is certainly the most beautiful of them all. Rising sheer out of the greatest depths of a sea that is usually of sapphire blue or profoundest ultramarine, its verdant valleys and lofty mountains rise higher and higher until the pale-green peaks pierce the fleecy clouds that hover over them.

Through the centre of each valley rushes and tumbles a mountain stream in a series of little cascades falling into deep bamboo-shaded pools. Where the streamlet enters the sea there is always a small bay, where a crescent of gleaming white sand separates the vivid blue of the water from the green and golden vegetation on the shore. In nearly every case clusters of little brown huts, thatched with russet cane-straw, nestle under the great pendant leaves of coco-nut palms or in the cool shade of gigantic mango trees. Long dug-out canoes and fishing nets lie on the snow-white strand and indicate that the happy native can get his food from the ocean depths as well as from his fruitful farm.

SIR HESKETH BELL, 1900 (see HESKETH BELL, 1946)

They say, they who know the islands, that Dominica is the most beautiful of all the Lesser Antilles, and in that they say well . . .

It is a worshipful place; 'a tabernacle for the sun'; a shrine of a thousand spires, rising tier above tier, in one exquisite fabric of green, purple and grey. The sea that lies at its feet is blue beyond comparison, a deep gentian blue. The same tint colours the haze that fills the inland gorges, as if the mist were but the blue sea vapourised.

SIR FREDERICK TREVES, 1908

Dominica, the southernmost and largest of the misnamed Leeward Islands, is also entitled to several other superlatives. Most of the West Indies boast themselves the 'Queen of the Antilles', but none with more justice than this tiny Porto Rico isolated between the two principal islands of 'French America'. It is the highest of the Lesser Antilles [and] the wettest, being habitually surrounded by blue-black clouds that pour forth their deluges by night or by day, in or out of season, even when all the sky about it is translucent blue . . .

Roseau, the capital, sits right out on the Caribbean, the mountains climbing directly, without an instant's hesitation, into the sky behind it. They are as sheer beneath water as above it, and the steamer anchors within an easy stone's throw of the wharves.

HARRY A. FRANCK, 1920

My first impression of Dominica was the amazing freshness and viridity, as well as virility, of the country. Everywhere the grass and foliage was of a vivid green colour, and luxurious growth abounded on all sides. This was undoubtedly due to the very frequent showers of rain, which suddenly without rhyme or reason descended from what a few minutes before had been a clear blue sky. But it was not objectionable rain; the shower would come, and a quarter of an hour later the sun would struggle through the passing clouds and all would be bright again. Though it generally left an impression of steaminess in its wake as the moisture which had not run off into the nearest stream (there were said to be 365 rivers, one for every day of the year, in Dominica) started to evaporate in the heat. A sort of Kew Gardens hot-house effect.

SIR REGINALD ST-JOHNSTON, 1936

Tyranny, extortion and vice

To rule some of the West Indian possessions in colonial times the British Government 'frequently', as the late Eric Williams – a man not known for pulling his punches – once observed, 'sent out rubbish as Governors'. Andrew James Cochrane Johnstone, who governed Dominica from 1797 to 1802, well deserves such contemptuous appraisal.

He was born in Scotland in 1767 as Andrew Cochrane, the eighth son of the Earl of Dundonald. At the age of sixteen a commission as an army officer was bought for him and he was packed off to India. In 1791, aged twenty-four, he was back in Scotland where family money and influence soon got him elected to Parliament as the Member for Stirling. Two years later, having married a daughter of James Hope Johnstone, the third Earl of Hopetown, he assumed the name Johnstone. It is not clear just why he did this, but from what is known of the rest of his life it is highly likely that it was done only with the accompaniment of a sizeable cash inducement.

Marriage and his duties as a Member of Parliament failed to retain his interest for very long, and within three years he was back on active service in the army – this time in the West Indies. In 1797 he was promoted to colonel and shortly afterwards offered the governorship of Dominica. He accepted at once. The opportunities it offered for him to make his fortune were too good to miss. His official duties were not onerous and he soon acquired one of the island's estates and entered enthusiastically into the business of buying and selling slaves, in the process setting himself up with a harem drawn from among the more attractive females. A year later he was appointed to the largely honorary post of Colonel of the 8th West India Regiment, then part of the Dominica garrison. As with all the other West India regiments the Eighth was composed of black troops under the command of white officers and senior NCOs. His appointment as Colonel opened up new possibilities for Johnstone and he quickly found a way, with the connivance of several of the regiment's officers, of defrauding the troops by diverting regimental funds and keeping their pay in arrears. Having sown the seeds of his destruction in this way the events which led to his downfall began early in 1802, when he received instructions from the Commander-in-Chief in the West Indies concerning the need for clearance and drainage work in the approaches to Fort Shirley, the island's main fortress overlooking an important anchorage some miles to the north of Roseau.

His orders contained specific reference to the extra pay soldiers were to receive if they were employed on this work instead of civilian labour. Johnstone was not a man to obey any order without first considering what advantage, if any, its execution might bring to himself, and a splendid opportunity to make easy money now presented itself. After entering into a syndicate which bought up uncultivated land in the vicinity of Fort Shirley he set the men of the Eighth to work on improving this, rather than on clearing and draining the marshy approaches to the fort itself. To then consider paying them extra, when they were not even getting the pay they were entitled to in the first place, was out of the question. The funds with which he had been provided for this purpose were diverted for his own use.

The soldiers, as soldiers do, put up with the situation for a while, but then as the weeks of extra and demeaning work with little or no pay began to run into months the less tractable decided enough was enough. On the evening of 9 April, after they had trudged back to their barracks inside the fort a full-scale mutiny was instigated, and within a couple of hours the mutineers were in complete control. In the general confusion that had taken place seven of their officers had been killed, one or two had escaped, and the remainder had been seized as hostages.

When news of the mutiny reached Johnstone in Roseau the next morning he sprang into action. Even if he was an out and out rogue he was no slouch when it came to organization. Within three days he had the island under martial law, had transported the island Militia and another British regiment by sea from Roseau to besiege the fort, and had had artillery and several hundred more troops brought from neighbouring islands. As a result, in the late afternoon of 12 April as he was about to storm the fort, he was informed that the mutineers had agreed to an unconditional surrender.

All might well have ended peacefully at this stage had he not, once he and his men entered Fort Shirley, decided to harangue the assembled mutineers and threaten them with loaded weapons in the gathering gloom. His remarks, delivered from the saddle, eventually turned what should have been a quick and painless operation into a bloodbath. Many of the mutineers had only a rudimentary understanding of English and could have had no idea what the man on the horse was bellowing about, and all of them must have been extremely tense and nervous. As they began to mumble with discontent Johnstone realized he had made a mistake and called out to them to surrender their arms. It was too late. Only a few men obeyed, and when one of the others shouted out some sort of warning, the troops accompanying the Governor, 'scarcely waiting for orders, fired a volley'.

At least seventy of the mutineers were killed or wounded. The remainder panicked; some returned the fire but the great majority attempted to flee from the parade ground. They were pursued through the fort out to the edge of the bluff on which it was sited and 'from the top of which, two or three hundred of them precipitated themselves into the sea'. Incredibly, very few were killed by their fall, and eventually all the others struggled ashore to be taken into custody. Some who managed to escape from the fort in the opposite direction avoided capture by hiding in the very swamps which Johnstone had been told to have drained, but eventually all were hunted down. By the time order had been restored and all the Eighth accounted for, fifty men were dead and another fifty had been wounded.

Three days later, after the ringleaders had been identified, seven soldiers were court-martialled, found guilty of 'exciting and joining in mutiny' and sentenced to death. Soon afterwards they and the rest of the regiment were transported to Martinique, then in British hands, where the executions took place. As it was not clear to the army authorities why the mutiny had taken place a Court of Inquiry was convened, and evidence taken from the surviving officers and some of the men. The subsequent report contained references to various irregularities in the way the troops had been employed and paid: at the time of the mutiny none had received the extra allowance he was entitled to, and most had not had their regular pay for several months.

Towards the end of May, by which time the Eighth had been shipped to Barbados, an investigation was begun into the state of the regimental accounts. The evidence this unearthed of unusual and irregular transactions, involving both pay and rations for the troops, was enough to show that the actions of some of the officers – and Johnstone in particular – had contributed greatly to the outbreak of the mutiny. This was given further confirmation in June, when another two dozen men were court-martialled, and it was asserted that 'short pay and want of money' were the general cry among the soldiers on the eve of the mutiny'. All those tried were found guilty and executed. Punishment of the rest of the regiment, now reduced to less than 400 men, took place later in the year. Nearly half were adjudged to have taken an active part in the mutiny and were sent as pioneers to British regiments, where no doubt being black they were soon worked to death. The remainder, considered not to have been directly involved, were drafted into some of the other West India regiments.

Out of the officers who could be held culpable only Johnstone and Major John Gordon, who had been in acting command of the regiment at the time, remained alive. Gordon was immediately sent back to England on half-pay. Johnstone, who was also put on half-pay having been dismissed from his post as governor, followed Gordon to England and, in a last attempt to revive his fortunes, accused his subordinate of embezzlement, misuse of public funds and general dereliction of duty. The subsequent court-martial of Gordon lasted two weeks and involved both men in trying to blame each other for what had taken place. In the end, although the major was acquitted on all charges, the officers who formed the court obviously reached their verdict with misgivings. In finding Gordon not guilty they recorded among other things that he 'procrastinated', showed 'culpable neglect', and was 'very irregular in not keeping an account of the monies which he received'. He remained on half-pay and was never employed again.

A year later, mainly as a result of the accusations made by Gordon at his own trial, Johnstone himself was court-martialled for various 'irregularities'. Largely because of the passage of time since the mutiny and the difficulty of obtaining evidence and witnesses, and because the accused was, if nothing else, a smooth-talker he was acquitted. In spite of this his army career was at an end. He remained on half-pay and was passed over for promotion to major-general.

In 1807 he resigned from the army and, finding the lure of the West Indies too strong, and with the help of family influence and string-pulling, secured a 'lucrative appointment' in the Virgin Islands. There he entered wholeheartedly into a fresh career of fraud, larceny and embezzlement which lasted for seven years. In 1814 he was the prime instigator of a plot to defraud the London Stock Exchange, in which he involved and ruined the reputation of his nephew, Admiral Thomas Cochrane, the tenth Earl of Dundonald. While awaiting trial for his part in this conspiracy Johnstone managed to escape and flee the country, presumably to pursue what the usually sober Dictionary of National Biography *records of his tenure in Dominica as a reign of 'tyranny, extortion and vice' in some other part of the world.*

Reminiscences of a redcoat

James Aytoun was another Scotsman who served in the army in Dominica, although some years before Johnstone arrived to blight the island and, as a private soldier, in a much more lowly position. He enlisted in 1786 and was very unusual for the day in being both literate and well-read. His memoirs, Observations, Recollections, Inferences, *which were written in 1829 contain a great deal of interesting information about all aspects of his life in the army both in the British Isles and abroad. He served in Dominica from 1788 to 1791 with the 30th (Cambridgeshire) Regiment (which in 1881 became the East Lancashire Regiment, in whose regimental museum in Blackburn his diary is now to be found), and recorded anything which caught his interest as is apparent from the following extracts:*

When in Dominica we had moderate duty, two or three nights in bed. The weather (with the exception of hurricanes) is pleasant but we were never sure of a fair day. Rain falls there very heavy but seldom continues a whole day. Our standing orders were three field days a week, drill six days a week. The regimental orders were on Sunday, 'A field day at 6 o'clock tomorrow if the weather will permit'. It often happened that the weather did not permit. I have been ready for a field day at five o'clock in the morning and every appearance of a fine day and in less than half an hour the rain would come from the windward side of the island. That stopped the field day. These interruptions obliged us to be ready for a field day every morning, Sundays excepted . . .

The crapo is a French name for a large sort of frog. The English call them bull frogs because they shout so loud you may hear them three quarters of a mile. They are protected as game but by what law I don't know. It is common to see the negroes selling them in parcels of six, tied together, in the market just as pullets. Here I once caught two of them and gave them to a soldier's wife. She skinned the hind legs and thighs and made a small quantity of stew equal to chicken broth. Unless I had tasted it I would not have believed it was so good. The French planters are very fond of the crapo. They do not frequent the water but have holes in banks and will leap ten or twelve feet when alarmed. The negroes catch them by torchlight . . .

I saw a mulatto woman's daughter. She was free. There is a practice with white men in the West Indies to purchase a steady black woman or mulatto freedom. Her children are free. It is not a free man but a free woman that gives freedom to the children. The girl I speak of was free. Her father had been white. She was not a common prostitute but hired herself to officers, etc., by the week or month, etc. One of our drummers offered to marry her but she would not. The drummer was fool enough to hang himself with his drum cord because the trollopse would not marry him and had not a soldier, whose name was 'Mylord Upchurch', cut the drum cord the drummer would have been in Kingdom Come in a few minutes. We had both laughs and jokes about cutting down the drummer. It was occasioned by Mylord Upchurch being confounded or surprised, that he had not the presence of mind to cut the cord above the drummer's head but he forced his finger inside the cord and cut both the cord and his finger. I have often heard Mylord swear about cutting down a drummer . . .

I never saw a beggar in Dominica except sailors but I forgot once having seen a black woman who had four children at one birth and she was allowed by her owner to carry the children about as a curiosity, but she did not beg. Our men gave her money. She carried two of the children herself and an old black man carried the other two. They all appeared to be in good health . . .

The small firefly is common in Dominica, but there is a larger sort about the size of the hive drones. The small sort show their light when flying, with what may be called a blink of light and then dark alternately but the large fly shows a constant light, flying or not. When not flying, the light they show is from a spot on the shoulder, about the diameter of a peppercorn. It appears in daylight of a whiteish color and of the appearance of fair hair but in the night it has a brilliant fierce light, more red than a farthing candle. If I recollect right, its wings are covered with something like the covering of the wings of the common beetle. The light they show when at rest is not equal to the light they show when on wing. When on the wing, a light across the under part of their body opens and shows a great deal of light, in proportion as much as six is to one against the light on their shoulders which, as observed above, is permanent, the light proceeding from the under part of the body being immediately closed when the fly is at rest.

It was, with the soldiers in our 30th Regiment, a custom to put some of the large flys into a vial bottle and hang the bottle on a nail by the side of their hammock and hang their watch beside the vial containing the flys, so that at whatever time they awoke they could see by the light of the flys the hour and minute. I have to observe that I read in my hammock, during the night, Smollett's translation of Don Quixote from beginning to end by the aforesaid flys, three of them tied together.

The man who was Chief Justice of Dominica at the time Aytoun was serving there, and who subsequently wrote a history of the island, also considered the firefly to be 'a wonderful insect':

. . . for it has a luminous quality in its head (above the eyes) under each wing, and in its tail; which, when the insect is flying, has the appearance of so many lights of candles moving in the air: or, the lights of a coach or post-chaise in a dark night, travelling towards you at a brisk rate . . .

Some of these flies are as big as the top-joint of a man's thumb, others are much smaller; and the latter have that luminous quality only in their tails . . .

The larger sort are often caught for the novelty of the light they give; if two or three of them are put into a glass, placed in a dark room, you may see distinctly any object there; or by holding a book close to the glass in which they are, you may see plainly to read the smallest print.

There is another quality remarkable in the fire flies, which is, that several of them being killed and mashed together will produce the same effect, and be as visible in letters marked out on the walls of a dark room, as if done with artificial phosphorous; and this for a considerable time after the flies are dead.

THOMAS ATWOOD, 1791

Over a hundred years later the Governor of the day found them equally remarkable, noting in his diary:

Rain fell this afternoon and the fireflies are extraordinarily numerous . . . But even more beautiful than the fireflies are the great luminous beetles that, now and again, fly across the clearings. The Creoles call them Les belles, in their French *patois*. In the daylight they are rather repulsive-looking things, almost black and about three-quarters of an inch long. But at night, when they fly serenely about among the tall trees, they are a beautiful sight. Their two very large eyes are then lit up like two gleaming emeralds, while under the thorax glows a vivid shield of the same extraordinary green light. Unlike the evanescent glow of a firefly, the illumination of these beetles is constant during flight, and so bright is it that it shines out to a considerable distance. I have sometimes, in the darkness, held one of these remarkable creatures between my finger and thumb and have been able to read by the glowing light.

SIR HESKETH BELL, 1904 (*see* HESKETH BELL, 1946)

Things worthy to be seen

Fireflies and luminous beetles are not the only things in Dominica which have attracted the interest of visitors over the years:

Dominica is one of the fayrest Islands of the West, full of hilles, and of very good smell. Whose singularities desiring to know as we passed, and seeking also to refresh ourselves with fresh water, I made the Mariners cast anker, after we had sayled about halfe along the coast thereof . . .

The place where we went ashore was hard by a very high Rocke, out of which there ran a little river of sweet and excellent good water: by which river we stayed certaine days to discover the things which were worthy to be seene, and traffiqued dayly with the Indians: which above all things besought us that none of our men should come neere their lodgins nor their gardens, otherwise that we should give them great cause of jelousie, and that in so doing, wee should not want of their fruite which they call *Ananas* [pineapples], whereof they offered us very liberally, receiving in recompense certain things of small value. This notwithstanding, it happened on a day certaine of our men desirous to see some new things in these strange countries, walked through the woods: and following still the litle rivers side, they spied two serpents of exceeding bignes, which went side by side overthwart the way. My souldiers went before them thinking to let them from going into the woods: but the serpents nothing at all astonied at these gestures glanced into the bushes with fearful hyssings: yet for all that, my men drew their swords and killed them, and found them afterward 9 great foote long, and as big as a mans leg. During this combate, certaine others more undiscreete went and gathered their *Ananas* in the Indians gardens, trampling through them without any discretion: and not therewithall contented they went toward their dwellings; whereat the Indians were so much offended, that without regarding anything they rushed upon them and discharged their shot, so that they hit one of my men named Martine Chaveau, which remained behind. We could not know whether hee were killed on the place, or whether he were taken prisoner: for those of his company had inough to doe to save themselves without thinking of their companion . . .

CAPTAIN RENÉ LAUDONNIERE, 1562.
In: *Hakluyt's Voyages Vol IX*

The same 'serpents' of 'exceeding bignes' are still around today, but were far more in evidence in the past. The 'remarkable circumstance' with which the following extract from a late eighteenth-century book ends seems to have assumed a life of its own: the same somewhat implausible story is now heard in any country where boas or pythons are to be found:

The principal and most remarkable of the reptiles . . . in Dominica . . . is that called by the French, 'Tete du chien', or Dog's-head snake, from its head, which much resembles that of a dog. Some have been caught in this island that measured upwards of twelve feet in length, and as thick as a man's leg. They have long, sharp teeth; their skins are scaled and beautifully spotted, and they have at the end of their tails a blunt-pointed, horny substance, which enables them to climb the trees.

The bite of these snakes is not venomous, nor is that of any kind of them in this island; but the tete du chien does mischief among the birds in the woods; and on the plantations they frequently devour the fowls and other poultry. They will swallow a full-grown fowl with its feathers; and several of them have been killed there with both a large fowl and an Indian coney entire in their bowels.

A remarkable circumstance, which happened in this island some time ago, deserves to be noticed in this place. A negro retiring from work one day at noon, instead of going home to get his dinner, fell asleep under a shady tree; and being missing at the time the other negroes assembled together to finish their daily task, it caused a suspicion that some accident had befallen him; they accordingly went in search of him, and found him asleep, with one of his legs, up to the thick part of his thigh, in the jaws of a large snake. Awakened by their noise, he was in the greatest terror, and struggling to get disengaged, was severely bit by the animal; to prevent this as much as possible, wedges were placed between its jaws, whilst they cut it to pieces; by which means only he could be released. This operation took some time, which together with the length of time, his leg and thigh had already been in the belly and jaws of the snake, reduced them almost to a state of digestion; and it was not till a considerable while after, that he recovered the intire use of them.

THOMAS ATWOOD, 1791

A peculiar bird which is described in the same book, and which was still common when it was written, managed to survive less well than the tête du chien it seems:

The diablotin, so called by the French, from its uncommonly ugly appearance, is nearly the size of a duck, and is web-footed. It has a big round head, crooked bill like a hawk, and large full eyes like an owl. Its head, part of the neck, chief feathers of the wings and tail, are black; the other parts of its body are covered with a milk-white fine down; and its whole appearance is perfectly singular. They feed on fish, flying in great flocks to the sea side in the night-time; and in their flight make a disagreeable loud noise like owls: which bird they also resemble, by their dislike of making their appearance in the day-time, when they are hid in holes in the mountains, where they are easily caught. This is done by stopping up some of the holes, which lead to their hiding places, and placing empty bags over the rest, which communicate under-ground with those stopped: the birds at their usual time of going forth to seek their food in the night-time, finding their passage impeded, make to the holes covered with the bags; into which entering, they are immediately caught; and great numbers of them taken in that manner in a short time. The flesh of the diablotin is much admired by the French, who used formerly to export great quantities of them salted, to Martinique and other French islands . . .

THOMAS ATWOOD, 1791

. . . the diablot – from which the mountain takes its name – a great bird, black as charcoal, half raven, half parrot, which nests in holes in the ground as puffins do, spends all the day in them, and flies down to the sea at night to fish for its food. There were once great numbers of these creatures, and it was a favourite amusement to hunt and drag them out of their hiding places . . . they were excellent eating. They are confined now in reduced numbers to the inaccessible crags about the peak which bears their name.

JAMES ANTHONY FROUDE, 1888

Dominica is famous among ornithologists as having been the home of an extraordinary bird called the diablotin. One of the highest mountains in the island is named after it. It seems that this bird was very numerous when the Europeans first came to Dominica, but, as it was extremely toothsome, and very easily caught, it quickly became extinct.

It was about the size of a pigeon and of black and white plumage. It had a hooked beak and webbed feet and was believed to go down to the sea at night in search of food. It nested in burrows, found in the soft clay on the mountainside, and was hardly ever seen in daylight. It was a mysterious bird and was credited with uncanny habits . . . old French and Spanish writers on the 'Caribbee' islands describe these diablotins in detail and wax enthusiastic on the exquisite flavour of their flesh. It is not surprising, therefore, that they should now be classed with the dodo.

SIR HESKETH BELL, 1902 (*see* HESKETH BELL, 1946)

Who can say whether the Diablotin . . . is really extinct in those mountain fastnesses? Once this bird was so plentiful that great numbers were killed and salted for export to Martinique. It is supposed that it has now been entirely exterminated by a species of carnivorous opossum, called *manicou*, which was casually introduced into Dominica; but within quite recent years there has been hot controversy over a single specimen, that fell wearily to earth one morning in the little town of Roseau. Was it a Diablotin as described by the Jesuit Father at the end of the seventeeth century, who wrote of it as 'about the same size as a pullet; with black feathers and strong black wings. The legs somewhat short; feet webbed like a duck; long thick claws; beak curved and pointed; extremely hard eyes, large and staring; can see in the dark, blind in daylight, lives on fish caught in the sea. Returns to the mountains where it lives in holes like rabbits.'

No mention is made of the beautiful, downy cream breast, which I especially admired in the bird, now stuffed and in the possession of Dr Daniel Thaly. It is supposed that its last midnight fishing expedition had been too long, and before it was able to regain its mountain fastness, daylight had blinded it.

HELEN CAMERON GORDON, 1942

Helen Cameron Gordon's 'mountain fastnesses' also contain another wonder of nature, but one which was not discovered until late on in the nineteenth century, by which time the poor diablotin was well on its way to extinction. Not a reptile, bird or animal, but an unusual body of water:

The Boiling Lake fills a small crateriform depression on the eastern slope of the Grand Soufriere Mountains. Sometimes the basin is empty, and then in the centre is seen the circular opening of a geyser. In times of activity boiling muddy water, heavily charged with sulphurous gases, is thrown up to a considerable height, until the accumulation in the basin forms the so-called Boiling Lake, and even then the position of the central orifice may be made out by the gyrating high mound of water caused by the ejective forces below.

HENRY A. NICHOLLS, C. 1875

Fenced in by steep, mostly indeed perpendicular banks, varying from sixty to a hundred feet high, cut out in ash and pumice, the lake rages and roars like a wild beast in its cage; the surface, to which such measurements as we could make assigned about two hundred yards in length and more than half the same amount in breadth, is that of a gigantic seething cauldron covered with rapid steam, through which, when the veil is for a moment blown apart by the mountain breeze, appears a confused mass of tossing waves, crossing and clashing in every direction – a chaos of boiling waters. Towards the centre, where the ebullition is at its fiercest, geyser-like masses are being constantly thrown up to the height of several feet, not on one exact spot, but shifting from side to side, each fresh burst being preceded by a noise like that of cannon fired off at some great depth below; while lesser jets suddenly make their appearance nearer the sides of the lake. What the general depth of the water may be would be difficult to ascertain; but a line stretched out over the edge from the end of a pole indicates a sheer descent of fifty or sixty feet within a couple of yards distance from the shore. The heat of the water, where it beats in seething restlessness on the cliff, is 185°F; we tied a thermometer to a stick and found the surface temperature at the distance of a few feet farther on to be almost 200°F. The height of the lake above the sea is a little over 2400 feet; an elevation which, at an average atmosphere temperature of 64°F, gives the boiling-point for water at 207°F, or near it.

WILLIAM GIFFORD PALGRAVE, 1887

... we reached the crest of the mountain and were confronted by a magnificent and awe-inspiring sight. In lieu of the soft, enchanting beauty of the green and blossoming mountain-side, a picture of grey and gloomy desolation lay at our feet. We were facing a huge circular crater fully a mile in diameter . . . It was the Abomination of Desolation.

The floor of the crater was fully a thousand feet below, and in the centre of it we could just discern a small circular basin, which, the guide told us, was our objective. To our disappointment, it seemed to be only full of pale, grey sand, with no sign of any lake, boiling or otherwise . . .

The scramble down into the depths below was rather a painful affair. The lower we went the hotter and steamier conditions became . . . Finally we got to the bottom, and found that the famous 'boiling lake' was merely a basin, about a hundred yards in diameter, covered with soft grey sand. A spring of warm water flowed into it from a crevice just above us, but the liquid sank almost immediately into a soft spot in the centre of the basin.

By this time we were very hungry and heartily consumed a picnic breakfast which we had brought with us. We had just finished our meal when the guide pointed out that the water was no longer disappearing into the centre of the space before us but was spreading rapidly over the sand . . . It was evident that large quantities of water were coming up from below, and we soon saw movements, like small geysers, appearing on the surface. It was also plain that the water was becoming very hot, as steam was rapidly rising from it. The volume of water increased so swiftly that we found it prudent to watch further developments from a spot higher up and farther from the eruption.

It was a wonderful and rather terrifying sight, and made one realize something of the extraordinary forces that were working just under our feet. In less than an hour the whole of the inner crater had become a seething cauldron of water boiling furiously. Five or six formidable geysers bubbled up in the centre to a considerable height and dense clouds of steam rolled off the broken surface . . . The guide told us that the water would soon go 'off the boil' and would disappear entirely into the depths below, leaving the basin merely a surface of dull grey sand, just as we had found it. During our painful climb up to the top of the outer crater we saw, on looking back, that it was so, and by the time we reached the crest the Boiling Lake had entirely disappeared. We were told that it usually repeated its 'turn' twice a day.

SIR HESKETH BELL, 1899 (*see* HESKETH BELL, 1946)

This interesting remnant

Henry Hesketh Bell, who was Governor from 1899 to 1905, was probably the most able colonial administrator Dominica ever had. As well as getting to know the island as well as he could by undertaking trips to places like the Boiling Lake, he also devoted a great deal of time and effort to the welfare of its people. Among the less fortunate of the population were the members of the last remaining Carib community in the entire Caribbean. Regrettably his efforts to protect their way of life, by putting their Reservation in the north-east of the island on a proper legal and administrative footing, did little to stem the decline in their numbers, or to halt the deterioration of their way of life, both of which had set in as soon as the first Europeans stepped ashore – something which has been all too well chronicled over the centuries:

. . . wee were come so neere aboard the shoare, that wee were met with many Canoes, manned with men wholly naked, saving that they had chaines and bracelets and some bodkins in their eares, or some strap in their nostrils or lips; the cause of their comming was to exchange their Tabacco, Pinos, Pantins, and Pepper with any trifle if it were gawdie . . . They are men of good proportion, strong, and straight limmed, but few of them tall, their wits able to direct them to things bodily profitable . . . Besides their Merchandise for exchange, every one hath commonly his Bowe and Arrowes; they speak some Spanish words: they have Wickers platted something like a broad shield to defend the raine, they that want these, use a very broad leafe to that purpose, they provide shelter against the raine because it washeth of their red painting, laid so on that if you touch it, you shall finde it on your fingers . . .

A Captaine or two watering neere the place where [we] anchored, found a leasure to rowe up a River with some guard of Pikes and Musketers, till they came to a Towne of these poor Salvages; and a poore Towne it was of some twenty cottages rather than Houses, and yet was there a King, whom they found in a wide hanging garment of rich crimson taffetie, a Spanish Rapier in his hand, and the modell of a Lyon in shining Brasse, hanging upon his breast. There they saw their women as naked as wee had seene their men, and alike attired even to the boring of their lippes and eares, yet in that nakedness, they perceived some sparkes of modestie, not willingly comming in the sight of strange and apparelled men: and when they did come, busie to cover, what should have bin better covered. The Queene they saw not, nor any of the Noble wives, but of the vulgar many; and the Maidens it should seeme they would not have so squemish, for the King commanded his Daughters presence, with whom our Gentlemen did dance after meate was taken away . . . It seemeth that themselves are wearie of their nakedness, for besides the Kings apparell they are exceeding desirous to exchange any of their Commodities for an old Waste-coate, or but a Cap, yea or but a paire of Gloves.

. . . The haire of men and women are of like length, and fashion . . . their meates are their fine fruites, yet they have Hennes and Pigges, but it should seeme rather for delight, then victuall: their drinke is commonly water, but they make drinke of their Cassain, better of their Pines (and it should seeme that might be made an excellent liquor) but the best and reserved for the Kings cup onely of Potatoes: their Bread is Cassain. The last report of them shall bee what I have seen in experience, namely their great desire to understand the English tongue; for some of them will point to most parts of his body, and having told the name of it in the language of Dominica, he would not rest till he were told the name of it in English, which having once told he would repeate till he could either name it right, or at least till he thought it was right . . .

GEORGE CLIFFORD,
A Briefe Relation of the Severall Voyages
of George, the Earl of Cumberland, 1598

The Indians, natives of Dominica, are descended from the ancient inhabitants, who were found there when this island was first discovered by Europeans, and are the people properly called 'Caribbes'. Of these there are not more than twenty or thirty families, who have their dwellings on the east part of the island, at a great distance from Roseau, where they are seldom seen.

They are of a clear copper colour, have long, sleek, black hair on their heads; their persons are short, stout, and well made; but they disfigure their faces by pressing flat their noses, which is done in their infancy. They are a very quiet, inoffensive people, speak a language of their own, and French, but none of them speak English.

They live chiefly by fishing in the rivers and the sea, or by fowling in the woods, at both of which they are very expert with their bows and arrows. They will kill the smallest bird with an arrow, or transfix a fish at a great depth in the sea; and are very serviceable to the planters near their settlement, whom they chiefly supply with fish and game. They are also very ingenious, making curious wrought panniers, or baskets, of silk grass, or the bark of trees.

It is much to be regretted that since this island has been in the possession of the English, so little pains have been taken to cultivate a union with these people, as they might be capable of essential service to its internal security, especially against the accumulation of runaway negroes in the time of peace; and in war they might be induced to join in its defence, should it be invaded. Yet they are permitted to roam wherever their fancies lead them, as much unnoticed as if no such people were in existence. They are men as well as we, are both with the same degree of sensibility; and by proper encouragement might be of material benefit to a country which was originally their own.

THOMAS ATWOOD, 1791

The original native or as they are called, 'Caribs', are inoffensive and are not many. The race appears to be hastening to extinction. They mix with neither black nor white. I never knew of a Carib man or woman being married nor being a servant nor in any way connected except among themselves. They are so scarce in Dominica that during three years I was there I had not more than two opportunitys of seeing them, I believe not more than twenty-four in all. I cannot say that they are giants like the Patagonians neither believe that they are pigmies such as Heroditus tells his jokes about. They were sitting on Adam's floor and seemed to be as much at anchor as Noah's Ark was before the flood. The young women were of fine cream colour, not the sickly yellow of ill-health.

JAMES AYTOUN, 1829 (see AYTOUN, 1984)

A century of peaceful avocations has completely metamorphosed the Carib. Instead of a bloodthirsty, man-eating savage, he is now as law-abiding and mild a subject as any the King has. He no longer paints crimson circles of roucou round his eyes and stripes of black and white over his body, but – and

I state it with sorrow – on high days and holidays, he wears a tall hat and a black coat. His Zemis have been scattered among collections of curios, and instead of yelling round a sacrificial stone, the Carib of to-day goes to confession to the parish priest, and tells his beads with edifying fervour. The picturesque abode depicted by Peter Martyr, where faggots of human bones represented most of the furniture, and a bleeding head hung on a post like a picture, has been replaced by the less romantic, if more comfortable, shingled cabin . . . The stone implements, with which in the old days he used to brain an adversary or hollow out his canoe, have long ago been replaced by the hoe and the axe from Birmingham . . .

The hundred years of peace and protection have arrested, almost at the last gasp, the extinction of this interesting remnant of one of the world's races. The 20 or 30 families reported at the beginning of the century are still with us to-day, if we count only the Caribs of pure breed, while at the last census, the returns showed, as the population of the Reserve, nearly 400, who 'claimed' to be Caribs. It is to be regretted, from an ethnological point of view, that the breed is suffering much from the admixture of negro blood. Out of the 400 who are settled on the reserve, I doubt whether more than 120 are full-blooded Caribs, and those are undoubtedly the last survivors of their race in the West Indies.

HENRY HESKETH BELL,
Report on the Caribs of Dominica, 1902

. . . there are still Caribs on Dominica, though they . . . have long been extinct in the other islands. Here, in the last Carib Reserve, [in] bygone days . . . the men and women did not speak the same language. We would have been told, had we inquired, that the Caribs' forefathers were a branch of the mainland Galibi. Driven from their lands, they had set sail . . . landed in these islands where, after killing the native warriors, they had taken their women to wife. Since that time, their daughters had preserved something of their mothers' tongue . . .

It is in the past 40 years that this small group has suffered what is perhaps its greatest loss of integrity – its language, or languages. Doubtless to some extent mutually corrupted, these two idioms subsisted side by side until about the end of the first decade of this century. Both succumbed before the French Creole patois of the West Indian Negro and 'coloured man'. Even today, when their memories of what they laconically term 'the language' are jogged, old men and women of the Reserve still often give different words for the same concept. But with the last Carib speakers there doubtless disappeared many cultural links with the past that can never be replaced. The use of a common idiom leads inevitably to a community of notions and mental attitudes. And so it is that the Island Carib of today knows little of his own culture and nothing about our culture except, as it were, through Negro eyes . . .

The girls no longer take easily to the old ways, and demand, like their coloured sisters, hats, shoes, and sewing machines. The boys learn just enough at school to lose interest in the old pursuits, and far too little to have a chance of success at the new ones . . .

DOUGLAS TAYLOR, *Columbus Saw Them First*, 1941

The mixed descendants of the last Island Caribs who inhabited the Lesser Antilles live on the north-east coast of Dominica . . . It was only in 1970 that a motorable road was cut through the area and telephone and electricity followed in the 1980s . . .

The position of the Chief is less romantic than most visitors like to believe. In 1952 a Carib Council was created as part of a local government system for the whole island . . . There are elections every five years and the chairman of the council is designated the 'Chief' . . .

It is a sad irony that this tribe of seafarers, after whom the waters of the Caribbean have been named, should end up in a corner of the island where access to the sea is almost impossible. There are only two difficult landing places on this wild and dramatic shoreline . . .

The strongest link with the past . . . are the Carib baskets which are sold in little craft shops all along the road through the Carib Territory. The brown, white and black designs of the larouma reed have been handed down from generation to generation. The square paniers and side bags are made in two layers with heliconia leaves in between. This waterproof design is a remnant from the days when food and goods had to be kept dry from sea spray in the open canoes and from rainfall along the forest trails across the mountainous interior. Such a basket is the most authentic souvenir you can get of the Caribbean and of the people who gave the region its name.

LENNOX HONYCHURCH, 1998

Endpiece

During the time that General Farquharson (the man who was too mean to pro-vide Bishop Coleridge with a bed for the night in 1832) was Governor of St Lucia

it is most unlikely that members of that island's society ever received many in-
vitations to Government House. The General, after all, was notorious for his
parsimonious habits. This was something which could never have been said of
the man who inhabited the administrator's residence in Dominica in the early
years of the twentieth century; although it seems, from an entry he made in his
diary in September 1901, Governor Bell had his own problems with men of the
cloth to put up with:

Our fortnightly receptions are usually held in the gardens which are an
admirable frame for them. The big shade-spreading trees shelter 'birds of a
feather' and prevent those sinister rows or circles of chairs which are the
bane of a host of hostess. The only drawback to the Government House
gardens is the near proximity of the RC churchyard. It is only just on the
other side of the wall, and the lugubrious intonations of a priest, reciting the
Burial Service, have more than once depressed the tone of our parties. Worse
still is the fact that, owing to the overcrowded state of the cemetery, the
defunct are often not interred at an adequate depth. The result is an
effluvium which, when the breeze is coming from that direction, has obliged
me, more than once, to send a protest to the Cathedral authorities.

10 Isla de Aves

'Island of the Birds'

Some said it was an island no one had ever seen and perhaps one that had just been created; but the captain and pilot maintained it had to be the small Island of the Birds.

JEAN BAPTISTE LABAT, 1722

Père Labat going once from Martinique to Guadeloupe had taken a berth with Captain Daniel, one of the most noted of the French corsairs of the day, for better security. People were not scrupulous in those times, and Labat and Daniel had been long good friends. They were caught in a gale off Dominica, blown away, and carried to Aves, where they found an English merchant ship lying a wreck. Two English ladies from Barbadoes and a dozen other people had escaped on shore. They had sent for help, and a large vessel came for them the day after Daniel's arrival. Of course he made a prize of it. Labat said prayers on board for him before the engagement, and the vessel surrendered after the first shot. The good humour of the party was not disturbed by this incident. The pirates, their prisoners, and the ladies stayed together for a fortnight at Aves, catching turtles and boucanning them, picnicking, and enjoying themselves. Daniel treated the ladies with the utmost politeness, carried them afterwards to St Thomas's, dismissed them unransomed, sold his prizes, and wound up the whole affair to the satisfaction of every one.

JAMES ANTHONY FROUDE, 1888

The island on which the gallant French corsair picnicked with his prisoners early in the eighteenth century is about 125 nautical miles west of Dominica, its closest neighbour. At that time, and until the middle of the following century, it was unclaimed territory. Its only visitors were shipwrecked mariners or seafarers calling to collect turtles and birds' eggs. Such collectors, because the prevailing winds made it difficult for a safe return journey to be made to any of the islands to the east, came from either the Dutch island of Saba to the north or Venezuela to the south.

This eventually led to a dispute about ownership between Venezuela and The Netherlands which came to a head in the 1860s, when Queen Isabella II of Spain was asked to arbitrate. The Queen, a wayward woman with a scandalous private life which led to her being deposed in 1868, was perhaps – in view of Spain's long involvement in Caribbean history – not the ideal choice of a person required to make a wholly impartial decision between Spanish- and Dutch-speaking claimants. In 1865 she found that as 'all the islands of the Caribbean Sea were discovered by Spaniards' Venezuela was the country that 'succeeded Spain in all its rights to the island', and so it remains today.

However, regardless of who may lay claim to it, Aves is a shrinking asset. In Labat's day it was a reasonably large island, reputedly some 15 metres in height and nearly 12 kilometres in circumference, with a couple of smaller islets to the west and north-west. It then supported plenty of bushes and trees, and fresh water could be found by digging. It was home to vast flocks of seabirds and the breeding place of a considerable number of turtles. While the birds are still there in large numbers, and some of the Caribbean's greatly reduced population of turtles still return to breed, the island is now little more than a crescent-shaped sand cay, only 1 or 2 metres high, with no vegetation other than ground-hugging creepers.

In 1972 the islet, as it now must be termed, was declared to be a faunal reserve by the Venezuelan Government. Six years later, in an attempt to prove it capable of supporting human life – and thereby influence the delineation of the country's territorial waters – a small naval base was established for 'surveillance and safeguard duties' near the south-western end. The two-storey prefabricated base, called Simon Bolivar, consisting of little more than an accommodation module and a helicopter landing pad, was mounted on piles in the sea with a long catwalk on to the cay. Twenty years after it was erected it was reported as being manned by eight naval personnel, with a single scientist studying the turtle population. It is more than possible that in the not too distant future, given the rate at which the islet is being eroded, the Simon Bolivar *naval base will be all that is left of Aves above the surface of the sea.*

11 Guadeloupe

'A braue frutfull Iland'

. . . at daylight this moring wee ware within a leag of the Esternmost Ind of Gordalupa. It being inhabited with french: they fiered to gonnes: we supposing it was to give an alarom to the Contary. This is a very high Land and full of mountaines. It is a braue frutfull Iland: heare is a very good harbor for shippes. This Iland doth yeld Shugar, and tobacco, and Cottaine, and Indiccoe: here wee lay beecalmed.

HENRY WHISTLER, 1655

Higher and higher ahead rose the great mountain mass of Guadaloupe, its head in its own canopy of cloud. The island falls into the sea sharply to leeward. But it stretches out to windward in a long line of flat land edged with low cliff, and studded with large farms and engine-houses. It might be a bit of the Isle of Thanet, or of the Lothians, were it not for those umbrella-like Palmistes, a hundred feet high, which stand out everywhere against the sky. At its northern end, a furious surf was beating on a sandy beach; and beyond that, dim and distant, loomed up the flat farther island, known by the name of Grande Terre.

Guadaloupe . . . consists, properly speaking, of two islands, divided by a swamp and a narrow salt-water river . . . the westward island, rising in one lofty volcanic mass which hides the eastern island from view, is perhaps, for mere grandeur, the grandest in the Archipelago.

CHARLES KINGSLEY, 1871

This island, like others in the chain of the Lesser Antilles, is volcanic, but although subject now to occasional disturbance, smoke in the day and flashes of fire in the night, the forces of nature are quieter than they were at one time, the last great earthquake being in 1843. The violence of the original eruptions may be gathered from the fact that the island contains a volcano of a very great height. The rainfall on the hills contributes to the rivers, which are numerous. It is a natural feature worthy of note that Guadeloupe is divided into two parts by a small sea canal about 30 yards wide, navigable by small vessels, and connected with good bays at both ends . . . Guadeloupe (or Guadaloupe) was so called by Columbus from the resemblance its mountains bore to some he knew in Spain of the same name . . . It is said that Columbus first saw the pine apple here.

C. WASHINGTON EVES, 1889

. . . between Dominica and Guadaloupe [there is] a blue-water channel. It is called The Saints Passage, not on the surmise that it leads to Heaven, but because athwart it lie Les Isles des Saintes as well as little Marie Galante. Here was fought between Rodney and De Grasse, the bloody and momentous battle of April 12, 1782. It was an engagement upon which hung the fate of Great Britain in the West Indies, for it was a fight for the mastery of the sea.

SIR FREDERICK TREVES, 1908

Guadeloupe – if I may be allowed an unpleasant comparison – is shaped like a pair of lungs, the left one flat and low, the other expanded into splendid mountain heights. They are really two islands separated by the short Salt River, across which is flung a single wooden bridge . . .

Basse Terre, the capital, is a modest little town on the southwest corner of the mountainous half of the island bearing the same name. Dating from the early days of French colonization, it once enjoyed a considerable importance, most of which disappeared with the founding of Pointe-à-Pitre, in a similar corner of the flat and more productive Grande Terre . . .

The commercial capital is situated at the mouth of the Salt River, in one of the hottest and most uninviting spots in the West Indies . . . It is a deadly flat town, with wide, right-angled streets, fairly well paved in a kind of crude concrete, with here and there a corner that recalls Paris, as do the street names.

HARRY A. FRANCK, 1920

Were it not for the innate cheerfulness of its inhabitants who share the French *joie de vivre*, Pointe-à-Pitre would be a depressing place. It is half circled by a dismal mangrove swamp, and is consequently afflicted by mosquitoes to an almost unbelievable extent . . .

Returning to Pointe-à-Pitre, after our visit to the historic fort [of Fleur d'Epèe], we sampled the cooking of the chef of the Hotel Moderne at a dinner given in a *salle privée* by some American fellow-passengers, and the evening ended in uproarious fashion, a staid official of a Government Department in the United States performing a *pas de cafard* to the strains of a gramophone, and killing at each wild step one of the monstrous cockroaches which were racing across the floor . . .

SIR ALGERNON ASPINALL, 1927

The death of Captain Faulknor

The mighty clash of British and French fleets in the channel between Guadeloupe and Dominica referred to by Sir Frederick Treves was the famous day-long Battle of the Saintes. Involving over seventy ships it was not only the largest naval battle of the eighteenth century, but the only one of any decisive significance ever fought in the Caribbean.

Thirteen years after it had taken place, and as a minor episode in one more of the many wars between France and Britain, another naval battle took place in the same sea passage which, even though it involved only two ships, was just as hard-fought. As with numerous other single-ship engagements that had taken place all over the Caribbean throughout the previous 300 years, its outcome was of no great significance other than to the officers and men involved except when, as in this case, it brought one of the participants entry into his country's pantheon of naval heroes.

In April 1794 Guadeloupe was occupied by the British, the French defenders' brief stand coming to an end when Fort Fleur d'Epée (the fort guarding Point-à-Pitre which Aspinall visited before his somewhat dubious meal at the Hotel Moderne many years later) was taken by means of a combined naval and military assault. Foremost among those storming the fort was the commanding officer of the frigate Blanche, *the newly-appointed and only very recently promoted 32-year-old Captain Robert Faulknor. As the son, grandson, great-grandson, nephew and cousin of senior naval officers Faulknor knew better than most the way to make his name in the Royal Navy of the late eighteenth century. He had been promoted from lieutenant and transferred from the command of a much smaller vessel a month earlier, as a direct result of his daring and outstanding leadership in attacks on Martinique and St Lucia, and was determined to make the most of any opportunity for further glory which might come his way as captain of the 32-gun* Blanche, *as his part in the attack on Fort Fleur d'Epée had shown.*

After having been sent away during the hurricane season the Blanche *returned to the Caribbean in October to find the French had retaken Guadeloupe and stationed a large 38-gun frigate, the* Pique, *off Point-à-Pitre. For the next three months Faulknor remained in the vicinity of the island, cutting off French communications and biding his time until the* Pique *was forced to make a move. Nothing happened until the morning of 4 January 1795, when the French frigate was seen to be underway and heading out very cautiously into the open sea.*

Having given the Pique *the whole day to get well clear of the land by keeping well to the south of the Isles des Saintes, Faulknor brought the* Blanche *around at dusk and the two ships were within range of each other's guns just after midnight. In the action which followed the* Pique *was handled in a very professional manner, with her captain constantly attempting, between the exchange of broadsides, to lay alongside and board the* Blanche. *Faulknor was just as adroit as a shiphandler and even more determined to avoid being overwhelmed by a crew it was obvious was larger than his own. After three hours of banging away at each other from a distance, during which the* Blanche *lost two of her masts, the two ships finally closed – but in such a way that Faulknor saw immediately was to his advantage. By securing the French vessel's bowsprit to his own ship not only would her crew be prevented from boarding, but none of her guns would be able to be brought to bear while his own quarterdeck armament would have a clear field of fire. What happened next is well stated in the sparse but telling words of the* Dictionary of National Biography:

The Pique then ran on board her on the port quarter, and Faulknor, intending to keep her there, exposed to the raking fire of the Blanche's guns, proceeded to lash, with his own hands, her bowsprit to the Blanche's capstan. While so doing he fell dead, shot through the heart by a musket-ball. Other hands secured the lashing, and the Blanche, paying off before the wind, dragged the Pique in her wake, keeping up a steady fire into her bows, which the Pique was unable to return.

Two hours later the French crew indicated they had had enough and the Blanche, *now under the command of the first lieutenant Frederick Watkins, hove-to so that a prize crew could be put aboard the disabled* Pique. *As both ships had had all their boats destroyed, and transfer by means of the hawser connecting them proved impossible, the boarding officer and ten men were obliged to swim across. They were greeted on board the* Pique *by a total shambles, the deck littered with the remains of masts, spars and rigging, and two-thirds of her crew either dead or wounded. Fortunately, expert dockyard assistance was close at hand, and a day or so later, under a makeshift jury rig and accompanied by the almost equally battered and unhandy* Blanche, *the* Pique *was brought into English Harbour in Antigua.*

Both ships were repaired, re-masted and re-rigged. The French survivors went into captivity as prisoners of war, and the Pique, *retaining her name as was the custom, entered service as a ship of the Royal Navy. Neither vessel spent very much longer in the Caribbean and both were lost before the end of the century; the* Pique *being wrecked on the French channel coast in 1798, and the* Blanche *on the Dutch island of Texel a year later.*

Long before this, however, Faulknor had become a national hero. The news of his death and the circumstances under which it had taken place caused a sensation in England, giving 'unwonted celebrity to this brilliant frigate action'. Until then no single ship action had caused so much excitement, nor had the deeds of any naval officer so caught the public imagination. Nelson, although he had already lost an eye in the service of his country, was still only a captain and had yet to achieve the first of the string of victories which would make his name, and the war as yet had not produced any other naval hero. In no time The Death of Captain Faulknor *had become the subject of paintings, engravings, poems, and stage performances, and his immortality was assured when, within a few weeks of receipt of the news of the fight between the* Blanche *and the* Pique, *the House of Commons voted a sum of money for the erection of a suitable memorial. Today, just as was recorded in the* Dictionary of National Biography *over a century ago, 'a monument by Rossi, erected in St Paul's Cathedral at the public expense, still keeps alive the memory of one whose early death but crowned the glorious promise of his young life'.*

12 Montserrat

'Shamrock island of the Caribbean'

... this little island ... was first planted by a small colony from St Christopher's, detached in 1632 ... Their separation appears indeed to have been partly occasioned by local attachments and religious-dissensions; which rendered their situation in St Christopher's uneasy, being chiefly natives of Ireland, and of Romanish persuasion. The same causes, however, operated to the augmentation of their numbers; for so many persons of the same country and religion adventured thither soon after the first settlement ...

BRYAN EDWARDS, 1793

Some communities are conspicuous for their respectability, others are notorious for their vice, but the general opinion here is, that Montserrat is the most disreputable place in the West Indies. There seems to be no villainy, no rascality, which the white inhabitants do not practice on each other, and on the others whom they chance to meet. This is particularly the case with the official people placed in authority, and by authority, over negroes and their fellow whites, as their moral guides. They are swindlers, drunkards, and debauchees. The highest in position are commonly spoken of as the 'artful dodgers', and publicly shown up ... as notorious defaulters. What shall we say to those moral ministers at home, who, affecting to be conscientious, and even pious, keep such notorious reprobates in high places. Of three Montserrat men whom I met, two were infamous for their utter want of principle and character. The third was an exceedingly forward, fast young man, associating apparently with all the *mauvais sujets* of Antigua.

CHARLES W. DAY, 1852

Plymouth is more than half hidden in the rich foliage that fringes the wonderfully wrinkled green of the hills at their base; it has a curtain of palms before it. Approaching, you discern only one or two facades above the sea-wall, and the long wharf projecting through an opening in the masonry, over which young palms stand thick as canes on a sugar plantation. But on reaching the street that descends towards the heavily bowldered shore you find yourself in a delightfully drowsy little burgh – a miniature tropical town, with very narrow paved ways, steep, irregular, full of odd curves and angles, and likewise of tiny courts everywhere sending up jets of palm-plumes, or displaying above their stone enclosures great candelabra-shapes of cacti. All is old-fashioned and quiet and small. Even the palms are diminutive, slim and delicate; there is a something in their poise and slenderness like the charm of young girls who have not yet ceased to be children, though soon to become women . . .

LAFCADIO HEARN, 1890

To the regret and shame of an Englishman

Whether the ill-tempered and intemperate remarks of Charles W. Day concerning those in authority in Montserrat in the middle of the nineteenth century were justified or not is open to question, but it is probably just as well that he was not writing fifty years or so earlier, when an incident occurred which he would have found well exemplified 'want of principle and character' among the island's officials.

Joseph Dombey was born in Macon in France in 1742. Although his name is now virtually unknown outside the land of his birth, in his day he enjoyed a considerable reputation throughout Europe as a botanist and a 'traveller of much celebrity' best known for the collections of plants he made in South America between 1778 and 1782. While in Chile he discovered 'the majestic tree, of the tribe of Pines, 150 feet high, now named after him Dombeya, of which the Norfolk island pine is another species'.

In January 1794 he was sent by the revolutionary Committee of Public Safety to North America 'in order to purchase corn from the United States, and to fulfil some other objects of public importance, especially relating to science and commerce'. To avoid being caught up in the war between France and England which had begun the year before he took passage in an American ship. All might have been well had this vessel then not sailed by a route across the Atlantic which took it into the Caribbean:

A tempest obliged him to take shelter at Guadaloupe, and that ill-fated island was then in as distracted a state as its mother-country. Having been sent out by the French republic, he was consequently odious to the royalist governor, and on being summoned into his presence, he rather preferred making his escape on board a vessel freighted by some republican deputies for Philadelphia. But before he could embark he was seized and thrown into prison. This violence excited a public commotion in his favour, and the governor thought proper to release him. In labouring to appease the tumultuous mob, which threatened vengeance on his enemies, he was thrown accidently into the river, and the consequences were nearly fatal to his life. When recovered he waited on the governor, and though found innocent, was ordered to quit the colony in the American vessel in which he came. That vessel was no sooner out of the harbour, than it was attacked by two privateers, and taken. Dombey, disguised as a Spanish sailor, was thrown into a prison in the island of Montserrat, where ill-treatment, mortification, and disease, put a period to his life on the 19th of February 1796. It must ever be the regret and the shame of an Englishman that a man like Dombey perished in a prison where English laws were known. It has justly been the pride of civilized society in our days that science, being exclusively of no nation, has suspended even the horrors of war in favour of its cultivators, but the horrors of war are much more commonly found to brutalize all nations in common. There must surely have been some persons at Monserrat who could read and write; some who, though slave-dealers, professed Christianity, but it was all in this case, as in many others, to very little purpose; for a man, the pride of his species, who went about doing good, and whose whole life was devoted to the service of useful science, perished unheeded among them!

ABRAHAM REES, 1819

A gift of blarney?

Bryan Edwards, who wrote about Montserrat near the end of the eighteenth century, mentioned that the island was originally settled mainly by 'natives of Ireland', and was content to leave it at that. This, however, for many visitors to the island after him, was something they seemed quite unable to do:

The negroes here have an Irish accent, which grafted on negro English forms the most diverting jargon I ever heard in my life.

HENRY NELSON COLERIDGE, 1826

It is a peculiarity of Montserrat that the negroes speak with a rich Irish Brogue. This phenomenon is explained by the fact that in the seventeenth century the colony was peopled almost entirely by Irish. The pious care with which this attractive dialect has been preserved for over 200 years is illustrated . . . in the following incident.

An Irishman fresh from Donegal arrives at Montserrat, and leaning over the steamer's rail addresses himself, in the following terms, to a coal-black nigger who has come alongside with provisions.

'Say, Cuffee, what's the chance for a lad ashore?'

'Good, yer honor, if ye're not afraid of wurruk. But me name's not Cuffee, an', plase ye, it's Pat Mulvaney.'

'Mulvaney? And do yer mean to say ye're Oirish?'

'Oi do.'

'The saints dayfind us. An' how long have yer been out here?'

'A matter uv tin year or so.'

'Tin year! An' yez black as me hat! Save me sowl, I tuk yez for a naygur.'

SIR FREDERICK TREVES, 1908

The population of the island is mainly negro-Irish, it having been settled by emigrants from the 'Old Sod', so that to this day Irish names predominate, freckled red-heads with African features are numerous, and the inhabitants are noted throughout the West Indies for their brogue and their gift of Blarney.

HARRY A. FRANCK, 1920

. . . at one time there were no fewer than three thousand Irish families in the island. They have left their mark in place names like Kinsale, and Harris

Village, and in such surnames as Daly, Burke, O'Gara, Ryan, and Curwen, and by the continued use of Irish idiom by the negroes, some of whom, it is said, even speak with a brogue . . . In this connexion an amusing story is told of an Irishman who, on his visit to Montserrat, hearing one black man shouting to another in the language of the Liffey, asked him how long he had been on the island. 'Shure, yer honour, and three years it is that I've been here', replied the black. Whereupon the Irishman, aghast, exclaimed, 'Glory be to God! And do ye turrn black in thot toime?'

SIR ALGERNON ASPINALL, 1927

At one time there must have been more than twenty-five hundred families of Irish extraction in the island. And true to the nostalgic spirit for their green Erin, which even to this day characterizes all people of Irish descent, these earlier Irish settlers saw to it that their trademark was left indelibly impressed for posterity at Montserrat. This showed itself not only in the surnames of the people, but also by the continued use of Irish idioms . . .

Even the physical characteristics prevail, so that one may meet a red-headed, freckled-faced colored person with a twinkle in his oft'-blue eye, on the Montserrat roads, who, in that delightfully free-and-easy Irish manner might be heard chanting silver-toned ballads . . . or, again, one might be hailed by a mulatto – a Mulcahy – who might be tossing off a few Slaintes at Erin in good old Donegal jargon in which might lurk much flavor of the brogue; and a brogue so thick that, figuratively, one could hardly cut it even with a Toledo blade.

It is a fact that everywhere on the island the Irish brogue is prevalent upon the people's tongues; and what is more, one is often startled by their names, so that pitch-black colored persons sport such delightful and musical names as . . . O'Hara and O'Malley . . . and a host of others too numerous to cover here . . .

All these might be speaking the Irish patois that they learned from earlier settlers, or they might be chiming their dulcet Irish diatessarons, with a merry Kerry twinkle in their eye, and bristling with wit and blarney, while panegyrizing their green Erin, the isle they have never seen . . .

In concluding . . . I am reminded of . . . an Irishman fresh from Erin, who, many years ago, was stopped on the road and addressed by a colored man in his own Gaelic dialect, his speech larded with the customary blarney and sporting a delightful brogue. Big-hearted Pat at once thought this fellow a son of Erin, so that he queried, 'Faith, my good man, what gift of the God may ye be and how long have ye been here?' 'One year' was the laconic reply. So that the true son of green Erin, his twinkling eyes almost popping out of his round face, exclaimed, 'By the ghost of St Patrick, glory be to God, if you can turn so black and so ugly in a year, I had better take to my legs, and return whence I came.' And friend Pat swung around on his heel and betook himself back to his ship, taking an oath never to set foot in Montserrat again.

HENDRIK DE LEEUW, 1957

It is apparent to anyone well acquainted with both Irish and African cultural milieus that most of Montserrat culture today is a composite of African retentions, European and regional borrowings, and internal innovations, of which Irish retentions and reinterpretations with African forms make up but a limited portion. The Irish heritage is manifested in the phenotypes of most islanders and in the English, and possibly in the creole, that they speak; in place-names and surnames which still are employed; and in certain customs . . .

There is no evidence that Gaelic was spoken in Montserrat, or anywhere else in the West Indies, after the 17th century, but I was told by several persons in Ireland that early in this century Irish tourists visiting Jamaica reported hearing Gaelic spoken by West Indians. A joke of racist nature occasionally heard in Ireland tells of an Irish tourist who, from the deck of a passenger ship, asked a Gaelic-speaking Kingston stevedore (from a nearby island who had come to Jamaica only a short time before, unknown to the Irishman) how long he had lived there; when told 'three months', the tourist insisted on leaving the West Indies immediately before he too 'turned black from the pitiless sun'. The creole speech of Montserratians is mainly a syncretism of English and African elements, although French, locally-invented, and maybe Irish words are incorporated into the vocabulary . . .

The most prominent retention of Irish pagan belief is the 'Chance Pond mermaid', a white-skinned maiden who is thought to reside in a shallow lake atop 3000 feet high Chance's Mountain. She has as a companion a 'diamond snake', and she sits from time to time on a rock beside the pool combing her long hair. If a person can seize her comb and run down the slope and wash it in the sea before being caught by the pursuing serpent, the mermaid's buried treasure becomes his. Every Easter at midnight a pilgrimage which attracts hundreds of islanders climbs the mountain by torchlight to arrive before dawn and surprise the mermaid . . .

JOHN C. MESSENGER, 1967

The idea of a black Irish enclave in a distant tropical island or another Emerald Isle with an Irish diaspora, sounds exotic and has prosperous possibilities for tourism, but it has no strong support from the historical evidence available to us.

It is not that there are no Irish links and social retentions. This would be odd since they were around for over 300 years; but the influence is not nearly as substantial as is supposed either by zealous Irish patriots in search of their roots or by Montserratians, who, mimicking smiling Irish eyes in North American cities, are anxious to regale themselves in green and wave the shamrock on St Patrick's Day.

... It is possible that the storied white-skinned mermaid of Chance's Pond had Irish connections, but to say ... that 'every Easter at midnight, hundreds of islanders climb the mountain by torchlight to arrive before dawn and surprise the mermaid' is to be basking in the realm of imaginative literature.

HOWARD A. FERGUS, 1994

Half our sorrow

One Montserratian who was prepared to claim Irish ancestry when it suited him, and who certainly had enough blarney to support the claim, was a novelist born on the island in 1865.

Matthew Phipps Shiell, who wrote under the name of M.P. Shiel, had his first book, a mystery story called Prince Zaleski, *published in London when he was thirty. It was followed by nineteen others in as many years, earning their author high-flown praise from contemporaries such as H.G. Wells and Arnold Bennett. His output included historical and romantic adventures, as well as more mysteries and what, today, would be considered science fiction stories. None remains in print.*

Some idea of why Shiel's books are no longer read, and are for the most part unreadable, can be gained from the preface to This Knot of Life, *a romantic novel published in 1909 at the height of his career. A passage chosen almost at random provides a good example of his style:*

... for the realization of space or of time, especially of time, pours over my soul a fainting rapture of the most potent opium, the most ravishing hashish. Ah, the obscure musics my heart has psalmed – moon-funerals dishevelled, brawlings of Baal-orgies, bodings, Obiah-blasphemies, breast-beatings by Babylon streams, threnodies of Redeemers cosmic-dreaming on their cross: so that I have felt that I must be the singer-ape par excellence in the human wood, that never man sang as I sing . . .

With his reputation based on such preposterous tosh it is hardly surprising that the only too-real brawlings, bodings and breast-beatings of the First World War proved too much for it. He published nothing between 1913 and 1923 and very little after that. The plots of his few later books were just as outlandish as those of his earlier ones, and did nothing to re-establish his pre-war reputation. He was awarded a Civil List pension in 1935, and died in lonely and lowly circumstances in Chichester, England, twelve years later.

The distancing of his writing from reality increased steadily throughout his life, and his final years were spent 'doing a book . . . in which is some detective work, proving, for example that the Apostle Paul was that Lazarus who, in his anti-Sadducee craze for resurrection, stayed four days in a tomb; and this book, I fancy, is my top-note . . .' Shiel always had a fondness for peculiar religious ideas and ideals, combined with a high opinion of himself and a very vivid imagination. In 1901, when he was thirty-six years old, he wrote:

by the time I was eleven . . . I had devoured . . . most of what is written in Greek. About the same time it occurred to me that English is a far greater language than Greek: and had never been written! Why, therefore, should not I be the child to write it?

Some such impulse drove me, about the age of twelve, to my first book; but, instead of writing English, I soon found myself caring for nothing on the earth but the imbroglio of phantoms in which my fancy involved me.

He remained embroiled with illusions to the end of his life, as is all too evident from his writing, but in nothing is it more obvious than in the connection he wrought between himself and the small islet of Redonda, which is situated to the north-west and well in sight of Montserrat. In an article About Myself, *composed for a brochure issued in 1929 to advertise the reprinting of some of his pre-war books, he wrote that 'I name myself "a native" of the West Indies, whither I was transported to commence to draw breath – to Montserrat', before going on to state:*

on my fifteenth birthday my father had me crowned King of Rodundo, a day of gala and of a great meeting of ships and people, many of them the worse for drink, the ceremony being performed by Dr Semper, then Bishop of Antigua, whose palm daubed me with the balm of anointment . . . Rodundo is a rock-island of scarcely nine square miles, and my subjects were troops innumerable of boobies swooping steeply into the sea like meteors streaming, with eleven poor men who gathered the boobies' excrement to make 'guano' (manure). And these were American people! When I imposed a nominal tax upon them, they each and all refused to pay, nor had I any means to compel them. Moreover, not long after my coronation the British Government, apprehensive that America might 'annex' the rock, 'annexed' it itself.

A second version of this tale, written later the same year but not printed until 1932, when it appeared as part of Shiel's entry in a writers' directory published in New York, contained some significant additions and one startling variation:

I was born in Montserrat, West Indies, preceded by eight sisters. After each female birth my father had a drawing-room prayer-meeting, conducted by the Wesleyan minister, to give thanks, but with hints to the Deity that a male birth next time would be appreciated; and finally I, Nature's last effort, was sent. My father being a preacher (not for money), 'religion' was my atmosphere . . . Moreover, my (Irish) father, 'descended from kings', had – wildly unlike his only-begotten son! – an admiration for kings, and on my fifteenth birthday had me crowned King of Redonda by Dr Mitchinson, Bishop of Antigua, with no little celebration, amid a gathering of ships (he was a ship-owner) and of tipsy people – Redonda being a small island that no Government had yet claimed.

At the time he wrote these two pieces Shiel was sixty-three years old. He had left Montserrat over forty years earlier, so the fact that he seemed unable to recall the name of the bishop who performed the 'coronation', or even how to spell the name of 'his' island, could fairly be put down to faulty memory. In any case, few ever queried these inconsistencies, and even fewer seem ever to have doubted that the events described did in fact take place. For the rest of his life Shiel stuck to his story and styled himself 'King Felipe I of Redonda', while conferring ridiculous dukedoms and knighthoods on some of his literary acquaintances.

The 'Realm of Redonda' which he created in this way undoubtedly would have expired with its founder, had 'King Felipe' not included among his 'courtiers' the now all-but forgotten poet and critic John Gawsworth. As Shiel's literary executor Gawsworth (whose real name was Terence Armstrong) decided to perpetuate the 'monarchy' by assuming yet another pseudonym, that of 'King Juan I of Redonda', and to expand the Redondan honours list. Among those he selected for one of his bogus knighthoods was his own literary executor, an English publisher who, long after the demise of Gawsworth, resuscitated Shiel's prize 'phantasm' and assumed the title of 'King Juan II' – so perpetuating the whole charade until the present day.

That the 'Realm of Redonda' was created by Shiel in order to boost his faded image as a writer, just at the time when there appeared the prospect of a revival of his fortunes, cannot be proved absolutely, but there are enough distortions, half-truths and plain untruths in the two versions of his 'coronation' to throw great doubt on the whole thing. He also wrote more than enough elsewhere to show that more often than not he preferred illusion to reality.

The reason for this, given his background and upbringing in a small, backward Caribbean island in the latter half of the nineteenth century, together with his determination to make good as a writer, is not too hard to understand. Details of family circumstances and early life are important factors in every writer's work. In Shiel's case, nearly sixty years after his death, they remain vital to whatever still remains of his reputation. To understand why this should be so it is necessary to analyse his accounts of the proceedings on Redonda, and the various statements which he makes in them.

As well as being unsure whether the island was called Rodundo or Redonda, he obviously had no idea of its true size, its population, or of its political status in 1880, when the 'coronation' was said to have taken place. Far from being 'scarcely nine square miles' in area, the island covers less than a quarter of one square mile. Phosphates had been mined there since 1869, and by 1880 several thousand tons were being removed annually by an American company employing a hundred or more workers. These employees, who nearly all came from Montserrat, lived on the island for months at a time. Because of this activity Redonda had been annexed to Antigua in 1872, and royalties had been paid by the mining company to the Federal Colony of the Leeward Islands (the seat of government of which was in Antigua) from then on.

With regard to the ceremony described by Shiel, no Dr Semper or Dr Mitchinson was ever Bishop of Antigua, and the first episcopal visit to Redonda did not take place until some time after 1882. In any event, regardless of names or dates, it is just as hard to envisage a senior Anglican cleric, at the height of the Victorian era, entering into some drunken frolic among piles of high-smelling guano, as it is to imagine such a personage 'crowning' the son of a Methodist lay preacher king of even the tiniest fragment of the British Empire.

In 1881, the year after his 'coronation' was supposed to have taken place, Shiel left Montserrat for Barbados. For the next three years he attended Harrison

College, a school with which the then Bishop of Barbados, Dr John Mitchinson, had close connections, and from which he, Shiel, matriculated in 1884. A year later he left the West Indies for England, where he remained for the rest of his life.

To at least one of his contemporaries on the London literary scene in later years Shiel was considered to be 'an inveterate liar'. On the strength of the details of his 'coronation', which the 'King' passed off as facts during the latter part of his life, this opinion of the novelist Arthur Machen may not have been too harsh. It is certainly borne out by various statements Shiel made about his parentage and background.

In the early 1930s, in a letter to a New York book dealer who had written to ask if he was, as the dealer suspected, 'a Negro writer', Shiel replied:

I'm afraid I am an Irish Paddy – very mixed blood – Andalusian, Moorish – but perhaps no 'Negro' except in so far as Roosevelt, the Mikado, that so 'Aryan' Hitler, are Negro . . .

His answer was disingenuous: Montserrat still awaits its first Spanish or North African settlers, and although the island had come under various Irish influences since the seventeeth century his claim to be an Irishman was just as fanciful as his claim to a throne.

Shiel's mother was born in 1828. From details in the parish records it is clear that she was a member of what was then known as the 'free coloured' community. In about 1850 (official records in Montserrat prior to 1863 are very scant) she married Matthew Dowdy Shiell, the man who became the writer's father. At that time, not so long after the abolition of slavery, and when the island's population of perhaps 7000 would have been rigidly divided into 'Black', 'White' and 'Coloured', it is difficult to believe that her husband could have been anyone other than a 'man of colour'. Added weight to this proposition is provided by Matthew Shiell's religion, as in the mid-nineteenth century not too many white Montserratians, particularly those who liked to think of themselves as Irish, would have professed Methodism. Any Irishness Matthew Dowdy Shiell may have inherited is much more likely to have stemmed from a liaison between an eighteenth-century plantation owner and one of his female slaves.

Some understanding of M.P. Shiel, the writer and fantasist, can be obtained from a similar understanding of the mores of a colonial backwater like Montserrat and a metropolitan centre like London in the late nineteenth century. He left the island as Matthew Phipps Shiell, a 20-year-old, well-educated, coloured colonial, with little other than a vivid imagination and a determination to become an author. He emerged in London a decade later as, in Hugh

Walpole's words, 'a flaming genius' of, in his own words, 'Irish parentage' whose birthplace was – again in Shiel's own words – 'like the burial-place of Moses, wrapped in mystery'. In other words, like many others of his sort of origins and complexion before and afterwards, he had to reject his background and change his name in order to get his talents recognized and to be accepted in white society. If there is anything which remains 'wrapped in mystery' it is why he felt that dropping the last letter of his surname made any difference, and how he supported himself during his first ten years in England.

Some idea of the anguish his 'passing for white' may have caused him is evident in a letter to one of his sisters (possibly the one the novelist Arthur Ransome mentions being introduced to in his autobiography, and whom he describes as 'a smiling negress'), written around the time his first book was published. Perhaps just as revealing as its frank sentiments is that they are expressed in clear, plain language, far removed from his normal florid literary style:

Some time ago I went to see a gentleman, and on the wall was a picture . . . of Negro men and women loading a Jamaican schooner with coconuts. Then I knew quite suddenly – THAT I am no Englishman. My heart leapt to them with love . . . They laugh knowing God. It was like a revelation to me . . . I greatly love the Negro Race: it is only the half-breeds that I think hateful and despicable.

Regardless of whatever pangs of conscience or feelings of alienation he may have felt during his early years in England, by the time he had become established as a novelist it was as a white *novelist that he was recognized and accepted by the London literary world. Even after his reputation faded and he fell back on boyhood memories to help revive his name (the 'coronation' was probably no more than some tomfoolery among relatives, perhaps mocking his story-telling abilities and over-active imagination, during a trip to Redonda given him as a birthday treat), those who believed in his fictitious kingdom also accepted his Irish 'descent from kings' without question.*

In the Caribbean today the name of M.P. Shiel is virtually unknown and his achievements as a writer completely ignored. The major collection of his papers, letters and manuscripts is held far away in Texas, and it is doubtful if more than a handful of his books could be found among all the Caribbean libraries. Even in Montserrat his name is all but forgotten. Outside the region appreciation of some of his work is expressed now and then by science fiction buffs, otherwise he is known only in connection with his ludicrous 'Kingdom of Redonda'.

This is bitterly ironic. By rejecting his ancestry Shiel did manage to achieve considerable success as a writer. Unfortunately he was of the wrong age and temperament to cope with the changes in the tastes of the British reading public brought about by the First World War, and his literary reputation expired long before he did. But had he not indulged in so much obfuscation about his background, or even if he had renounced his bogus Irishness and all the other sophistry later in life, there is every chance he would now be remembered and honoured – if not in England still – then at least in that part of the world from which he came.

M.P. Shiel was, in the parlance of his day, a coloured West Indian novelist, and surely today worthy of a place in the pantheon of Caribbean authors? That his books, with one exception, had nothing to do with the West Indies, and all today are virtually unreadable, is neither here nor there. Who is to say that in the latter half of the present century the novels of some of the current expatriate West Indian writers will not be considered equally arcane?

Whether or not his books were ever the romantic, imaginative masterpieces that Bennett, Wells and Walpole said they were, Shiel certainly made it as a writer and deserves to be remembered as one of the earliest, if not the first, West Indian novelist. That he is not, but instead is usually thought of as nothing more than a shadowy eccentric connected in some way with a make-believe Caribbean kingdom, is something to be regretted. As for the man himself, who once wrote poignantly 'But to believe fantasies is what causes half our sorrow, as not believing realities causes half . . .', it is probably no more than he would have expected.

Like job on a heap of ruins

Between 1987 (some years after I had left the Navy) and 1995, when we were forced to abandon our home there because of the eruption of a volcano (the top of Chance's Peak and the myth of the mermaid all being blown away in, dare I say it, the twinkle of an eye), my wife and I lived in Montserrat. The disaster brought about by the eruption was not the first we had suffered, as six years earlier our house – along with most of the others on the island – had been severely damaged by the never-to-be-forgotten Hurricane 'Hugo'.

Previous to that Montserrat had not suffered any serious hurricane damage for over sixty years, and in 1989, as the island waited for 'Hugo' to arrive, there were not too many people still alive who could recall just what they were in for. Reading an appeal which the resident Roman Catholic priest had written shortly after the 1928 hurricane would not have eased anyone's mind:

Dear Friends,

A most violent hurricane has swept over Montserrat, terrific and destructive far away beyond anything of the kind within the memory of those living in the land.

The Catholics have been the greatest sufferers in several respects. My church is a heap of ruins, hardly is a stone left upon a stone. Altars, statues, chandeliers, pulpit, tabernacle, everything has been crushed to bits. It has taken a week of strenuous work to discover a trace of the Holy Vessels and the Consecrated Hosts. Only the battered bell tower is standing as a lonely sentinel on a field of ruin and destruction. My school has been blown away in a thousand pieces to the neighbouring field.

My Chapel-of-ease is a heap of stones. The greater part of the Convent of the Sisters is carried away, and the other part is uninhabitable. The galleries of the Presbytery and a part of the roof have been torn off with unimaginable violence. The force of the gale was so irresistible that a part of the roof of the Convent was raised up in the air and crashed down before my door, a distance of 300 feet.

And our poor people, how much they have suffered! Forty-two dead have been found under the ruins of their houses. Hundreds of wounded, attended to in the best possible way have suffered cruelly. Scarcely two or three families of our Catholic Community in the southern district have a roof over their heads – a flock without a fold. At one of those huts still standing I found one evening one hundred and sixty-eight persons assembled for a shelter. My house serves as church, as Convent for the Sisters, as Presbytery, and as a shelter of relief. I am like Job on a heap of ruins, and it is easy for me to read in that heap of stones, of bent iron and shattered timber the life and works of Job, an edition revised and frightfully increased. I trust generous hearts will come to the rescue, otherwise what to do and where to turn my head, and how to begin? My people have nothing left, not a penny, no bread, no shelter, no garments to cover themselves.

And what a day, and what a night that fatal 12th September! A howling, a breaking, a tearing, a cracking, a flaming sky, a roaring ocean and torrents of water. It was to us like Death howling at the doors, hammering up the floors, shaking the walls to and fro, and battering down the roof with iron sledges. My boy fell on his knees for a hasty confession, and so did his little sister and my old servant. I confessed to Almighty God with a complete and sincere Contrition; never in my life have I made so many acts of contrition within so short a space of time. I had to satisfy myself with this Contrition, having no one to whom to confide my fears, my tremblings, and my consternation. How small, how powerless, how insignificant one feels, when around us everything is breaking, tearing, tumbling down and flying away through the sky. Never had I imagined that one could see and hear in so short a space of time a like accumulation of things so frightful, so nerve-racking, and so terrifying.

And now I am seated here as one absorbed in a lasting dream, unable to return to the cold reality, that cold reality which is a heap of stones, of bent iron, of broken timber, of ruin and of misery. Is it true, is it possible, is it imaginable? No church, no school, no altar, nothing except a faint spark of trembling life, and what is life without anything else?

F.E. PETERS, 1928

13 Antigua

'Near to perfection'

Antigua, as 'tis much the largest, so it is the most beautiful and best Inhabited of the [Leeward] Islands; of a fruitful Soil, but to be wrought with a good deal of labour; contains a great number of safe and commodious Harbours, which are well defended by Forts and Batteries erected on them for their Security: The Island is very healthy, and were it not for the excessive heat of the Sun, it would be in all things agreable to life.

GOVERNOR JOHN HART. In: *Letter to the Board of Trade*, 1722

Antigua is a fine Island, tho' it has not one Single Spring of Water in it: So that in times of drouth when all their Ponds are dry, and their Cisterns almost empty, they are obliged to fetch their fresh water from Montserrat, in times of War; or, in times of Peace from that and Guardaloup a Neighbouring French Island.

EMANUEL BOWEN, Note on his map of Antigua, *c.* 1750

I was very pleasantly surprised with the look of the country. Antigua is so generally spoken of as a dry and adust place where the earth refuses to yield water for the use of man, that I received more than ordinary pleasure in gazing on the gentle wooded hills and green meadow vales which decorate the interior of the island. Antigua . . . is formed . . . without any central eminences, but for the most part ramparted around by very magnificent cliffs, which slope inwards in gradual declivities. From some of these rocks, especially near the parsonage of St Philip's parish, one of the finest panoramic views in the world may be obtained . . . The heart of the island is verdant with an abundant pasturage or grassy down, and the numerous houses of the planters, embosomed in trees, have more of the appearance of country mansions in England than almost any other in the West Indies. The shores are indented in every direction with creeks and bays and coves, some of them running into the centre of the plantations like canals, some swelling into estuaries, and others forming spacious harbours. Beyond these, an infinite variety of islands and islets stud the bosom of the blue sea, and stand out like so many advanced posts of defence against the invading waves.

HENRY NELSON COLERIDGE, 1826

It is singular that in the island of Antigua there is not one spring of fresh water. Consequently the inhabitants are dependent for their supply of this necessary article on the rains, which fall at certain periods in torrents, and are caught in tanks, with which the barracks, as well as the generality of the better class of houses, are provided. From January until June 1804, scarcely a drop of rain fell; so that for many weeks we were on an extremely small allowance of water. Even this would have been still more limited, had not several sloops been constantly employed, during this drought, in bringing barrels of water from the neighbouring island of Montserrat, and thereby replenishing the tanks. Although the members of the corps to which I had the honour to belong, were by no means addicted to the use of water as a beverage, we nevertheless suffered severely from its scarcity.

LIEUTENANT-COLONEL J. LEACH, 1831

St John's, the capital of Antigua, is . . . well arranged, covers a space of about 150 acres of land; most of the streets are wide and well-kept, and intersect each other at right angles – the principal ones running in a straight line down to the sea. There is one peculiarity attending the construction of these streets, which is, that there are no causeways; and consequently, the pedestrian traveller has to elbow his way amid trucks and hand-barrows, gigs, carriages, and horsemen, droves of cattle, or cargoes of mules, just landed from other countries, cattle-carts, or moving houses.

At the corners of the different streets are seated hucksters (black or coloured women); some with their shallow trays, containing cakes of all descriptions, parched ground nuts, sugar-cakes, and other confections, and varieties of fruits and vegetables; others have piles of cottons, coloured calicoes, bright-tinted handkerchiefs, etc., placed by them, or carefully spread along the sides of the most frequented streets, to attract the eye of the passer-by. As most of the Antiguan houses are raised a few feet from the ground, which necessarily requires the use of a step or two, the hucksters are very fond of monopolising such appurtenances; and it is no uncommon thing to be obliged to wait until they remove their different wares, before you can enter the house, or else take the chance of breaking your neck over heaps of potatoes, or come in closer contact than is advisable with bottles of ginger-drink, or pots and pans of gorgeous colours, from the well-known English potteries.

MRS LANAGHAN, 1844

. . . Antigua is dependent on the rains that fall for the supply of water [and] although it is not quite correct to say, as is often done, that there are no springs in this island, still there are very few, and those that are to be found are very inconsiderable . . .

But it is only those who entertain northern notions of what is called 'rainwater', who would regard this fact as an objection to a residence in the island. Whether it be that the absence of smoke causes the rain to reach the earth in a state of greater purity, or that more attention is paid to its purification and safe keeping after it is gathered into tanks, I know not; but this I know, that I never felt the want of good pure water while I sojourned in Antigua . . . The want of spring water in Antigua is, therefore, not felt to be a want even by those who do not belong to the class of the West Indian, who, when applied to to decide a dispute as to the salubrity of water in an island in which he had resided for seventeen years, answered – 'Water, gentlemen! – water! I really don't recollect ever having tasted *the water*.'

R. BAIRD, 1850

There is one street in St John's known as Scotch Row, from its being inhabited chiefly by Scotch shopkeepers, who are mighty *nonchalant* in manner, whilst their shopboys, mostly from some high flat in the Gallogate, are often absolutely rude, invariably omitting the 'sir', when addressing a customer, and bandying about the 'yes' and 'no', in terms of offensive familiarity. They are lazy withal. One morning at half-past six, an hour when in the Tropics all mankind ought to have been up, I walked out to make a purchase, and found not a single store open. At last one solitary shopman drove into town in his gig! Thus are trading matters arranged in Antigua. Several of the merchants are confirmed drunkards. One, for a week at a time, is never sober; another rarely quits his bed, but lies drinking rum and porter from morn 'till dewy eve, and eve 'till morn again. Canny Scotland indeed seldom shews itself to advantage in the West Indies.

CHARLES W. DAY, 1852

Antigua is lower, longer, and flatter than the other islands. It carries no central peak: but its wildness of ragged uplands forms, it is said, a natural fortress, which ought to be impregnable; and its loyal and industrious people boast that, were every other West Indian island lost, the English might make a stand in Antigua long enough to enable them to reconquer the whole. I should have feared, from the look of the island, that no large force could hold out long in a country so destitute of water as those volcanic hills, rusty, ragged, treeless, almost sad and desolate – if any land could be sad and desolate with such a blue sea leaping around and such a blue sky blazing above.

CHARLES KINGSLEY, 1871

As the steamer enters St John's Harbour, where the largest men-of-war may safely lie at anchor, though its entrance is difficult and at times dangerous, on account of hidden rocks and a sandy bar, the spectator is at once struck with the exceedingly pleasing appearance of the capital town, with its regular and well-laid-out streets, and signs of commercial activity; and all praise is due to the indefatigable Antiguans, who certainly deserve 'the palm of merit' for their industry and perseverance in the face of such difficulties as have never been experienced by any of the other islands. When I state that they have absolutely no rivers, and but few springs, and that up to a few years ago they were dependent upon the rainwater collected in tanks and ponds for their own use, and for purposes of irrigation, and yet that every acre available for cultivation is or has been farmed, and with former very great success, my readers will understand under what apparently insurmountable difficulties the Antiguans have both toiled and succeeded.

O.T. BULKELEY, 1889

Antigua is a complete contrast to Dominica. It is an island of coral formation ... and most of it is very flat. It much resembles Barbados. The greater part of its area is under sugar-cane cultivation, and the broad fields of green canes, with the plantation buildings nestling in clumps of tall trees, dotted here and there, make a landscape that reminds one rather of wheat-growing districts in the Homeland. In fact the island is very 'English' in many ways, and the coloured folk, instead of speaking a French patois, as in Dominica, talk in a queer clipped English in which one finds many old words only used in the days of the Georges. The island, having been settled for more than 250 years, has a long history behind it, and there is about it an air of gentility and conservatism that is missing in the colonies that have been under more than one flag.

SIR HESKETH BELL, 1905 (*see* HESKETH BELL, 1946)

To-day Antigua is a very different sort of place, and the capital, St John's, is quite an imposing little town, though still somewhat old-fashioned. Fortunately it had its wide streets laid out in regular lines by some wise eighteenth-century town-planning expert, and subsequent generations have benefited more than he could ever have dreamed ...

... and in many ways Antigua is very conservative, and for many reasons, but not all, one is perhaps glad that she is. There is a friendly spirit everywhere such as is seldom found in these hurrying, scurrying days: in fact I once heard Antigua described as being rather 'eighteen-sixtyish', and that it was all like a big family party. Indeed, a prominent coloured Civil Servant said recently – much to the embarrassment of the lady, not long out from England, to whom he was talking – 'Yes, Ma'am, you'll find Antigua a very pleasant place to live in. We are all in the family way out here!'

SIR REGINALD ST-JOHNSTON, 1936

Antigua is near to perfection, but it is not in the accepted sense of the word tropical. There is no lush magnificence of vegetation even in the hot, low-lying part of the island where coconuts and swamps fringe the sea. There are – in exchange for thickly forested mountains, tree-ferns and abundance of flowering trees, habitual from Tobago or Grenada to Jamaica – a number of beautiful harbours, each with its tale of battle, personal or national, with ragged coasts so that rock and island seem to be carved out of the sea.

ROSITA FORBES, 1949

Antiguan style . . .

The 'air of gentility and conservatism' noted in Antigua by Hesketh Bell in 1905 (when he was living there for a while as Acting Governor of the Leeward Islands), and which was still very much in evidence during Sir Reginald St-Johnston's time as Governor thirty years later, had disappeared long before I first set foot on the island in 1959. It had been greatly disturbed by the establishment of American navy and air force bases there during the Second World War, and afterwards any residue had been blown away completely by the advent of mass tourism. But another well-established aspect of the Antiguan character, which the war and the arrival of tourism had done nothing to modify, was still very much in evidence in the middle of the twentieth century, and has become even more pronounced since. This was that Antiguans felt themselves, and made no bones about claiming, to be a distinct cut above their neighbours. If today it would be difficult to find many in Bell's 'Homeland' prepared to subscribe to the view of Cecil Rhodes, Remember that you are an Englishman, and have consequently won first prize in the lottery of life, *it would prove just as hard to find anyone in Antigua who did not consider that to have been born an Antiguan was to have won the jackpot in the lottery of West Indian life (and, dear Reader, who better to know this than someone married to an Antiguan?).*

In 1900 Hesketh Bell, a year after taking up the post of Governor of Dominica, was provided at first hand with perhaps not the ideal example of this facet of the Antiguan character:

I returned yesterday from an extremely interesting jaunt through one of the wildest parts of the island . . . So that some of the men, who have just come out from England with the idea of becoming planters, might have a look at this part of Dominica I invited four of them to accompany me . . .

One of the planters, near Layou, kindly provided us with ponies for the first part of the journey, and, as we had to spend a couple of nights in the forest, we had to take rather a lot of camping outfit with us. What with the porters and other hangers-on we were quite a large party. The only unhappy member of it was my temporary servant. My own man, hearing that we were bound for a long trudge through the forest, had, of course, suddenly developed an acute pain in his foot and declared his inability to walk. He had, however, provided a substitute in the shape of a tall black man from Antigua. This man was a recent arrival in Dominica and was evidently determined to show the greater 'distinction' of the people of the northern island as compared to what he called the 'bush people' of Dominica. The natives of the various islands are extremely insular in their pride, and constantly try to assure each other of their relative superiority. The coloured folk of Barbados claim to be the most up-to-date, but the people of the Leeward Islands consider that they run them pretty close. I was speaking to my Antiguan, on that subject, on our way up to Layou, and was amused to hear him say: 'Oh, yessah! Barbados may be all very well for eddication, but it is Antigua for de polish.' This man, who rejoiced in the name of Williamson, had rigged himself out in a garb that was entirely unsuited to bush work. He had a very smart suit on and a bowler hat. On his feet were the largest pair of patent-leather boots I think I have ever seen, and he carried a small, black and shiny portmanteau with his initials in large white letters thereon . . .

When we started on our journey the weather was lovely, but the sky soon became overcast and it was evident that we were in for a storm. The track became so bad that we had to send back our ponies and proceed on our flat feet. In many places the undergrowth beneath the gigantic forest trees became so dense that our men had to hack a way through for us . . .

After three hours of such progress even the youngest of us began to feel the strain of the effort, and especially was this the case with my unfortunate Antiguan. At one place I found him sitting at the foot of a huge tree, looking the picture of misery. He had discarded his patent-leather boots and they were hanging round his neck. His beautiful suit was covered with mud and there was a large dent in his 'bowler'. When I tried to cheer him up he only looked up plaintively and exclaimed: 'Oh, sah! Had I the wings of a dove!'

That the assumption of an air of superiority in Antigua has never been confined to the members of any one level of society, or to people of one particular colour, or even to just those born on the island, was demonstrated long before the unfortunate Mr Williamson lost some of his style in the forests of Dominica in an episode related in Antigua and the Antiguans, *a book published in the first half of the nineteenth century:*

A resident of Antigua, who, in days of militia glory, served in the dragoons, went to a neighbouring island, of which he was a native, to pay a visit to his friends. In order to astonish the inhabitants, and create a 'sensation', Mr – determined to land in full uniform. The dress of the dragoons was very smart, and the swords and steel scabbards they carried, very long and heavy. Fancy then, our brave *militaire*, who, bye the bye, is a very short and corpulent personage, with a redundancy of colour, landing upon a sandy beach, beneath a burning sun, in all the glory of blue cloth and yellow worsted, with his Goliath-like weapon, scarcely twelve inches shorter than himself, dangling, or rather dragging, gracefully by his side. Although of little stature, he is big of heart; and proudly erecting his head, and settling his shoulders, he marched along, amid a herd of astonished boatmen and sea-side loiterers, with all the dignity of a commander-in-chief. The news spread like wild fire – astonishment was at its height – for rich and poor, black, white, and coloured, all thought their *ci-devant* neighbour was Fortune's child, and had been promoted governor of his native island. Before, however, any procession could be formed, or salute fired to welcome his arrival, his real rank was discovered; and as the truth became known, the assembled multitude one after another departed, and left our gallant dragoon 'alone in his glory'.

MRS LANAGHAN, 1844

A most convenient and commodious place

Most of my time in Antigua in 1959, as the most junior surveyor on board HMS Vidal, was spent in assisting with a survey of St John's Harbour, in preparation for the dredging and construction work which was to take place when deep water port facilities were created there during the next decade. The survey was interesting enough, particularly as the inner harbour in those days was too shallow to provide an anchorage for anything larger than the traditional West Indian trading schooners. With such craft in plentiful evidence along with a variety of other wooden boats, as well as the barges which were used to ferry bulk sugar out to ships lying in the outer harbour, it presented an appearance which could not have changed greatly in over 100 years.

On the opposite side of the island was another much smaller harbour with even more of the air and aspect of a bygone era. This, because of its long association with the Royal Navy, those of us with an interest in history found even more appealing. By that time English Harbour had ceased to be the silent, deserted, almost forgotten place which a visitor like Helen Cameron Gordon – who is quoted later in this chapter – had seen shortly before the Second World War, but it was still very far from the bustling hub of the Caribbean yachting world it was soon to become:

Whereas English Harbour in this Island is by nature a port of the utmost safety and security for His Majesty's ships against violent storms and tempests, and at the same time a most convenient and commodious place for refitting and cleaning any number of ships that His Majesty may think fit to send to his American plantations, either for the protecting them or annoying his enemies in these parts, the which being taken into consideration by the Legislature of this Island, they, out of duty to His Majesty and regard to their country, have, at very great charge and expense to the public of this Island, caused a wharf to be built at the said harbour for the use of His Majesty's ships and erected a fort at the entrance of the harbour to defend the same, of which His Majesty in his great wisdom hath already so far approved that he has at his own charge been graciously pleased to cause storehouses to be built there, and withal to supply us with cannon and several stores of war for the use of the said fort, for which, as well as the rest of his tender and paternal care of us his distant and remote subjects, we the Governor-in-Chief of these his Leeward Caribbee Islands in America, and the Council and Assembly of Antigua (with hearts of unshaken duty and loyalty) do humbly beg leave to return our utmost unfeigned and hearty thanks.

Preamble to an Act of the Antigua House of Assembly, 1733

... we proceeded to English-harbour, where the only dockyard of importance on this station is established. This harbour is large, and deep enough to admit ships of any size, although the entrance is so narrow, that they are obliged to be warped in. It is agreeably situated, surrounded on all sides by lofty hills covered with shrubs ... Ships of war seldom come here but for the purpose of refitting, as this is one of the most unhealthy spots in the West Indies; at least, there are more seamen die here every year than in the whole Leeward Island station besides, with the exception of Barbados. The situation itself is unhealthy, being so surrounded that the ventilation is impeded, and the heat becomes intolerable. Indeed, there seems to be no spot in these countries but what is from time to time visited by the yellow fever, which renders them the grave of Europeans. But the causes of fever here are accumulated: the men are employed at severe labour in the dock-yard beneath a vertical sun; and, in spite of the severest discipline, find the means of procuring rum at an easy rate – a temptation no sailor can withstand. If they see a single individual of sober habits fall a victim, it is a sufficient argument to them that temperance is no security, and they may as well enjoy the luxuries while within their reach.

J.A. WALLER, 1820

It was hard work the whole way to English Harbour, where we arrived ... a little before sunset ... The entrance is exceedingly narrow, and every preparation was made to moor the ship in the event of the wind baffling her. An attempt to tack would infallibly run a vessel ashore. However we glided in gently to our birth between the two quays of the dockyard, and fastened the ship by hawsers to rings on the shore on either side.

This is without exception the prettiest little harbour I ever saw; the extreme neatness of the docks, the busy village which has grown up in their vicinity, the range of hills of various shapes and colors which encircle the inland sides, and the rocky Ridge which frowns over the mouth with its Union and cannons and ramparts, present such a combination of tropical beauty and English style and spirit as I never saw elsewhere in the West Indies. The harbour is said to be unhealthy, and from its inclosed situation such a circumstance seems probable; at the same time I have not heard of any instance in which the crews of ships have materially suffered during their stay there. Indeed it is a season of great merriment with them: they live on shore, and after their regular dock labour, dance and sing all the evening to their own abundant content. The officers have a large and commodious barrack to themselves, and in most cases find it a very agreeable place of relaxation from the wretched confinement on board ship in this perspiring climate. St John's, the capital of Antigua, lies on the opposite side of the island, and this distance, which is perhaps a little annoying to the more urban part of the lieutenants and midshipmen, is an excellent quality in the harbour with regard to the common sailors. There is a devil in the West Indies called New Rum, which has killed almost as many stout tars as the French have, and he looks so like an angel of light in Jack's eyes, that it is not in the poor fellow's heart to refuse him any thing.

HENRY NELSON COLERIDGE, 1826

The dockyard presents a fine and noble appearance; and ... everything seems to be conducted in the best possible manner; while the yard itself is kept so beautifully clean, that a walk through it affords real pleasure ...

The storehouses upon St Helena are principally used for storing coals, and in consequence, her majesty's steam-vessels frequent more that side of the dock. The largest ships of war (that visit these seas) can go alongside this wharf when necessary ...

The last-erected part of this naval establishment, or 'the dockyard', as it is more generally called, is separated from St Helena by the blue waters of the dock, and contains various buildings ...

. . . I must be allowed to remark, that, although in my life I have visited many public buildings in England, as well as in other parts of the globe, I never met with more politeness, from the lowest to the highest of the officials, that I experienced at this English Harbour naval establishment.

MRS LANAGHAN, 1844

A more picturesque or more uncanny little hole than [English Harbour] we had never yet seen . . . Past low cliffs of ash and volcanic boulder, sloping westward to the sea, which is eating them fast away, the steamer runs in through a deep crack, a pistol-shot in width. On the east side a strange section of gray lava and ash is gnawn into caves. On the right, a bluff rock of black lava dips sheer into water several fathoms deep; and you anchor at once inside an irregular group of craters, having passed through a gap in one of their sides, which has probably been torn out by a lava flow . . . This first basin is for half of its circumference circular, and walled with ash beds . . . To the left it leads away into a long creek, up which, somewhat to our surprise, we saw neat government-houses and quays; and between them and us, a noble ironclad and other ships of war at anchor . . . But right ahead, the dusty sides of the crater are covered with strange bushes . . . while on the cliffs around, aloes innumerable . . . send up their groups of huge fat pointed leaves from crannies so arid that one would fancy a moss would wither in them. A strange place it is, and strangely hot likewise . . .

CHARLES KINGSLEY, 1871

The undying interest of Antigua centres in and about the famous English Harbour . . . on the south coast . . .

No place I have visited has brought back to my imagination more vividly scenes that must have been enacted in the past. Perhaps it is because all the buildings are enclosed within a comparatively small area; or else, that the now deserted harbour is shut away and distinct from all the world: entirely individual, entirely self-effacing, as it must have been, and so extraordinarily well suited for its splendid purpose – headquarters of the Admiralty in the West Indies during the French wars.

All still, all silent now, but vibrant with recollections of famous, fearless men.

HELEN CAMERON GORDON, 1942

Events large and small

On the 12th of June, 1842, a very bright and beautiful meteor passed over the town of St John's, in a direction from east to west. Its form was globular; and as it passed rapidly along the heavens, it emitted bright spiral flashes of fire, which gilded the sky, and threw deep shadows upon the earth. During its progress, it was attended by a rushing noise, sufficient to call the attention of those who did not even notice its extreme brilliancy . . .

The next great event to be recorded, is the awful earthquake, with which Antigua and many of the other Leeward Islands was visited, on Wednesday, the 8th of February, 1843 . . . a low, hollow, rumbling sound arrested the attention, and announced, in its own peculiar solemn tone, the coming of an earthquake. Immediately after this awful warning, a tremor of the earth was felt, which gradually increasing in violence, led the frightened inhabitants to rush from their houses, and seek safety in the open air. Heart-rending were the screams, fervent and numerous were the calls for mercy, from the assembled groups. The air was darkened with the dust from the falling buildings, as well as from the sulphureous exhalations which issued from the opening earth, and almost stopped respiration . . .

The excess of terror occasioned by this awful throe of Nature was so great, that many individuals threw themselves over the wharfs, and sought refuge in the treacherous waves. Still their fears were not allayed; for the sea was so turbulent that they were under the necessity of again seeking dry land to save themselves from being engulfed in its yawning abyss . . .

MRS LANAGHAN, 1844

The vast majority of the people who have visited Antigua since Mrs Lanaghan's day have gone there without witnessing anything nearly as dramatic as a heavenly fireball, or suffering breathlessness from anything resembling 'sulphureous exhalations', but few will have left without having at some time been disturbed by something much more insignificant. That almost always this will have been a far less fleeting experience than seeing the flash of a meteor or feeling the shock of an earthquake is made evident by the account of one irate visitor, a near-contemporary of the author of Antigua and the Antiguans:

My first acquaintance with the West Indian musquito was made during a week's residence in an indifferent lodging-house in St John's, Antigua, where, in consequences of my not being protected from their attacks by the almost indispensable musquito net, I was peculiarly exposed to their assaults; and, judging from my experience at that time, I would have supposed, not only that they were a legion in point of number, but that they were the worst of the many species into which the famous Cubans divide those to be found in their island. Indeed, it was not till an after period of my journeyings, when in the Spanish colonies, and also in the southern states of America, that I found any of the musquito tribe more annoying than those encountered in Antigua. First impressions are, however, always the most acute, if not always the most lasting; and it is therefore during the first weeks of his sojourn that the invalid will feel most annoyance from the cause referred to. Moreover, and the assertion will seem a strange one, almost as much discomfort is produced by the buzz or humming of the insect as by its bite . . . The humming sound, produced by the motion of the wings of the insect, and which impresses the mind with the conviction that it is only selecting a soft and sensitive point of attack, often proves very annoying, particularly to one debilitated by illness. Indeed, the bite of the insect is scarcely felt at the time; nor is it productive of much annoyance at any time, provided only the party operated upon can refrain from rubbing the part that may be affected.

R. BAIRD, 1850

14 Barbuda

'Such a barren rocke'

. . . the last yeare 1628, Master Littleton (a planter of St Christopher), with some others, got a Patent of the Earle of Carlisle to plant the Isle called [Barbuda] thirty leagues northward of St Christopher; which by report of their informers and undertakers for the excellencie and pleasantnesse thereof they called Dulcina, but when they came there, they found it such a barren rocke, they left it.

CAPTAIN JOHN SMITH, 1630

Barbuda bears due north from [Antigua], and is about thirty miles distant. It is so low and level that I at least could not distinctly make it out, till we were within four miles from it. The coast is beset with shoals and reefs under water, and it was a matter of some anxiety to see how the vessel insinuated itself, as it were, between these rocks, a man standing on the bowsprit and giving his directions to the helm. We got to land in about six hours from our setting out.

Here some of the party mercilessly oppressed the sides of certain macilent and cat-ham'd creatures which the natives from ignorance suppose to be horses; they are ten hands in height and their necks and heads fall from the shoulder in an angle of forty five degrees below the horizon. Four of us invaded the state carriage which came down from [Codrington] for the express purpose of importing us . . .

In this vehicle we sat an hour under one of the most undeniable tempests of rain I ever was caught in, whilst we painfully moved on at a foot's pace over the grassy track which led from the shore . . . The vegetation on either side . . . appeared here more like a young forest, the trees and bushes being so high as to preclude the possibility of seeing twenty yards to the right hand or left of the road. The surface of the country is at the same time such a dead level, except an inconsiderable hillock at the other end of the island, that none but the veteran woodsman can traverse it with certainty. The forest is well stocked with uncommonly fine deer, and a certain number of the slaves are the recognized gamekeepers of the island . . . They generally possess a horse each, a duck gun and dogs, and I believe have little else to do except maintain themselves and procure venison whenever it is wanted. The worst is, the fellows always fire with slugs; so that usually the haunch is lacerated in sundry places in a manner vexatious to the cook, and inconvenient to the consumer. Some of us were up to a regular chase, but upon an inspection of the universal stud of the colony, we found there was no horse of more than two miles-an-hour power, and besides, the thickets were so close that riding after a stag would have been impracticable . . .

We arrived at [Codrington] as wet as water can make the outside lendings of men. Our bags and portmanteaus were nearly in the same condition . . .

HENRY NELSON COLERIDGE, 1826

Verily, gentlemen of Antigua, your corn-fed mutton is excellent; you moreover evince much philosophical acumen in your piscivorous propensities. Your crawl-nurtured *corramor* is a competitor with the salmon, and for the recondite process of stewing, your mud-fish surpasseth the pond-fed carp; and then your groupers, yellow-tails, mullets, and snappers, your trunk lobsters and cockles, and that delicate tantalizing dainty, the mangrove oyster, are all superlatively good: but where, in the name of Apicius, do you get your venison? It comes from the neighbouring island of Barbuda: which lies nearly due north of Antigua, about twenty eight miles, but so low, that in hazy weather you are close in with the shore, when only the tops of the trees appear above the horizon as if growing out of the water.

T. WENTWORTH, 1834

The Island of Barbuda lies between the latitudes of 17° 32′, and 17° 44′ N.... it is low and flat, with a rocky shore, somewhat elevated toward the East, N., W., and North-West; it is well inhabited, and fertile, producing cotton, corn, sheep, fowls, fruit, pepper, indigo, and tobacco; but good water is scarce. The greatest extent of Barbuda from NW to SE is 15 miles, and its highest land is not to be discerned on any side more than 6 leagues off; the greater part of its shores are rocky, foul, and extremely dangerous; for you will frequently find at the prow of your vessel 50 and 60 fathoms water, while at the stern there will only be 4 or 5 fathoms, so steep and hazardous are the reefs that surround it ... This island did belong to the *Codrington* family, one of whom bequeathed its revenue to the Society for propagating the Gospel. Its present inhabitants are about 1500 negroes, who, under the direction of a few white people, are employed chiefly in raising stock for the neighbouring islands. Citrons, pomegranates, oranges, figs, raisins, and a variety of herbs and roots are cultivated with much success, and the island abounds with the finer sorts of woods.

JOHN W. NORIE, 1836

Barbuda Island was for years known as 'the sportsman's paradise', and at one time deer, and duck, and wild guinea-fowl were numerous ...

Sir Sydney Armitage-Smith, whom I took over with me on one occasion in HMS *Dauntless*, was a keen deer-stalker, and had shot them in the Highlands, in the Carpathians, and in other parts of the world. Reading in a guide-book of 'the sportsman's paradise', and of the Barbuda deer, he had brought with him to the West Indies various rifles, many cases of ammunition, and, in spite of my warnings, much optimism. I had some official business to attend to that afternoon, and had to leave him to his own devices. I did, however, see that he had the best guide available. The haunt of the deer was a long way off and could only be reached by walking, mostly along the beach as there were no roads and but few tracks through bush. But his zeal was still alight and off he went. It was about sunset when I returned to the ship, and I was sitting comfortably on deck with [the captain], enjoying a whiskey and soda, when we looked shoreward and observed a dejected-looking figure carrying a rifle at the slope and heavily ploughing through the loose sand. It was poor Armitage-Smith, and he *was* cross when he at last arrived on board; and it was not until he had had a drink or two that we could get a word out of him but subterranean murmurs and curses. It appeared that he had fought his way all day through scratchy bush, surrounded by clouds of flies and mosquitoes, and once he *thought* he had seen a deer!

SIR REGINALD ST-JOHNSTON, 1936

Delicacies and dangers

Had Armitage-Smith, a retired senior civil servant turned great white hunter, bothered to read anything which previous visitors to Barbuda had written – other than of its somewhat dubious reputation as a 'sportsman's paradise' – he might not have been quite so keen to venture into the bush:

The mosquitoes are so terrible [in Barbuda] that there was no sitting in peace, till some oakum was lighted and green leaves thrown upon it, which produced a great smoke and effectually banished them. It would require some familiar acquaintance with these gents the mosquitoes to believe that this lacrymose smoke was an exchange for the better. But he who once has heard that shrill hostile clang about his nose or cheeks, and knows that the winged wretch only waits till he has found out the softest and most delicate cranny of your face, in which to fix his cursed proboscis, and there out suck your Christian blood, leaving behind him redness and swelling and itching and pustule . . . this man would rather sit in the smoke of a brewery than be at the tender mercy of these unwearied plagues of fallen man.

HENRY NELSON COLERIDGE, 1826

To have obtained one of the island's other great delicacies would have been far easier and, if we are to accept at face value the rapturous approbation of someone who had sampled it while visiting Barbuda 100 years earlier, far more satisfying:

Let the corporation of London only purchase the fee-simple of the island of Barbuda, and elect annually from among themselves a viceregent duly qualified, and they may each in turn feast to their heart's content, and bestow their benison on the primitive excellencies of indigenous turtle. He who has never tasted of this amphibious triad in its native latitudes, has no comprehensive idea of the generous redundancy of relish, the cherishing and invigorating stimulus it imparts to the percipient gourmand. The West Indians practise, with scientific distinction, a more scrupulous exactness in modifying the trichotomous divisions of fish, flesh, and fowl, than your *artiste* of the kitchen in England, whose skill attains only to confounding their distinctive properties in the masquerade of soup. He has no conception of the unsophisticated excellence of turtle steaks; of the emollient and salubrious qualities of green fat, asserting its own supremacy, and the incomparable goût of fresh turtles' eggs! besides, the animal wastes in flesh, and the viscosity of its juices become empoverished on the voyage.

T. WENTWORTH, 1834

The general appearance of Barbuda, and especially the track from the landing place on the south coast to the village of Codrington as described by Coleridge in 1826, had changed little by the time I first visited the island almost a century and a half later. In 1974 I was in command of the delightfully-named survey ship Fawn, *and had been given the task of charting the waters all around Barbuda to a distance of about ten nautical miles offshore. Surprisingly, in the written instructions I had received concerning the survey not only was no mention made of charting the waters close inshore, but I was specifically forbidden from taking the ship within less than a mile of the coast. Once I had read about the island in the modern version of Norie's Caribbean sailing directions, traversed it in the ship, and then had a walk around some of the shoreline (leaving* Fawn *at anchor more or less where Governor St-Johnston had sipped his whisky and soda on board HMS* Dauntless *many years earlier), the reason for this prohibition was all too clear.*

That Barbuda was a place to be given a wide berth had been made apparent to mariners long before the mathematician and hydrographer John Norie had compiled his West India Directory. *By the 1830s, when his sailing directions were being written, the island – because of its position and extremely low profile – had been a danger to shipping for over 300 years. It had begun to claim ships, lives and cargoes from the early sixteenth century, soon after the time of Columbus, and was to remain a serious hazard for nearly another century after the* Directory *was published. If it became less so during the twentieth century it was only because of the development and increasing use of modern position-fixing aids such as radar and satellite navigation receivers.*

The total number of vessels which have grounded or been wrecked on Barbuda is unknown, but nearly 150 were recorded between 1685, when the island was first settled, and 1927, when the last one of any size to be lost ran ashore on the east coast. Some of those that landed up on the west or south coasts, which are reasonably rock-free, could and did manage to haul themselves off again with the loss of little more than minor damage to the hull and a major blow to the master's pride and reputation. All of those that ran on to the reefs which protect the north and east coasts were doomed to stay and break up there. A Spanish galleon, the Santiago de Cullerin, which foundered off the south-eastern point of the island in 1695, while undoubtedly not the first wreck, is the earliest about which anything is known.

Those that followed, year in and year out, for the next two centuries or more ran into the island from all directions, many after ocean passages from places as far away as Sweden, Italy, Surinam and Massachusetts. Nearly all were cargo vessels, ranging in size from small wooden schooners to, in later days, large iron steamships, loaded with anything from slaves to sulphur, coal to coffee, manure to machine parts. Sometimes the entire cargo was lost with the ship, but more often than not some if not most of it could be saved, and salvage work provided the Barbudans, whether as slaves or free men, with a major occupation. It also provided the lessees of the island – the Codrington family mentioned in Norie's Directory who possessed the valuable 'Right to Wreck' – with a considerable source of income. The 44-gun frigate HMS Woolwich, which was lost off the north coast in 1813, provided little in the way of salvage money as all the crew were saved and they stripped the ship of everything of value before she was abandoned. For many years afterwards, however, so much of her copper sheathing was recovered that even when Coleridge visited the island in 1825 he was able to record that the remains of the frigate were 'now commonly called Sir Bethel Codrington's copper mine'.

For the men who carried out such salvage operations the work was not without its risks, as was made all too apparent in 1847 after a French vessel, Le Nouveau Justin, had gone aground. The master complained that the salvors, anxious to save as much of the ship and cargo as they could, had acted without his consent, and in a violent and dishonest manner. The matter was blown up into a diplomatic incident which was not resolved until after it had been taken up at government level in Paris and London. That salvage work was also not without its unexpected compensations was probably best demonstrated sixty-odd years later when a large schooner, the Ruth B Cobb, ran on to the south coast. As she was laden with nothing but rum and cocoa the salvors needed very little time to decide on which portion of the cargo to direct their attention, nor later on how best to bamboozle the Receiver of Wreck concerning the number of barrels recovered.

The last ship, as opposed to a boat or yacht, to be wrecked was the steamship, Amersfoort, a large Dutch-registered freighter which ran aground on the east *coast in 1927. In spite of it having been pounded ever since by the Atlantic rollers which crash on to the windward coast, a part of the hull was still very much visible during* Fawn's *survey in 1974, and remains so today.*

15 Redonda

'A mere volcanic peak'

A storm-tossed, iron-bound coast; frowning cliffs towering upwards to the height of a thousand feet; rocky slopes so precipitous that even the wild goats can scarce gain a foothold thereon! Such are the points which will strike you most about Redonda as you view it from the deck of the ramshackle little sugar drogher which has brought you hither.

But perchance you have never heard of the place, do not know its position on the map and are unaware of its claims to distinction. And if this be so it is hardly surprising, for it is a spot so little known, so far removed from the path of the most ubiquitous globe-trotter, that even a schoolteacher might be pardoned for being ignorant of its whereabouts, its products and its population.

By way of introduction, then let it be said that the island in question is one of the smallest of the leeward Antilles, and that it is situated some fifteen miles to the northward of Montserrat . . . A mere volcanic peak rising sheer from the ocean bed, it remained for unnumbered ages in the possession of sea-birds, no one thinking it worthy of settlement; but about thirty years ago it was accidently discovered to contain rich deposits of guano, and since that time it has been persistently hammered, drilled and blasted in order to make it yield up the mineral.

Dorothy Harding, who began an early twentieth-century magazine article with these words, was the third child and only daughter of a British merchant marine officer, Captain Jesse Ham Harding, and his wife Maria. She was born on board her father's ship, the barque Traveller, *in the Indian Ocean in 1880, two years before the captain retired from the sea in order to take up the unusual (but for a man accustomed to commanding an all-male body of workers in confined circumstances, not inappropriate) position of Superintendent of Redonda, in charge of the phosphate mining operations.*

The Harding family, except during infrequent visits to England or brief periods in some of the islands round about, particularly Montserrat, remained on Redonda until Captain Harding's death in 1904. Although Dorothy and her brothers received no formal schooling, but were taught by their parents, until they were well into their teenage years, none suffered from what must have been a most unusual childhood. Both boys became doctors, and Dorothy from the age of about twenty was able to support herself in England as a writer and journalist. Her account of life on Redonda was published a year before she married and moved to the United States, where she died in 1939. It remains, other than two articles published by her mother, the only eye-witness account of life on Redonda during the time it was inhabited; a period which came to an end in 1929:

At the present day [*c.* 1902] the population is a floating one, varying according to the season from as many as two hundred and fifty to as few as ten or a dozen souls, but of these only three are white – the Superintendent, his wife and his assistant. Furthermore, it should be understood that, in this instance, mankind does not, as in legal phraseology, embrace woman, for with the one exception already mentioned the feminine element is entirely wanting. This is a state of affairs which never fails to evoke the amazement of the stranger, but a very few words will suffice to explain its *raison d'être.*

When, nearly twenty years ago, Captain H———, the present manager, went to take charge of the mines, he found the community seething with rebellion and civil war (the two most fertile causes of trouble being native rum and 'destructive, damnable, deceitful woman'), and being a man wise enough to know his limitations the first step he took towards establishing peace and order was to stop the supply of liquor for all time and to banish every petticoat beyond the seas. Since then not a single black woman has set foot on his dominions, though he and Mrs H——— are always ready to give a hearty welcome to any white ladies who may wish to pay the island a visit.

It is usually a source of great surprise to members of the fair sex that labourers are willing to come and work in the mines, seeing that in doing so they must leave their wives and families behind them; but, strange as it may appear, this rule has never given rise to complaint.

The men, nearly all of whom come from Montserrat, are expected to remain on the island for three months before going home, but many of them stay longer than this without asking for a holiday, notably a little, wizened, white-wooled negro, named George Washington, who once put in a two years' spell of continuous work without going away for a single day. They are a happy, irresponsible, light-hearted race, these darkies, seeming to be quite unaware of the existence of such things as worry or discontent. Their hours are long, their wages small, their fare none too dainty, and their amusements, save such as they can create for themselves, absolutely nil, yet they never complain and are invariably cheerful and merry.

They begin work at 6 AM, and continue until 5 PM with an interval of one hour only; yet after wielding sledge and pick all day in the blazing sun, they have hardly swallowed their evening meal of pea soup, salt meat, sugar and bread, before they collect in the largest room at their disposal and begin to dance with great vigour and grace to the strains of concertina, tin can, tambourine, bones and triangle. Very often the sounds of the music, the rhythmic stamp of naked feet, the snatches of song and wild bursts of laughter, can be heard issuing from their barracks far into the night, altogether giving one the impression that the lack of female society does not cause them any very great amount of distress.

The government of Redonda may be described as an unlimited monarchy, all power, both spiritual and temporal, being vested in the Superintendent. This omnipotent individual carries the entire code of laws in his head – a plan which possesses the double advantage of enabling him to add or subtract clauses without anyone being a bit wiser, while if an offence should be committed for the punishment of which there is no precedent, it doesn't take him more than five minutes to invent an entirely new law to fit the case.

Truth to tell, however, his administrative faculties are taxed but lightly, for anything approaching serious crime is absolutely unknown in this unique little colony.

But, as the novelists say, we anticipate. You must imagine that after a three hours' sail from Montserrat, your sloop has run under the lee of the island, and, dropping anchor, now lies tumbling to and fro in the cross swell. You are not allowed much time for noting your surroundings. Almost before the main-sail has come flapping down about your ears a boat is alongside, and thankful to say goodbye to your cramped and none too savoury quarters, you tumble into her and are rowed ashore by two perspiring stalwart negroes. There is no harbour at Redonda strictly speaking, and if the sea be at all rough landing is neither an easy nor a graceful performance. The boat, stout of rib and plank and as broad in beam as a Dutch frau, is backed rapidly in towards the wharf on the crest of a wave the while you stand uncertainly poised in the stern sheets. There is a swish and swirl of water, and a rope dangles before your eyes . . . you clutch at it frantically, at the same time making a wild spring in the air, and the next moment, to your secret amazement, you find yourself safe and sound on 'terra firma'.

But do not congratulate yourself too warmly; there is worse to come. You are now standing on a narrow strip of beach at the foot of the cliffs, and the only way of reaching the settlement on the higher slopes is by means of a cobwebby aerial tramway which extends up a rocky gorge for a distance of eight hundred feet. It is a very simple, not to say primitive contrivance, primarily intended for the conveyance of mineral from the quarries down to the shipping ground.

There are two standing wires of steel, on either of which runs a trolley with a huge iron bucket hung therefrom, the trolleys being connected by an endless checkrope, also of steel. In order to bring up the lower bucket it is therefore only necessary to weight the one at the top with stone or water ballast, the speed being regulated by a brake at the head of the wires. As you stand on the edge of the tub, clinging nervously to the carriage (*the orthodox manner of making the ascent*) you feel that this is an extremely wobbly and insecure mode of transit, and your host, who accompanies you, probably receives somewhat random answers to the flow of small talk wherewith he strives to divert your mind during the upward journey.

It is said that in this as in everything else except earthquakes familiarity breeds, if not contempt, at least indifference, but those who travel on the wires for the first time generally give a sigh of relief as the bucket comes to rest at the top and they step off on the platform.

The aerial flight accomplished, you find yourself in the negro settlement – a score or so of wooden buildings clustered in a narrow gully – but a few minutes scramble up a rocky pathway brings you to the Superintendent's bungalow, and from this point you obtain an excellent and comprehensive view of your surroundings.

A desert island truly, but not such a one as is dear to the writer of fiction! Here you do not find all the fruits and vegetables of the earth growing side by side in the greatest profusion and with a charming disregard of climate. The only vegetation is a coarse kind of grass and a particularly healthy variety of cactus – a prickly pest which spreads and flourishes exceedingly in the dry, hot soil seeming to find foothold for its roots in every crack and cranny of the cliffs.

Furthermore, Providence has been neglectful in the matter of livestock, for the fauna, though varied and interesting, is not likely to conduce to the comfort or well-being of the ship-wrecked mariner. Rats, mice and cockroaches abound, iguanas lurk among the rocks, centipedes and scorpions may cross your path at any time, and land crabs must be picked out of your bath before you can take your morning tub with any degree of comfort.

A few wild sheep and goats there are certainly, and though they are small and poor, compared to their English forebears, yet their flesh pleasantly varies a monotonous diet of tinned meats. The capture of these animals is effected in a manner peculiarly West Indian. When the larder needs replenishing, the stately negro cook makes a muster of the kitchen hangers-on and sallies forth at their head with firmness in his step and murder in his eye. Mounting upon one of the huge boulders with which the ground is strewn, he gazes round in much the same way that the Israelites of old may have surveyed the Promised Land, and then, having spotted the most likely looking mutton, he swiftly gives the word of command. In response his whippers-in form a circle round the unfortunate beast, bounding from rock to rock like antelopes, until finally penning it into a corner, the leader of the band swoops down like the Captain of the Assyrian host and grips it by the scuff of the neck.

Since Redonda produces no crops whatsoever, all foodstuffs have to be imported. Fresh meat and vegetables are brought twice a week from Montserrat, while groceries and such things as salt, beef, flour, peas, etc., for the workmen's mess, are sent straight from England or New York, in quantities sufficient to last five or six months. To avoid complications in the Commissariat Department it is necessary to be extremely previous in ordering these stores, and even with all the forethought in the world a hiatus will sometimes occur between the consumption of one consignment of provisions and the arrival of the next. It is whispered that on one occasion the store room shelves were bare save for two or three tins of tripe, and half a dozen of sour champagne, while at yet another period the only articles of diet in stock were corned beef and blacking!

It is not, however, the fluctuation of menu which most impresses the stranger with regard to a prolonged residence at Redonda. He is struck rather by the excessive loneliness of the life, for the white folk get no society whatever, save such as is afforded by visits from friends in neighbouring islands, or by the captains of ships calling there for cargoes of phosphate. Another point which makes a distinctly unfavourable impression on him is the impossibility of getting medical aid in case of illness, but this fact does not seem to greatly trouble the islanders themselves. For the liver and all its ills they look to calomel as their sheet anchor, while if fever be the trouble they fly to the quinine bottle. Beyond this they are practically at sea, but if the symptoms are too vague for diagnosis their usual procedure is to begin at the left hand side of the medicine chest and work round to the right, hoping, rather than expecting, to hit on the proper remedy in time.

No, it is impossible to deny that interesting and attractive as it may appear to the outsider, life at Redonda is not without its drawbacks. Given a contemplative disposition and a fondness for one's own society one might perchance be very happy there, but the majority of folk will probably agree with the Frenchman who, when he had thoroughly grasped all the peculiarities of the situation, raised his hands and eyes to heaven and exclaimed with pious fervour: '*Mon Dieu! Que c'est affreux*'.

DOROTHY HARDING, 1903

16 Nevis

'A Quakeress in the company of Spanish dancers'

Now mark my scheme! Nevis is the most lovely as well as the most healthy island in the West Indies . . . Now I and my family and you and Edith, and Wordsworth and his sister might all go there and make the Island more illustrious than Cos or Lesbos. A heavenly climate . . . a heavenly country . . .

SAMUEL TAYLOR COLERIDGE. In: *A Letter to Robert Southey,* 1801

The appearance of Nevis is perhaps the most captivating of any island in the West Indies. From the south and west it seems to be nothing but a single cone rising with the most graceful curve out of the sea, and piercing a fleecy mass of clouds which sleeps for ever round its summit. It is green as heart can conceive, perfectly cultivated, and enlivened with many old planters' houses of a superior style and churches peeping out in the most picturesque situations imaginable. A complete forest of evergreen trees grows like a ruff or collar round the neck of the high land where cultivation ceases. On the north and east the cone is not so perfect; it falls off in one direction in a long slope which terminates in a plain towards the Narrows of St Kitt's, and is broken to windward into one or two irregular hills.

HENRY NELSON COLERIDGE, 1826

... little Nevis, the conical ruin, as it were, of a volcanic island ... A single peak, with its Souffriere, rises to some 2000 feet; right and left of it are two lower hills, fragments, apparently, of a Somma, or older and larger crater. The lava and ash slide in concave slopes of fertile soil down to the sea, forming an island some four miles by three, which was in the seventeenth century a little paradise, containing 4000 white citizens, who had dwindled down in 1805, under the baneful influences of slavery, to 1300; in 1832 . . . to 500; and in 1854 to only 170. A happy place, however, it is said still to be, with a population of more than 10,000, who . . . are well-ordered and peaceable, industrious, and well-taught, and need, it is said, not only no soldiers, but no police.

CHARLES KINGSLEY, 1871

Nevis . . . is prim and neat, a dapper island. Its sea margin describes a decorous oval. Its surface is smooth. In its precise centre is a precise hill, cone-shaped and modest, while at either end of the oval is a smaller mound of the same pattern. Thus it comes about that Nevis appears staid, old-maidenly and most genteel when compared with the brazen-faced islands around – a Quakeress in a company of Spanish dancers.

SIR FREDERICK TREVES, 1908

Nevis was an island of strange contrast in prosperity to St Kitts, and that contrast was caused almost entirely by the Nevis mountain. In other words, here was a small circular island with such a high mountain (3600 feet) – for the size of the island – that its steep sides ran straight down to the sea, leaving very little flat land, and therefore very little land of easy methods of transport for agriculture . . . And . . . the mountain was merely a quiescent volcano, and in comparatively recent geological time it had erupted millions of separate boulders of stone, which littered every yard of the island in a remarkable manner, so that it was almost impossible to do any ploughing.

The result was that under modern conditions this steep and dry and stony island could not compete at sugar-growing for the world markets, and there was really no other drought-resisting crop that was a paying one. In consequence Nevis . . . today is almost derelict.

SIR REGINALD ST-JOHNSTON, 1936

Among the recent pioneers in the Leeward Islands is Mrs Mary Arrigo, thirty-six-years-old interior decorator and a wartime British special agent. She has bought a coconut plantation in the island of Nevis and intends to establish a cottage colony there. In Nevis there are only three other white women. There is no bank, hotel or shop, but life is cheap enough with servants plentiful at 8s. a week, and gin and rum at 5s. a bottle.

DONALD MCCORMICK, 1950

A fitting resort for people of quality

By the time I managed to visit Nevis for the first time a little over a hundred years after Charles Kingsley had sailed past, although the population remained the same size as in his day other statistics appeared to have changed. The true height of the mountain had been established as 3232 feet, and the proper dimensions of the island were more like eight by five miles. In addition, the boulders which had been noted by St-Johnston during his time as the Administrator of St Kitts and Nevis no longer seemed to litter 'every yard', and it was obvious that since 1949 the number of white female residents must have risen at the same rate as the price of a bottle of rum.

To a casual visitor like myself in the early 1970s the island looked more as it had appeared to Sir Frederick Treves at the beginning of the century – prim, staid, neatish – than it had to St-Johnston, who saw only abandonment and dilapidation. At the same time there were some signs of dereliction, with none more apparent than those surrounding a large building on the southern outskirts of Charlestown. This had been built towards the end of the eighteenth century, but was connected with something which had been a natural attraction of Nevis from the time of the first settlement:

In this Island there is a hot Bath, which as well for the reports that I have heard, as also for that I have seene and found by experience, I doe hold for one of the best and most sovereigne in the World. I have heard that divers of our Nation have there been cured of the Leprosie, and that one of the same persons now, or lately dwelt at Woolwich neere the River of Thames, by whom the truth may be knowne, if any man desire to be further satisfied therein. As for my own experience, although it was not much, yet the effects that I found it work both in my selfe, and other of my company in two dayes space, doe cause me to conceive the best of it. For at my coming thither, I was grievously vexed with an extreme cough, which I much feared would turne me to great harme, but bathing in the Bath, and drinking the water, I was speedily cured; and ever since that time I have found the state of my body (I give God thankes for it) farre exceeding what it was before, in strength and health.

ROBERT HARCOURT, 1625

I own that it contributed not a little to my Health and Vivacity. I usually went in at nine a Clock at night; and observed, That in two minutes time the sweat was ready to blind me, and that in about three minutes more I was obliged to quit it through faintness of spirit. Upon stepping out of it into the green bank, the wind blew so exceedingly cold that I should almost have fancied myself instantaneously transported to Nova Zembla, or Greenland; that is to say, we have a perpetual breeze of the Trade-wind that runs from East to West, which refreshes us in the Day, but is cool enough in the Night, and of course must prove intensely cold when we just come out of so hot a bath. I do not mean that it blows directly from the East Point; for it varies from North-East to South-East, according to the place and position of the Sun, and in October it generally blows directly from the North; we have no Land and Sea Breezes, as is usual in Jamaica. However, half a pint of strong Madeira Wine enabled me to cloath, put on my Riding Coat, and go briskly home; the next Morning I was almost as nimble as a Mountebank's Tumbler.

THE REVEREND WILLIAM SMITH, 1745

To the south of the town, at half a mile's distance, are situated the mineral baths on a rising ground near the margin of the sea. The establishment is very large, and can afford, as I was told, accommodations for forty or fifty boarders. An invalide with a good servant might take up his quarters here with more comfort than in any other house of public reception in the West Indies . . . There are three spacious plunge baths on terraces one above the other and varying in their temperature from 50° to 100° Fahrenheit. The lowest and largest is now given up to the boarders and others as a turtle crawl. There the poor flat gawky creatures flounce about till they become sulphuretted to a certain culinary degree, which is known by the Eatable beginning to lose his equilibrium, and, instead of lying level on the water, to sink half his body edgeways under, and leave the other half an upright semicircle in the air. When this sign of the times appears, the fortunate owner, impatient of the joy, erects his head and snuffs the coming soup . . . and now Turtle cannot reasonably expect any thing better than death and dressing.

HENRY NELSON COLERIDGE, 1826

On Nevis certain hot springs were discovered, close to Charles Town. Now a hot spring was the one thing needed to make the islands a fitting resort for people of quality, for at the commencement of the eighteenth century the life of a man of taste and breeding could not be supported without a spa.

At Nevis, therefore, a spa was established; and here, to this Tunbridge Wells of the Caribbees, came all the fashionable of the West Indies – the rich merchants with their wives and daughters, the planters, the majors and captains who were invalided or on leave, and the officers of any ship of war that could make an excuse to anchor within sight of Booby Island . . .

Alas! all this has passed away. The spa is silent and in ruins. The roof of the great building has fallen in, while the balconies and verandahs, which witnessed so much simpering and such play of fans, have vanished to build cart-sheds . . .

SIR FREDERICK TREVES, 1908

. . . residents from the neighbouring islands came to Nevis to take the cure at its thermal baths. The old Bath House is still standing . . . and after having been closed for many years has again been opened as a hotel . . . The waters are said to resemble those of the Wildbad Springs in Würtemberg, and many remarkable stories have been told of their efficacy. According to one they cured a negro boy of leprosy though he had broken out 'in running sores or ulcers all over from head to foot' . . .

Stories of the rank and fashion of the West Indies assembling at these baths, and of local Beau Nashs, must be accepted with reserve, for the Bath House was not erected until the end of the eighteenth century, when the fortunes of Nevis were already on the decline.

SIR ALGERNON ASPINALL, 1927

The Nevis arms depicted two young ladies apparently pouring out from a cocktail-shaker a Nevis rum-punch for a third one, who has presumably reached the 'sliding on the floor' stage. Actually it is intended to represent the offer to an ailing person of a draught of Nevis curative waters, but as these waters are only taken in the form of hot baths, which one doesn't, or shouldn't, drink, the design is not quite accurate . . .

Today there stands, and is still in good use, a large stone hotel over the hot springs . . . in its day a fashionable resort as a spa, on the lines of English spas of those times, for inhabitants from all the other West Indian islands . . . The waters are said to be radioactive, and also contain large amounts of magnesium, sodium, and sulphur. Both my wife and myself found them of considerable benefit to rheumatic tendencies when we went over to Nevis on my frequent visits of inspection.

SIR REGINALD ST-JOHNSTON, 1936

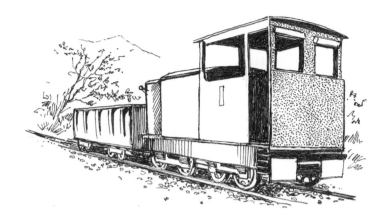

17 St Kitts

'A highly cultivated garden'

The vale of Basseterre in softness, richness and perfection of cultivation surpasses any thing I have ever seen in my life. Green velvet is an inadequate image of the exquisite verdancy of the cane fields which lie along this lovely valley and cover the smooth acclivities of Monkey Hill. This hill is the southern termination of a range of great mountains which increase in height towards the north, and thicken together in enormous masses in the centre of the island. The apex of this rude pyramid is the awful crag of Mount Misery, which shoots slantingly forwards over the mouth of a volcanic chasm like a huge peninsula in the air. It is bare and black and generally visible, whilst the under parts of the mountain are enveloped in clouds. The height is more than 3700 feet, and is the most tremendous precipice I ever beheld. But the ruggedness of this central cluster only renders the contrast of the cultivated lands below more striking, and the entire prospect is so charming, that I could not help agreeing with the captain's clerk who said he wondered that Colon, who was so delighted with this island as to give to it his own name, should not have made a full stop upon its shores. I do not uphold the pun, but upon the whole it was well enough for a hot climate and a captain's clerk.

HENRY NELSON COLERIDGE, 1826

The approach to St Christopher's from the north-west, is highly interesting. The northern part of the island is mountainous and clothed with forest; and as we drew near to the coast, it was delightful to observe the brows of the hills and plains below, bright and verdant with the sugar-cane – the settlements of the planters looking neat and prosperous – some of the wind-mills turning – companies of negroes seen in the distance, at work in the fields – neat places of worship visible – eight large vessels, with other smaller ones, in the harbor of Basse-terre, we presumed, for their cargoes of sugar. A more remarkable prima-facie evidence of prosperity, I have seldom witnessed.

JOSEPH JOHN GURNEY, 1840

Moored in another blue harbour, a great semicircular basin, bounded by a high billowing of hills all green from the fringe of yellow beach up to their loftiest clouded summit. The land has that up-tossed look which tells a volcanic origin. There are curiously scalloped heights, which, though emerald from base to crest, still retain all the physiognomy of volcanoes: their ribbed sides must be lava under that verdure. Out of sight westward – in successions of bright green, pale green, bluish-green, and vapory gray – stretches a long chain of crater shapes. Truncated, jagged, or rounded, all these elevations are interunited by their curving hollows of land or by filaments – very low valleys. And as they grade away in varying color through distance, these hill-chains take a curious segmented, jointed appearance, like insect forms, enormous ant-bodies . . . This is St Kitt's.

LAFCADIO HEARN, 1890

St Kitts will impress the visitor as being not only well-to-do but comfortable. Almost every available part of it is cultivated, for fields of sugar-cane climb far up the mountain sides. The island possesses excellent roads; its villages are neat, while there is about them little of that squalor or air of dejection which is conspicuous in neighbouring islands. After the experience of such wild islands as St Lucia and Dominica, St Kitts will be welcome, since it is, in happy measure, free from the untidy tangle of the tropics, from the ever-repeated savage gorge and tree-bristling precipice. It is welcome to those who, in their journey among the islands, have become surfeited with the 'everlasting hills' and the exigency of the restless and importunate jungle,

SIR FREDERICK TREVES, 1908

Though St Kitts was the first island of the West Indies to be settled by the English . . . its capital bears the French name of Basse Terre . . .

We had the misfortune to first land [there] on a Sunday. Basse Terre was as dead as if a general funeral were just over. It was not simply that we bemoaned with the tourist-minded fellow-countryman from the steamer the fact that every 'liquor Store' was tight and genuinely closed; the dreary lifelessness of the whole place got on our nerves. The very trade wind seemed to refrain from any unnecessary exertion; the citizens appeared to have given even their minds a holiday and replied to the simplest question with a vacant stare. It was a 'holy day' as truly as a French or Spanish Sunday is a 'day of feast', or 'festival'. I imagine heaven is much like an English community on a Sunday – so piously dull that a new inmate would soon be on his knees imploring the gatekeeper to let him go to the only other place available.

At eleven o'clock four species of church service broke out, the Anglican, Catholic, Moravian, and what [was] referred to in a Sunday whisper as the 'Whistling'. We went. One was forced to, in self-defense and for the utter absence of any other form of amusement. Then we understood why the community could endure the apparent lack of recreation and exercise of its deadly Sabbath. Negroes striving to maintain the cold, calm, rather bored English manner from the opening hymn to benediction supplied the former, and the ups and downs of the Anglican service furnished the latter.

HARRY A. FRANCK, 1920

Narrow gauge running

St Kitts, as every visitor who did not arrive there on a Sunday has noticed, is an exceptionally fertile island, as its original Amerindian name of Liamuiga *denoted. In the latter half of the eighteenth century it was considered to be one of Britain's most valuable possessions because of the amount of sugar it produced, and sugar has dominated the economy ever since.*

All the arable land was divided into estates, and for something like 250 years each processed its own crop of sugar-cane using a wind-driven, and later a steam-operated, mill to extract the cane juice, together with a boiling-house to clarify and crystallize the sugar. This was a slow, laborious and far from efficient operation, but one which worked well enough in the boom years of the eighteenth century and up until slavery was abolished in 1834. After that such production methods threatened ruin for the estate owners, so much so that by the beginning of the twentieth century many were close to bankruptcy and St Kitts was facing economic collapse.

The situation was saved in 1910 when some of the estate proprietors decided to establish a factory capable of processing the whole of the island's sugar-cane crop, and of marketing the raw sugar in bulk. Within two years a modern factory, designed to produce 60 tonnes of sugar an hour had been built near Basseterre. It has been greatly enlarged and modernized since, but throughout its existence its operation has depended on the efficient daily delivery of vast quantities of sugar-cane. This has been achieved very successfully by the use of a narrow gauge railway connecting it with all the estates.

The railway has a history slightly longer than that of the factory, the first stretch of line being laid from a pier at the main harbour to a site about one and a half kilometres inland. All the building materials and equipment for the factory were then taken by rail to the site as they were landed from the ships which brought them from Great Britain. The gasoline-driven locomotive which hauled these trains is still in existence, though long out of service. It can be found, more or less complete and with its distinguishing number, 8, just about readable through the rust, in a disused and overgrown siding near the factory.

At the same time as the factory was being built two more lines were laid down. Because of the central mountain mass the only practical route for these – like that for the main roads – was on the relatively level ground close to the sea. The east and west feeder lines were run in opposite directions from the factory marshalling yard, to connect it with estates on each coast, and by the time sugar production started in 1912 there were about twenty kilometres of track in use. In 1925 the two feeder lines were extended to complete a circular track all around the island, bringing the total length to nearly fifty kilometres, and connecting the factory with all the estates. Another sixteen kilometres have been added since in the form of transfer sidings with passing loops, and in extensions to the marshalling yard.

Because of the narrowness of the coastal plain the road and railway run side by side and there are many manually-operated level crossings. During 'crop time' between February and July, when the factory is in full operation, these crossings are manned continuously. At other times they are operated by the crew of any train using the line. A distinctive feature of the landscape of St Kitts is the number of river beds, called ghuts, which form deep gullies across the coastal plain, Nearly all are dry for most of the year, but fill up very quickly after a rainstorm. Their presence made it necessary to build a total of twenty-six bridges for the railway, and these – ranging from 2 to 110 metres in length – are found on both coasts.

The rolling stock consists of 19 locomotives (not all of which are in service at any one time), over 700 cane wagons, 49 mud wagons, 25 bagasse wagons, and 18 raw sugar bins, together with a few flat-bed bogies and molasses tankers. The locomotives range in size from two 40 hp Rustons used for yard shunting to a 150 hp Hunslet which is the largest of the main-line haulage engines. The remaining haulage locomotives comprise seven 101 hp Hunslets, five 100 hp Rustons, and two 145 hp Whitcombs. All are diesel engines except the two shunters, which are gasoline-driven. A single 125 hp Armstrong is used solely for hauling raw sugar from the factory to the port.

Each engine is known only by a number painted on the side of the cab, with one exception. The railway's one and only 145 hp Davenport, which is used for main-line short haul work, was given the number 13 when first taken into service. It suffered so many breakdowns and mishaps while operating under this number that eventually a name was substituted, and Churchill *(which perhaps gives some indication of its age) became the first and only named locomotive in the railway's history.*

Every year each of the thirty-odd estate managers provides the Railway Superintendent with an estimate of how much cane he expects to harvest during the forthcoming 'crop time'. Using these figures the Superintendent then calculates the amount needed from each estate to make up the 2700 tonnes which the factory requires each day. A schedule is prepared showing the number of cane wagons to be allocated to each of the twelve transfer sidings to collect the daily quotas. These sidings, which are all named, are about three to five kilometres apart, and each services between one and six estates. The cane is brought from the fields in large trailers towed by powerful tractors, and is then loaded mechanically into the wagons.

A train is made up of a maximum of twenty-seven wagons, each with a three-tonne capacity; which means that at least thirty trains a day are needed to meet the factory's demands at the height of the harvest. Even with the high rate of juice extraction achieved by modern grinding methods it requires between nine and ten tonnes of cane to produce a single tonne of raw sugar. As the annual production is around 30,000 tonnes it can be seen that the railway has to deliver anything up to 300,000 tonnes of cane to the factory each year. During the harvest this means that trains are running by both day and night. Raw sugar is carried in five-tonne bin wagons along a spur from the factory to a bulk sugar store near the port, from where it is then transported by road to the wharf for shipping.

That its final product is hauled along the same stretch of track that was used, all those years ago, in the erection of the factory seems most appropriate. And it may well be that, just as the railway was there before the factory was constructed, it will still be there after it has been demolished. The amount of sugar produced by St Kitts each year is an almost infinitesimal proportion of the total world output, and has been produced at a loss for many years. Neither the nationalization of the industry in 1976, nor the island's achievement of independence in 1983, did anything to increase the annual output or to turn a profit. The time may well not be too far off when sugar production will cease. In which case it is not too difficult to envisage a modern version of lo-comotive No. 8 hauling parts of the factory back to the port for shipping abroad as scrap.

When, if ever, this melancholy event takes place it need not follow that it would also mark the end of the railway. A tour of St Kitts is a pleasant and in-teresting experience, and one which of necessity has to be made by road fol-lowing the coastline. Given the undoubted appeal of narrow gauge passenger railways all over the world, there seems to be no reason – with some new or suitably converted rolling stock – why in future an even more interesting tour could not be made by rail.

Awful commotions

Mrs Lanaghan's 'awful earthquake' which struck Antigua in February 1843 was also felt in many of the other islands, particularly in Guadeloupe where it de-stroyed Point-à-Pitre and killed several thousand people. In addition:

St Christopher's also suffered very severely, the damage done being immense. The stone dwellings and stores in Basseterre, the capital of the island, fearfully shook and rent ... The square was crowded with a concourse of persons of every age, sex, and condition – pride, rank, power, were alike forgotten – as upon bended knees, or with clasped hands and pallid lips, they invoked the aid of that Great Being ...

At Johnstone's, or French River, a melancholy catastrophe occurred. It is a spot chosen by the washerwomen of Basseterre as the scene of their necessary avocations; and upon the eventful morning of the earthquake, about ten of these females were busily employed in washing, in a natural basin (formed by huge rocks) at the moment of the shock taking place. Seven of these women fortunately escaped by flight; but the three, who were exactly underneath the cliff, met a more melancholy fate. At the commencement of the awful commotion, an immense rock parted from this cliff, and fell into the stream below. The affrighted females fled from the scene of danger; but, alas! the increased oscillations of the earth caused it to rebound with fearful velocity, and striking against a larger rock, it split into three or four pieces, and thus dealt destruction to each of the poor panic-stricken women!

MRS LANAGHAN, 1844

A few years after this the island was visited by a man who, during the total of five years he spent in the West Indies rarely found anything to his liking, or had a good word to say about anyone he came across. He quickly found something else to complain about, having it would seem soon after his arrival experienced one or two other forms of 'awful commotion':

In St Kitts, the highest legal authority in point of rank during my sojourn in the island, played the flute in a wretched style at half dollar public concerts, when he got hired. He also danced quadrilles very execrably, and had danced 'Jim Crow' in Dominica. He played 'Dr Pangloss' in private theatricals. Such is the manner in which the dignity of the high seat of justice is sometimes sustained out here.

CHARLES W. DAY, 1852

Copious libations to Bacchus

In March 1809 a ship transporting the 23rd Regiment of Foot from the Caribbean to North America stopped briefly at St Kitts. Among those who went ashore was the young officer who had had the unnerving experience with the tarantula in Martinique a month earlier (see pages 71–72). In doing so it seems he let himself in for a hazardous encounter of a different kind:

The appearance of St Kitts is that of a highly cultivated garden, crowned with a high mountain, called Mount Misery, which is also a volcano, and smoke is not infrequently seen, issuing from its crater. There is another high rock in the island called Brimstone Hill, on which are erected barracks for a Regiment, and quarters for Artillery and Engineers. The regiment in these barracks was the 25th, old friends of ours, and they sent immediately to invite us all to dine with them on the hill. Weak as I was, I could not resist joining my brother Officers in the party, and to dinner we went. The meeting of two old Regiments who had seen hard service together was not likely to take place without copious libations to Bacchus, and this meeting was certainly one of the most distinguished of that description. It was followed up by a similar invitation for the next day, which was also accepted, and celebrated pretty much in the same manner. Two such days could hardly be spent in this climate, without producing their consequences, and two of our Officers were taken ill of fever and were obliged to be left behind when we sailed. One of them afterwards died. Whether the 25th left similar memorials of our meeting or not is more than I can tell. The view of the sea from Brimstone Hill is quite magnificent. Halfway down the rock are quantities of Monkies, established there in times long gone by, and who enjoy a similar exemption from annoyance as those at Gibraltar, and are not allowed to be shot at. They are consequently very bold and impertinent.

CAPTAIN THOMAS HENRY BROWNE,
Napoleonic War Journal, 1807–1816

HMS Vidal, *the ship in which I first went to St Kitts, arrived in Basseterre Bay some century and a half after the 23rd Regiment's bacchanalian visit. By then the barracks at Brimstone Hill had long been deserted, and the island maintained no naval or military establishment of any kind to afford us the type of reception given to Browne and his fellow officers. Even so, as all on board soon found out, a similar degree of hospitality – although perhaps of a less formal nature – was far from lacking. The ship anchored off Basseterre late on Saturday 7 November and sailed again early the following Monday morning. Only the briefest outline of what transpired during the intervening Sunday appeared in the commanding officer's official report of proceedings later sent (as it was at the end of each month) to the Admiralty Hydrographic Department:*

On Sunday 8th November about thirty ratings and ten officers attended the Armistice Day Service at the Cenotaph and I laid a wreath in company with many others. This simple and moving ceremony was attended by a great number of people, many of them ex-servicemen.

I spent most of the rest of the day at an ex-servicemen's get-together on a sugar estate with the Administrator, His Honour Colonel the Honourable Henry Howard. There were some interesting medals. One old man had served under General Pershing, and had one medal secured with a ribbon off a chocolate box and a safety pin, apparently commemorating the owner's ascent of the Eiffel Tower. Very wisely the Estate Manager had organised a cricket match, players unlimited. This cut down on the consumption of rum to some extent, but it was still extremely difficult to call 'time, gentlemen, please' at about 8.00pm.

CAPTAIN R.H. CONNELL, ROYAL NAVY
HMS Vidal's *Report of Proceedings
for the Month of November 1959*

18 St Eustatius

'The Golden Rock'

From one end of the town of Eustatia to the other is a continued mart, where goods of the most different uses and qualities are displayed before the shop-doors. Here hang rich embroideries, painted silks, flowered Muslins, with all the Manufactures of the Indies. Just by hang Sailors' Jackets, trousers, shoes, hats, etc. Next stall contains most exquisite silver plate, the most beautiful indeed I ever saw, and close by these iron-pots, kettles and shovels. Perhaps the next presents you with French and English Millinary-wares. But it were endless to enumerate the variety of merchandise in such a place, for in every store you find every thing, be their qualities ever so opposite.

> JANET SCHAW,
> *Journal of a Lady of Quality: Being the*
> *Narrative of a Journey from Scotland to*
> *the West Indies in the Years 1774 to 1776*

St Eustatius may have been in eruption, though there is no record of it, during historic times, and looks more unrepentant and capable of misbehaving itself again than does any other crater-cone in the Antilles . . .

> CHARLES KINGSLEY, 1871

St Eustatius – generally called Statia for short – is a little Dutch island with a remarkable past . . .

The only town is Orange Town, which lies partly on the beach and partly on the cliffs adjacent. The two divisions communicate by a long, steep, sloping road. On the brink of the cliff stands an ancient and ruinous fort, Fort Orange, where still, it is said, a few rusty and dismounted cannon are to be found among the cactus and acacia. Recent visitors to the island speak of the town as poverty-stricken, dilapidated, and melancholy, its church and chief houses as decayed, and its business as well-nigh invisible. Along the beach in its whole length, are the ruins of warehouses and stores, together with other relics of what must have been an immense shipping trade.

SIR FREDERICK TREVES, 1908

St Eustatius is . . . an extinct volcano with its top cut off and rising from the sea in magnificent white cliffs . . . Its anchorage is safe, and a steep path cut in the face of the cliff leads to Oranjestad, the capital, its old fort now used as court house, post-office, and prison, and the Dutch Reformed church rising above its ancient vaults. Once upon a time Statia was a rich and coveted prize, and many nations strove for possession of the 'Golden Rock'. First colonized by the Dutch, it was successively seized by the English, the French, then went on round the circle again, finally reverting to Holland. Today its glory is faded and gone, and with its deterioration its allegiance has become a bit unsteady. Emigration to the United States is unceasing, that to Holland is slight . . . The limited rains and consequent lack of water are largely to blame for its rapid depopulation . . .

HARRY A. FRANCK, 1920

In commemoration
of the
Salute to the flag of the United States
fired in this fort on 16 November 1776
by order of
Johannes de Graaff
Governor of St Eustatius
in reply to a national gun-salute
fired by the
United States Brig-of-War ANDREW DORIA

under Captain Isaiah Robinson
of the Continental Navy

———

Here the sovereignty of the
United States of America
was first formally acknowledged to a
national vessel by a foreign official

Presented by Franklin Delano Roosevelt
President of the United States of America

Plaque on Fort Oranje unveiled 12 December 1939

St Eustatius is the most desolate of the [Dutch] Windward Islands, and even its dramatic past is slowly being obliterated by the wind and the sea. Fort Oranje, which fired the first salute to the rebel flag of the American colonies, still looks down on the bay that was once crowded with blockade runners; but the warehouses, which played such an important part in American history, now lie in ruins, their disordered stones mingling with the spume and the fine black sand along the beach, in a losing battle against the encroaching sea . . .

The streets of Oranjestad have recently been paved. but beyond the town there are only a few dirt roads winding through the brown stubble and the sparse undergrowth . . . the sugar and the sisal plantations have been deserted and the upper slopes of the Quill are the only suggestion of green on the island. Everywhere else there is only dust and ruins and silence . . .

PHILIP HANSON HISS, 1943

Beads from the sea

The period during which St Eustatius was known as the Golden Rock, because of the vast amount of trade carried on there, began in the middle of the eighteenth century. It ended some time before the turn of the century, largely as a result of a brief occupation of the island by the British in 1781, during which the entire contents of the numerous warehouses admired by Janet Schaw were seized as booty and sold in a massive auction. Amid the turmoil which would have taken place along the narrow foreshore below Fort Oranje, as uncouth and uncaring soldiers and sailors broke into each building and dragged out its contents, damage to the more delicate items and to sealed containers would have been unavoidable, with anything of no apparent, immediate value being tossed aside. The latter must have included casks or boxes filled with glass beads, as such beads have been turning up on the beach in front of Oranjestad ever since.

Among the items of merchandise not mentioned, or perhaps not seen, by the indefatigable Miss Schaw were those goods intended for trading in West Africa in exchange for slaves, including glass beads of every size, shape and colour. Together with such things as silver bells, pewter ware, cowrie shells, bracelets and mirrors, these had been found to be highly prized in all the areas from which slaves were taken.

Initially obtained only from Venice, such beads had begun to be manufactured in Holland by the middle of the seventeenth century. Produced in the pre-industrial age, and made from long five- or six-sided glass tubes, no bead had truly regular facets or was identical in every respect to any other. It was quickly found that there was a preference in each region of West Africa for beads of a particular size and colour, and the Dutch were quick to produce whatever was wanted, to a better standard, and in greater quantities than the Venetians. Most, of course, would have been taken direct to West Africa from Europe, as part of the cargoes carried by slavers on the first leg of the notorious 'triangular trade', but not all. The Golden Rock in its heyday was known as a place where anything and everything could be bought and sold, and there is no reason to doubt that 'slave beads' did feature on some merchants' inventories – particularly for sale to slave traders from the American colonies.

Almost all the beads which turn up on the beach in St Eustatius, if not through the action of the sea worn down into oval or round shapes, are five-sided, between one and three centimetres in length, and blue, opaline or green in colour. They are found nowhere else in the Caribbean. Each one as it is recovered provides the finder with a direct link to a period in the history of the island which, given its gentle, peaceful appearance today, it is almost impossible to visualize. Each bead is also a tangible reminder of the much longer and far less innocent period during which a few handfuls of the things could purchase a human being.

19 Saba

'A healthy and prosperous sphere'

... Saba rises sheer out of the sea some 1500 feet or more, without flat ground, or even harbour. From a little landing-place to leeward a stair runs up 800 feet into the bosom of the old volcano ... They build boats up in the crater – the best boats in all the West Indies – and lower them down the cliff to the sea ...

CHARLES KINGSLEY, 1871

Close to St Eustatius is the island of Saba, a place so curious that it must rank with the islands of romance and not with things of this world ... Unlike any other West Indian island, the majority of the population are white, and not only white but Dutch, the good old-fashioned kind, with blue eyes, freckled, sandy complexion and flaxen hair. The inhabitants being Dutch speak English as their native tongue. The only town ... is on the mountain top, and being so placed it is called Bottom ...

Living aloft in their volcano, in a summit city called Bottom, these simple Dutch people who speak English reach the extreme of the improbable in the nature of their staple industry. They do not make balloons nor kites. They are not astronomers, nor are they engaged in extracting nitrogen from the atmosphere. They are, of all things in the world, shipbuilders, and shipbuilders of such merit that their boats and small craft are famous all over the Windward Islands. Let it be noted that fishing smacks are not only built in a crater, but on an island which has neither beach, harbour, landing stage, nor safe anchoring ground, where no timber is produced, where no iron is to be found, and where cordage is not made. The island has indeed, except in the matter of size, no more facilities for the development of the shipbuilding trade than has a rock lighthouse. The production of ships from craters is hardly less wonderful than the gathering of grapes from thorns or figs from thistles.

When the Saba ship is finished it is lowered down the side of the cliff, and has then apparently to shift for itself . . .

SIR FREDERICK TREVES, 1908

Saba . . . is only a mountain-top, towering three thousand feet above the Caribbean, and extending who knows how far below its surface, for the water is very deep all about this tiny patch of five square miles. Cone-shaped, of volcanic formation, it rises abruptly from the sea to the clouds, and one thousand feet up, in what must once have been a crater, is the only town, aptly named 'The Bottom'. . . One fantastic tale has it that supplies from the outer world and the inhabitants returning with them are hauled up the slope in baskets attached to a cable anchored in the town; the unromantic truth is that the former are carried up on the heads of the latter, or on the little horses which are equally skilful in climbing the rock-cut 'Ladder'. Strangely enough, Saba is famed for the boats it builds, which are constructed not at the water's edge, but in 'The Bottom'. If he is set on remaining in Dutch territory, there could be no finer place in which to house the war lord of the twentieth century than the island of Saba.

HARRY A. FRANCK, 1920

Saba, the smallest of the three Windward Islands, has less than half the area of the island of Manhattan. Its volcanic slopes plunge abruptly into the sea. It is the greenest of the Dutch islands, the quaintest, and the most dramatic
. . .

The men of Saba are excellent sailors, through years of experience in launching their small boats against the heavy seas and in beaching them under all conditions. They are also boat builders of some ability, but the myth that Sabans build sloops – or even schooners – on the tops of mountains and lower them over cliffs is ridiculous. A few boats are still built, but they are so small that they can be carried on the shoulders of a dozen men . . .

The legend of Saba as an island of beautiful, golden-haired women with blue eyes is in a class with the story about shipbuilding on mountain tops. It is simply not true. These stories doubtless originated with travelers who were astonished to find white women living in the Caribbean, and while it is true the women are white and that many are attractive, some writers have so far improved the story as to state that ninety per cent of the population are women, and that there is only one eligible bachelor on the island. Recently a young United States Navy flier on patrol duty, intrigued by this tale, dropped a letter addressed to 'the most beautiful girl in Saba'. His success was immediate, and weeks later he was still receiving answers from the various competitors for the title . . .

PHILIP HANSON HISS, 1943

Saba, you rise from the ocean
Decked with your tropical plants,
Verdure so rich without measure
Covers the high mountain lands.
The fog and the sea-breeze together
Mingle and freshen the air,
Making you, Saba, so precious
A healthy and prosperous sphere.

THE REVEREND SISTER WALTRUDA,
A verse of the Saban National Anthem, 1960

'Spanish work'

If Saba today has a reputation for any particular product it is something made by the ladies of the island in their own homes, rather than by their menfolk in lofty mountainside boatyards. This is the delicate and beautifully-wrought drawn-thread work, known there as 'Spanish work', for which they have now been renowned for a century or more. It acquired its local name from being introduced in the late nineteenth century by a young schoolteacher, Mary Hassell, who though born in Saba had been educated at a convent in Caracas, where she was taught the art by Venezuelan nuns.

Proficiency in this form of lace-making achieved wide popularity among Saban women, and their skill became more widely known in the early years of the twentieth century, after examples of their work which had been entered in exhibitions held in Holland and Denmark had found buyers and laid the foundations of a small export trade. A market, mainly in the United States, was developed on an individual basis by the simple and ingenious method of soliciting orders through the manufacturer of any product imported into Saba, by writing and asking for details of the writer's wares to be circulated among the company's employees. While many such letters failed to produce any response there were enough replies and requests for more information over the years to produce a flourishing cottage industry.

The trade which developed in supplying discerning American housewives with items such as lace-decorated tablecloths, sheets, pillowcases, cocktail napkins, handkerchiefs and blouses was given a boost in the 1920s when articles about the island, its crater-dwelling boat-builders and its 'golden-haired women with blue eyes' began to appear in American publications, but then tailed off badly during the Great Depression in the next decade. Saba suffered as much as the rest of the world from the effects of this and the Second World War which followed and by the 1950s, when the population was down to a little over 1000, the demand for 'Spanish work' had all but ended.

It began to be revived in the 1960s, after an airstrip had been constructed and the island developed into a select tourist destination. Prospective purchasers could then not only see at first hand the range and exquisite quality of the drawn-thread work available, but also come face to face with the individuals whose handiwork it was. Within twenty years of the opening of the airport 'Spanish work' had become one of Saba's largest foreign exchange earners.

Perhaps the only sad part of the tale is that the woman who started the whole thing off, Mary Hassell (or Mrs James Johnson, as she became in 1874), died long before the renaissance began, at the age of eighty-five in 1939. Her grave is to be found in the cemetery of the Roman Catholic church of St Paul's Conversion at Windwardside, while fine examples of the lace-work she is remembered for introducing to Saba are undoubtedly to be seen on the altar linen and priest's vestments inside the church.

20 St Barthélemy

'The little pebble'

St Barthélemy [is] colloquially called 'St Barts'. The inhabitants are chiefly white, and among them one finds the physiognomy, traditions, and customs of their Norman ancestors. Yet though they speak French, it is only badly, the prevailing language being English, or at least the caricature of that tongue which many decades of isolation have developed . . .

. . . of volcanic formation, the island suffers for the lack of trees and water, being forced to hoard its rainfall in large cisterns . . . Gustavia, the capital, was once rich and prosperous, being a depot of French and British corsairs, who carried on trade with the Spanish colonies. There are still immense cellars built to hold the booty and merchandise, and zinc and lead mines that lie unexploited for lack of capital. To-day the inhabitants live for the most part in abject poverty, getting most of their sustenance from the neighbouring islands and emigrating to Guadeloupe, where they are noted for their excellency as servants, despite their unfamiliarity with the native 'creole'.

HARRY A. FRANCK, 1920

The new Swedish colony

Before the latter half of the twentieth century the tiny island of St Barthélemy was almost totally ignored by visitors to the West Indies. The American Harry A. Franck, who shortly after the First World War travelled from one end of the Caribbean to the other, was unusual in devoting even a couple of paragraphs to a place which, as he makes clear, had long lapsed into obscurity. In his very brief, derogatory remarks about the island he made it clear that it was then (as of course it still is) a French possession, but his failure to question how or why it had a capital with the most unGallic name of Gustavia, would indicate that he had no knowledge of events which made the history of St Barts different from that of every other island in the Caribbean.

These events took place when the attempts made by the rulers of the Duchy of Courland to establish a West Indian colony during the seventeenth century (see page 39) were echoed towards the end of the next century by the ruler of another Baltic state, King Gustavus III of Sweden, who was envious of the Virgin Island possessions of his Danish neighbours. After an attempt to negotiate with Spain in order to acquire either Trinidad or Puerto Rico had met with a quick rebuff, he turned to France with a request to buy Tobago. This too was refused but soon afterwards, in exchange for special trading privileges for the French in the Swedish port of Göteborg, he was offered St Barthélemy instead. The King was very pleased to accept even though 'he had no notion of its value', and probably very little idea of its size or precise location. The French were even more pleased, as they had long realized the minute island they had owned since 1648 was practically worthless.

Sweden took possession in March 1785. The island then had a population of less than 1000 (of whom over a quarter were slaves) and was so poor that its principal asset was considered to be its goats, which probably numbered less than the people. The Swedish authorities immediately granted the island free port status in order to take advantage of the increased trade flowing through the Caribbean as a result of the recently concluded American War of Independence. The port itself, in the small natural harbour on the west coast, was renamed Gustavia and from then on trade became the island's main economic activity.

The announcement of the acquisition of a colony, and of its opening as a free port, had an unexpected effect in Finland, then a poor and backward duchy of Sweden, where it created the so-called 'Saint Barthélemy fever'. A rumour began to circulate in those parts of the country where many years of bad harvests had been experienced that the island was the promised land, where gold was to be found merely by scratching the ground with a knife. Many Finns came to believe that the Swedish Government was prepared to pay the cost of travel for those prepared to emigrate, and a considerable movement of people began, with farming families moving to the coast to take up the offer of a free passage. None ever managed to make the Atlantic crossing, but the 'fever' did not subside until the King issued a proclamation explaining that the new colony was no place for farmers, but only somewhere where trade was being developed. This was sufficient to attract other sorts of immigrants to the island, and within less than twenty-five years the population had increased to well over 5000.

In spite of the concentration on trade there was still some farming. Sugarcane was planted but without much success, and most agricultural activity took place in fairly small fields. The plantation system was never introduced and for most people outside Gustavia it is likely that life for both blacks and whites was not that different. Any agricultural work under the adverse conditions created by a difficult terrain and lack of fresh water must have meant nearly as much labour for the master as for the slave. Except briefly during the period of the island's greatest economic activity in the early years of the nineteenth century, the black proportion of the population never exceeded that of the white, and by the time Sweden abolished slavery in 1847 there were only 520 slaves left to be freed. Most of these soon left, as they could find no work as free labourers nor any land on which they could settle.

With the end of the Napoleonic wars in 1815 the economy entered a long decline. Trade decreased, forcing many merchants to sell up and leave, while a series of natural disasters – droughts, earthquakes and hurricanes – during the first half of the century speeded the ruination of the island. A fire devastated Gustavia in 1852, adding to the general distress, and by 1870 St Barts was moribund. To Sweden it had become a useless financial burden, and approaches were made to the United States, Italy and France in an effort to be rid of it. Only France showed any interest, and the population of the island was asked in a referendum to indicate whether or not they would accept a return to French rule. Out of the 352 people who were eligible or who bothered to vote (and from the available evidence it is not clear which), only one dissented.

St Barthélemy was returned to French sovereignty in March 1878. It made very little difference to the way of life or to the general standard of living, and the island continued to be a remote, forgotten and poverty-stricken place. That this poverty was not merely financial is surely borne out by the fact that it was not until the beginning of the twentieth century that the islanders started to import donkeys, to carry their goods along the trails which were then all that connected

Gustavia with the outlying communities. That it had taken until then for them to realize that these animals, which must have been in common use in all the other islands round about for the previous 200 years or more, could be used to relieve man's burden indicates either matchless obduracy or an incredible degree of apathy, if not stupidity, among the population of the day. Harry A. Franck's remarks in 1920 may not have been too unkind after all.

21 St Martin

'Land of salt'

Today, the 23rd of March 1648, have assembled Robert de Lonvilliers, Knight and Lord of this place, Governor of the island of St Maarten, on behalf of His Most Christian Majesty, and Martin Thomas, likewise Governor of the said island, on behalf of the Prince of Orange and the States General of Holland, and . . . have agreed upon the following:

(1) that the French shall continue in that quarter where they are established at this present, and that they shall inhabit the entire side which faces Anguilla;

(2) that the Dutch shall have the quarter of the fort, and the soil surrounding it on the south side;

(3) that the French and Dutch established on the said island shall live as friends and allies, and that, in case of either party molesting the other, this shall constitute an infringement of this treaty, and shall therefore be punishable by the laws of war;

. . .

(5) that the chase, the fisheries, the salt-pans, the rivers, the lakes, the fresh waters, the dye-wood, mines and minerals, harbours and roadsteads, and

other commodities of the said island shall be common, and shall serve to provide the wants of the inhabitants . . .

A portion of the Partition Treaty, 1648

The Island of St Martin . . . was originally settled by Englishmen, and tho' belonging, at the commencement of the French Revolution, to the French and Dutch jointly the inhabitants were, and still continue to be nearly all English . . . The Dutch and French are extremely few, and of these that have attained to any consideration, it has been by intermarriage and the facilities of the Revolution.

An Island thus inhabited by Englishmen could never have been expected to escape the horrors of the Revolution and it is scarcely necessary to add that it was almost ruined. The Dutch Government yielding the Island entirely to the Fraternity of French Republicans in 1795, more than one-third of the Sugar Estates were immediately sequestered as belonging to Englishmen, everything British, or that wore the semblance of being such, was in direct contravention of the most sacred engagements swept away at this melancholy period . . .

A portion of the Report on the Population, Culture, Revenue,
etc., of the late French part of the island of St Martin, 1815

Far to the north is St Martin, the possession of which France also shares with Holland despite its barely forty square miles of extent, making it the smallest territory in the world with two nationalities . . .

HARRY A. FRANCK, 1920

. . . the captain thought the weather so bad that it might be advisable to put into the Dutch island of St Martin's for the night . . .

The Dutch Lieutenant-Governor very kindly invited us ashore to dine . . . and we were most hospitably entertained at one of the longest dinners I have ever faced. Course after course came on, and out of politeness I did not like to refuse, but I felt almost too heavy to rise from the table at the end of it.

But all the same we spent a very pleasant evening afterwards with his family circle and some other friends whom he had asked in, singing choruses of all the latest English songs. The Dutch in these islands are nearly all old settled families, and from close association and intermarriage with neighbouring English islands their customary language has now become English . . .

I should have mentioned that earlier in the afternoon when we first went ashore the Governor had as a preliminary produced glasses of a rather sweet champagne which he insisted on our drinking with him, after which he had taken us round in his car to see the sights of Philippsville [sic], the capital. This did not take long, and then he said: 'Shall we now call upon the Governor of French St Martin's?' . . .

I was delighted at the opportunity, and after he had spoken on the telephone to his fellow potentate we started across the island for the short run of four or five miles to Marigot, the French capital. About halfway, on a lonely part of the road, was a Dutch sentry, complete with a coloured striped sentry box, and a little further on a French one, similarly housed. It looked rather like a scene in a toy theatre, especially as there was a comical looking palm tree between them, with a donkey and a pig, each tethered to a rope, contentedly lying under it. The contrast in the two halves of this small island was at that time very marked, as the Dutch capital and roads were very clean and well kept, whereas the corresponding French part was not; but in fairness I must say that I have heard there has been a vast improvement in French St Martin's in the last year or two.

Arrived at Marigot we duly paid our call on Msr Fleming, who despite his English name was a Frenchman, and [who] produced glasses of a rather sweet champagne! This was somewhat embarrassing, as it was only half an hour since the previous round, but we nobly did our duty.

On being taken round Marigot the impression we gained was of a small sleepy French town, with grass growing among the stone pavements and very few people moving about. In one shady street we saw a whole row of game-cocks, fighting birds, each tied well away from each other by one leg. I was subsequently told that the inhabitants made their living principally by breeding these for export to the Spanish islands; and also by a 'rake-off' on liquor brought in to this duty-free port and then re-exported to 'an unknown destination'. At that time prohibition reigned in the USA and also in the American colonies of St Thomas and Porto Rico.

SIR REGINALD ST-JOHNSTON, 1936

St Martin . . . is only twenty-one square miles in area, but despite its small size, it is shared by France and Holland. It is the only Caribbean island to be divided between two European powers . . .

St Martin epitomizes the condition of The Netherlands Windward Islands, which live with their memories of the past in a state of suspended animation. Many of its plantations are deserted, and the more virile elements of its population have emigrated. The people who have remained exist largely on money remitted to them by relatives in Curaçao, Aruba, and the United States. Many people are supported by government projects, and though they are not lazy, they have become apathetic.

The soil is not particularly fertile; much of it is tipped at an angle of forty-five degrees and many of the fields are covered with huge boulders. Sugar and cotton, cultivated during the days of slavery, have been abandoned, and only a small amount of hay is baled and shipped to Curaçao. Even the salt industry, which once made the island important, has all but vanished, due to competition from the neighbouring British island of Anguilla.

PHILIP HANSON HISS, 1943

The vanished industry

St Martin was known to its first, Amerindian, inhabitants as Sualougia, *the Land of Salt, and it was the ease with which salt could be obtained there that brought about its settlement by Europeans in the seventeenth century. Under the terms of the treaty which divided the island between the Dutch and French settlers the salt pans – the shallow ponds which were found behind some of the bays – became common property. Two of them, Great Salt Pond behind a large, well-sheltered bay on the Dutch south coast, and Grand Case, behind a smaller but equally safe anchorage on the French north-west coast, were ideally situated for the development of an export trade, and it was in these two places that the production of salt in commercial quantities was soon concentrated. The salt industry remained an important part of the economy for nearly 300 years, with the annual production peaking at around 35,000 tonnes in the middle of the nineteenth century. It began to decline after the turn of the century, with operations in the Great Salt Pond coming to an end in 1949, and those at Grand Case nearly twenty years later.*

Although the shallow ponds were the general property of the inhabitants, salt in commercial quantities could not be produced by individuals working alone, and both were soon divided up by dikes and dams into the smaller compartments called pans which could be managed by groups or associations working for the common good. Once a system of controlling the entry of sea water had been evolved, and the pond suitably subdivided, the salt-making process was very simple. Each pan was several feet below sea level and the shallow area of sea water it contained quickly evaporated to form a lake of brine, called pickle, under which the salt crystallized into a layer which was often up to twenty centimetres thick. Production could be ruined by heavy rainfall but, as it took from three to four days before rain and sea water would mix, this could usually be drained off or, in later years, pumped off using windmills.

The reaping of the salt was seasonal, often lasting for two or three months at a time. In the mid-nineteenth century, when the industry was all-important, the reaping of the Great Salt Pond alone provided work for up to 1000 men, women and children. The layer of salt in each pan was harvested by crews of ten to fifteen, each working under a 'captain' to fill rectangular, flat-bottomed barges known as 'flats'. The women in the crew were employed, using peculiar metal-tipped fingerstalls, to crack lumps of salt from the bottom while wading knee deep in the brine. The lumps were then rinsed off and passed in baskets to the men of the crew who broke them up as they filled the flat. Each fully laden flat was then poled ashore for the work of unloading to begin. This consisted of the men shovelling the salt on to trays which the women then 'headed' to piles which often rose to five or six metres in height. Further labour came later when, to provide a cargo for export, the salt from each pile had to be bagged and transported in carts to the beach for loading into the boats which took it out to a ship at anchor. As the 'heading' of the bags across the beach was normally done by small boys, the entire process of salt production and exportation was gruelling, degrading and often painful work for young and old alike, and was an industry which did not die a moment too soon.

It seems most appropriate that the disused salt pans have played a part in the rejuvenation of St Martin. Soon after 1949 the Great Salt Pond began to be filled in, in order to allow Philipsburg to expand beyond the confines of the two narrow parallel streets it had consisted of up until then; and within a few years of the end of operations in Grand Case a large part of it had similarly been filled in to create an airport runway. Both reclamation projects have assisted greatly in the development of tourism, something which although perhaps not ideal as the mainstay of any island's economy, is certainly better than the salt industry it eventually replaced.

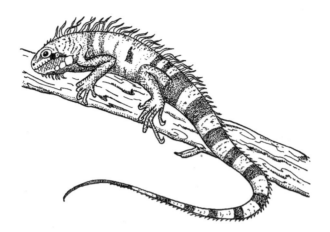

22 Anguilla

'The exact antipode of the large plantations of sugar'

Anguilla presents a very singular appearance for a West Indian island. A little wall of cliff of some forty feet in height generally rises from the beach, and when you have mounted this, the whole country lies before you gently sloping inwards in a concave form, and sliding away, as it were, to the south where the land is only just above the level of the sea . . . Seven tenths of the country are entirely uncultivated; in some parts a few coppices, but more commonly a pretty species of myrtle . . . seems to cover the whole soil . . . Indeed there were scarcely any of the usual features of West Indian scenery visible; neither of those prominent ones, the lively windmill or the columnar palm, was to be seen, and there was a rusticity, a pastoral character on the face of the land, its roads and its vegetation, which is the exact antipode of the large plantations of sugar.

HENRY NELSON COLERIDGE, 1826

The island of Anguilla, so called from its snake-like form, is said to have been discovered and colonized by the English [in 1650]: it was filled with alligators and other noxious animals, but the soil was good for raising tobacco and corn and the cattle imported multiplied very fast. It was not colonized under any public encouragement, each planter laboured for himself, and the island was frequently plundered by marauders.

CAPTAIN THOMAS SOUTHEY, 1827

... Anguilla, a small island, deriving its name, I presume, from its snake-like appearance ... We were sorry to learn that [it] is not in so prosperous a condition as many of the neighbouring British islands. How it fares with the laborers, I know not; but as it is a poor island, it is probable that many of them have been induced to quit it, under the temptation of higher wages in other colonies. With regard to the white inhabitants, we were told that they had expended their compensation money somewhat too easily, and were reduced to a state of no small poverty and distress. I believe there is some view entertained of converting it into a penal settlement.

JOSEPH JOHN GURNEY, 1840

Mariners all, the Anguillans in times of plenty had taken their surplus stock of peas, sheep, goats and cattle to the neighbouring islands and even to Trinidad. In times of scarcity emigration naturally followed the trade routes. Some went to Antigua, some to St Kitts, some to Trinidad and some to the Spanish Main. For all that, the greater portion clung tenaciously to Anguilla, their home, their fatherland.

Then came the Sombrero days in the middle 1860s, when a field of emigration more adapted to the mode of life of the Anguillan labourer was opened. For a part of the time he might cultivate his land and in good seasons have an abundant crop of provisions, then he could go to dig and dive for the phosphate rock in Sombrero; thus acquiring a sum of ready money to purchase clothing for the family. This led to the foundation of a higher standard of living in many an Anguillan home. Three good meals a day, a liberal ration of rum and molasses, and seven or eight dollars a month constituted good pay for the Sombrero labourer. But eventually even this failed, and similar drought and distress in the early 1870s forced Anguillans to become indentured labourers on the sugar plantations of St Croix.

S.B. JONES, 1936

Anguilla is an extraordinary place, quite different to the usual type of West Indian island. It is very flat, the highest 'mountain' being only about 200 feet, and is of coral limestone, providing a natural surface for excellent roads in all directions. The inhabitants are a sturdy, independent type, and at the time of my visit there were hardly a dozen young men in the place, because out of the 6000 inhabitants every available man had gone off, as usual, to work for the four or five months' season on the sugar-cane estates . . . of Santo Domingo. Here they used to receive good wages, and – *mirabile dictu* – to bring back the money each year, and with it they built houses or employed it in other useful ways at home. The result is that this large island of thirty-five square miles is covered with separate, well looked after holdings, each with a good substantial house in the centre of it, and each house well stocked with the amenities of life. During the remaining part of the year the people grow provisions on their lands, plant up cotton, and perform the operation known as 'reaping the salt ponds'.

SIR REGINALD ST-JOHNSTON, 1936

Waterloo money

Soon after 1815 and the end of the Napoleonic wars those Anguillan planters who had had their estates in St Martin seized by the French during the hostilities (see page 178) submitted claims through the British Government for compensation from France. Some claims were settled reasonably promptly, but negotiations about the rest were still continuing twenty-five years later.

Among those whose claim to an award of what came to be called 'Waterloo money', after the British victory which ended the wars, was William Richardson, whose late father's estate had been among those seized. In 1821, despairing of ever receiving any compensation in his own lifetime, and in a manner which throws a strong light on the – to say the least – peculiar moral standards of the day in Anguilla, he bequeathed his prospective share of Waterloo money by deed poll:

ANGUILLA, Know all men by these presents that, whereas certain of the produce and Emoluments belonging to the Estate of Richard Richardson Senior's Property situated in the Island of Saint Martin was in the French revolutionary Government sequestered and with held by the said Government, and whereas provision was made for the Payment and reimbursement of the same by a clause of the late treaty entered into between the English and French Government and, in the event of the said reimbursement being made, I William Richardson for the love, good-will and affection which I have and do bear unto my Coloured Children, Vizt: Benjamin, my Coloured Son borne of a Negro Woman called Loatsey (now in his Possession or given him, my said Son, by me); Mary, George, Richard, Maria, Hubert, John and Augustus borne of the body of a Negro Woman called Maricha; William, the Son borne of the body of a Negro Woman called Belinda; and unto the said Maricha ... have given, granted and Confirmed, and by these Presents do freely, clearly and absolutely give, grant and Confirm unto them . . . all and Singular the said Sum . . . to which I am entitled as one of the Heirs of said Richard Richardson Senior . . .

Whether his coloured progeny, along with his favourite concubine, ever benefited as a result is not known, any more than are the views his wife and legitimate children may have had of the bequest. Not surprisingly, perhaps, the surname Richardson remains common in Anguilla to this day.

23 Sombrero

'First outlier of the New World'

At noon we were only two hundred and ten miles from Sombrero, 'the Spanish Hat', a lonely island, which is here the first outlier of the New World.

CHARLES KINGSLEY, 1871

Sombrero (which Kingsley in fact never saw, as his ship passed it during the night) is a very small island about thirty-five nautical miles north-west of Anguilla, of which it is a dependency and to which it bears a remarkable resemblance in shape. It stands in the middle of the Atlantic end of the sea passage to which it has given its name. In separating Anguilla from the Virgin Islands, this sea passage forms one of the main routes for shipping into and out of the Caribbean. Sombrero is treeless, waterless and uninhabited except for the Anguillan keepers of the lighthouse which has been maintained there since 1867. Although it had been recognized as a hazard by generations of seafarers long before this date, Sombrero had first entered the wider public consciousness only sixty years earlier after one such seagoer had been deliberately abandoned there.

In December 1807 Robert Jeffrey, an armourer's mate on board the 18-gun brig HMS Recruit, *had so annoyed or upset his commanding officer, Captain* the Honourable Warwick Lake, while in the vicinity of the island, that he had been taken ashore and marooned. Being a resourceful character Jeffrey survived reasonably well on a diet of shellfish and rainwater for over a week before being rescued by an American vessel outward bound from the Caribbean for Massachusetts. Once ashore in the United States, and having had little trouble in finding work as a smith in order to support himself, he decided to remain there.

The story might have ended here, and all might have been well for Captain Lake had the putting ashore of an offender to die on an uninhabited island been a punishment sanctioned by whatever version of the Naval Discipline Act was in force at the time, but this was not the case. Word of his action soon got out and a search for Jeffrey was instigated. His whereabouts were not discovered until 1810, when a warship had to be sent to the United States in order to bring him back to England. There he was treated as something of a hero, and after receiving a considerable sum in compensation he made a living for a while by exhibiting himself in London. Captain Lake suffered the indignity of being court-martialled and dismissed from the Navy.

It is not known if it was the publicity attached to Jeffrey's marooning which prompted a visit to Sombrero by a geologist in 1811, any more than it is known whether the latter's report on the island brought about the start of the extraction of its phosphate deposits nearly fifty years later. What is known, is that the removal of phosphate began in the way it did because the island was uninhabited and its ownership undecided.

In 1856 the United States Congress passed the Guano Islands Act, authorizing the captains of American ships to claim sovereignty over any abandoned island with deposits of seabird manure which they knew of, or came across, during their voyaging. Sombrero was a prime example of such an island, and within three years an American-owned company was already busy there. A light railway had been laid down along half its length, connecting a large quarry with a landing place on the south-west coast, where there were workshops, a steam-driven rock crusher, accommodation for the supervisors, and barracks for the almost entirely Anguillan workforce.

By the time Charles Kingsley sailed past on his way, at last, to spend a Christmas in the West Indies, so much phosphate had been removed that the profile of the island (as he might have recorded had he been awake and able to see it) had already lost any resemblance it may once have possessed to that of a Spanish hat. By then too the dispute which had arisen between Britain and the United States about the sovereignty of the island had been resolved in the former's favour, and the Sombrero Phosphate Company was paying the Crown Agents £1000 a year in rent.

Once the surface deposits had been removed the phosphate became increasingly difficult to extract, being found in pockets which could only be worked by blasting. On an island which, once the low hill that had given it its name had been destroyed, was nowhere more than about twelve metres high such work was eventually being conducted below sea level, and divers had to be employed. As well as becoming increasingly arduous, phosphate mining now became that much more dangerous and expensive. Production reached its peak in 1881 when some 20,000 tonnes of ore were exported, but fell off rapidly thereafter and ended altogether in 1888. About 7000 tonnes were shipped that year, but by then the deposits were worked out and much of what left the island was rubbish rather than phosphate. The workings were abandoned two years later.

After that Sombrero's only inhabitants consisted, as they still do today, of the lighthouse staff of four keepers and a cook. It is surely not without interest, in view of the propensity for procreation shown by one of their white ancestors as revealed in his bequest of 'Waterloo money', to note that in the 1890s all four keepers were named Richardson, and that this remained the surname of at least one of the four until the end of the twentieth century.

24 Tortola

'A long way from the Isle of Man'

A skilful negro sailor, whom we picked up at St Thomas, piloted us along a somewhat difficult course, to Roadtown in Tortola. The island as we approached it presented a highly interesting appearance; its mountains peaked and picturesque, and the plains below clad with sugar-cane.

With some difficulty we found board and lodging at a tavern close by the sea, kept by a singular colored old lady, named McClaverty. Her rooms had been occupied up to that day by some of her relatives who had been dangerously ill with fever, and the children of the family were creeping about the house, in a most emaciated condition. No alternative offered but to take the apartments; we were assured that there was no danger, and we happily escaped without the least infection. The constant draughts of a delicious easterly breeze sweeping through the house, were indeed sufficient to prevent it; and that we were not in the way of starvation, was evident, from the sight which caught our eye, of a number of green turtles in a small reservoir of sea water, before the door of the tavern. These animals abound among the rocks and keys of the Virgin Islands, and are common fare at the tables of the gentry . . .

After regaling ourselves with a plentiful breakfast . . . we pursued our course through scenery of uncommon beauty – in parts almost of a Swiss character. From a mountain called Chateau Belair, we obtained a view, at once, of almost all the islands of the Virgin group, with their satellites or keys ... The scene was magnificent. There are no roads, on this island, for carriages – only rocky and precipitous mountain paths, for journeys on horseback or foot.

JOSEPH JOHN GURNEY, 1840

If you ask an Englishman where the Virgin Islands are, the probability is that he will stare at you blankly. A certain statesman to whom that question was put, replied that he could only say that they were a long way from the Isle of Man! ... Politically they form a presidency of the Leeward Islands, and on behalf of the Governor their affairs are controlled by a Commissioner [who] is Treasurer, Registrar of Shipping, Deputy Judge of the Summary Jurisdiction Court, Magistrate, Registrar, Provost-Marshall, Coroner, Registrar of Deaths, Civil Marriage Officer, and Postmaster, besides numerous 'etceteras' ... This veritable Pooh Bah was once expected to act as medical officer as well, and it must have been disconcerting to the King's representative to be called up at night to minister to the medical needs of his subjects! ...

The Virgin Islands are quite innocent of hotels; but motor-boats of any size can lie snugly in their secluded harbours, and a sportsman wishing to enjoy a novel holiday amid beautiful surroundings would find in this little archipelago a sanctuary where he would be completely free from the disturbing features of modern civilization.

SIR ALGERNON ASPINALL, 1927

We boarded the 'plane, which was manned by an American major and captain, and after taxying across the bay, we rose to a height and flew over a number of islands till we reached Tortola, and planed down into the water in Road Town Bay ...

On arrival in Road Town ... the Commissioner's boat came off and conveyed us and the American officers to Government House. As a seaplane had never before been seen in these waters, nearly all the inhabitants came down to the water's edge to see this curious sight.

The Commissioner (Dr Wailling) is not only responsible for the government of the British Virgin Islands, but is also judge and doctor, and both he and his wife are loved and respected by the people.

From the veranda in Government House we had a very fine view of Road Town and Bay, and to us they looked like one of the Highland lochs in

Scotland. We had a wonderful meeting in our church that night, people coming from all over the island. As there is only one road (of a kind) round the bay, the people had to climb over the mountain tracks, and these are what we should call at home dried mountain streams, composed of loose stones and bolders which are almost impossible to negotiate at night. Happily there was a full moon shining, which enabled us to have a packed church.

J. E. HENDERSON, 1939

Being conscious of one's conduct

In the eighteenth century Tortola was home to a sizeable community of the Society of Friends, better known as Quakers, a religious group whose members were firmly and courageously opposed to slavery. As they were frequently harried and persecuted for their beliefs it probably came as no great surprise to the rest of the community when in 1778 two of their number, Samuel and Mary Nottingham, who owned a plantation at Fat Hog Bay near the eastern end of the island, decided they had endured enough and were about to return to their home city of Bristol. What must have both astonished and infuriated their intolerant non-Quaker neighbours was that before they left for England, the Nottinghams not only manumitted all their slaves, many of whom they had taught to read and write, but made over the entire plantation to them as common property.

When the Quaker philanthropist Joseph John Gurney visited the plantation, called Long Look, in 1840 he found it in good order, well cultivated, and capable of supporting a community of around sixty 'respectable' and 'orderly' men, women and children. One of their most cherished possessions was 'A letter of Christian advice addressed to their predecessors' by the Nottinghams some fifty-eight years earlier, which they carefully preserved 'as a sort of title deed to the estate'. Fortunately for posterity Gurney made a copy of this document, the extremely moving contents of which speak for themselves:

Bristol, 30th of 9th month, 1782

Dear George,

Thy letter of the 8th of last 6th month we received, which was well pleasing to us to hear of the present good disposition of thyself, and the rest of our late servants, whose welfare and happiness, both here and hereafter we have much at heart. But we are sorry to hear of the removal of poor John Venture and Harry, though not without hopes of their partaking of that mercy which is extended to all, without respect of persons, whether white or black; so, George, remember what we write to thee, we write to all of you who once called us Master and Mistress. But now you are all free, as far as it is in our power to make you so, because none are free indeed, except they are free in Christ; therefore we admonish you, not as your master and mistress, but as your friends and benefactors, beseeching you to be conscious of your conduct, and circumspect in your behaviour to all, that none may accuse you of abusing that freedom which we, in the course of Divine Providence, have been permitted to give you; remembering also, that as free men and women you are accountable for every part of your conduct, and must answer for the same on your own persons if you do amiss, in which case, the laws where you are have provided a punishment, according to the nature of the offence; but do well and ye shall have praise of the same. And that you may be enabled to live honestly among men, we have given you our East End plantation in Fathog Bay, with every thing thereunto belonging, which we will endeavour to have secured to you by all lawful ways and means, that none may deprive you nor your offspring of it, but that you may freely cultivate and improve it, to your own benefit and advantage, and thereby be provided with a sufficient subsistence to live comfortably together in all friendliness and cordiality, assisting each other, that those more advanced in years may advise the younger, and these submit to the council of the elder, so that good order and harmony may be preserved among you, which will assuredly draw down the blessing of the Most High. But if you have not wherewithal to cultivate and improve the plantation yourselves, we advise you to hire yourselves for a season, to whom you please, as also the plantation, if you think it necessary, till you acquire a sufficiency to go on yourselves: but in every step you take of this kind, always remember the good of the whole. And as soon as you can make a beginning on the plantation yourselves, with cotton and provisions, we by all means would have you to do it, that you may not be scattered and too much divided, but endeavour to dwell together, and be content with food and raiment, and a blessing will certainly attend you, under the influence of such a disposition. Tell Dorcas Venterpool we are much obliged to her for her friendly care and attendance of poor John Venture and Harry, during their sickness. We shall be pleased to hear how you go on by any opportunity, and that you cautiously maintain a good report among the neighbours, live in love among yourselves: and the peace of God, which passeth all understanding will assuredly be with you and yours, which we earnestly desire and pray for, being your sincere friends and well-wishers.

SAMUEL NOTTINGHAM
MARY NOTTINGHAM

The way of the world being as it is the situation at Long Look as recorded by Gurney could not last, and when in due course the estate was broken up and separate titles were needed, the Nottinghams' bequest of a communal title served to create problems which it took until towards the end of the twentieth century to resolve completely. Be that as it may, descendants of the original free community still live in the vicinity of Fat Hog Bay today and can look back with some pride on their past. They can also recall with affection the white man and woman who once owned their ancestors – something which the descendants of another eighteenth-century Tortolan plantation and slave owner would find it extremely hard to do, and this whether they were black or white.

One man who was probably enraged more than any other by the action of Samuel and Mary Nottingham was Arthur Hodge, an irascible and brutal individual who belonged to a family long resident in the Virgin Islands and who, during the last decades of the eighteenth century, inherited the family estates in Tortola. He also rose high enough in what passed for society on the island of his day to be appointed a member of the Legislative Council.

Hodge was renowned for the ill-treatment of his slaves but nothing was, or indeed could be, done about this until 1811 when, following a violent quarrel with another council member, he was accused of having over the years brought about the deaths of at least twelve of them. As the killing of a slave had been made a capital offence under an act passed by the British Government in 1798, once he had been so accused the authorities had no option but to bring him to trial. This was something which went against the grain of the rest of the island's white society. Even though a number of his employees, including a white overseer, swore affidavits testifying to Hodge's cruelty and to a number of deaths he had caused by excessive flogging, and in one case by pouring boiling water down the throat of a female slave, it was by no means certain that a judge and jury drawn from among his fellow planters would even consider finding him guilty.

This being so the Governor of the Leeward Islands, Hugh Elliot, proceeded to Tortola from his headquarters in Antigua in a warship to witness the trial for himself. The previous year Elliot had found himself powerless to ensure that justice was done in a similar case brought against a barbaric slave-owner in Nevis by not attending the trial in person, and he was not prepared to let such a thing happen again. On 29 April, in a special court set up by the Governor, Hodge was charged with a single murder caused by flogging, but with eight more indictments drawn up in case this charge failed. At the end of a marathon twenty-two hour sitting, and after taking an hour and a half to deliberate, the jury found the defendant guilty but, as this automatically invoked the death penalty, with a strong plea for mercy.

In some fear of public disturbance Elliot immediately declared martial law, and asked the captain of the ship in which he had arrived to prepare to land sailors and marines to maintain order if needed. Such precautions were all that proved necessary. The small white population of Tortola, regardless of what thoughts they may have harboured about the relative importance of black and white lives, were in no position to defy the Crown in the shape of the Governor and the Royal Navy, and no disturbance took place. Elliot rejected the plea for mercy and Hodge was hanged on 8 May – the first white man to be executed for the murder of a slave anywhere in the British West Indies.

The surname Hodge remains common in the Virgin Islands to this day, like that of Richardson in Anguilla – and for very much the same reason. One man who bore the name, but with considerably more honour than the slave-murderer who may well have been one of his ancestors, was born in Tortola in about 1840 and spent all of his short adult life as a soldier in the 4th West India Regiment. This, like the 1st in British Guiana (see page 17) and the 8th in Dominica (see page 79), was a regiment in which all ranks up to and including that of sergeant were black, and all officers and senior NCOs were white. After the end of the Napoleonic wars the four such regiments which remained in being were all used not only to provide garrisons for the British colonies in the Caribbean, but also for those in West Africa.

In 1866 Private Hodge was serving with his regiment in the Gambia when, as part of a punitive expedition against one of the interior tribes, a detachment was ordered to storm Tubab Kolon, a village on the River Gambia about thirty kilometres from the open sea. Under the command of the Governor of the colony, Lieutenant-Colonel George D'Arcy, the troops attacked first of all with field artillery, but this was too light to have much effect on the high, stout stockade surrounding the village. D'Arcy, impatient to get the job done, called for volunteers to assist him in creating a breach by hand. Two officers and fifteen men – one of whom was Hodge – answered his call and, as soon as the necessary axes had been issued, all set off towards the stockade in the face of very heavy musket fire.

The two officers were shot and killed almost instantly, and only D'Arcy and two of the soldiers avoided being wounded before the rest of the party reached the high fence. Hodge and another soldier named Boswell were then the only two able to set to work with their axes. As soon as they had made a hole big enough for them to pass through Boswell was shot dead. Hodge followed his commanding officer through the gap, only to be hit and badly wounded just as he had finished hacking open the fastenings of a gate. D'Arcy, who seems to have led a charmed life, remained unscathed and was able to direct the fighting which then took place as the remainder of his force poured in through the open gate. The defending tribesmen put up a fierce resistance, not giving up until they had suffered several hundred casualties. The 4th West India Regiment's losses amounted to two officers and four men killed, and some sixty wounded. Among the latter of course was Private Hodge, whom D'Arcy later praised warmly in front of the rest of his troops.

The Governor also took further action, and in the London Gazette of 4 January 1867 it was announced that:

The Queen has been graciously pleased to signify Her intention to confer the Decoration of the Victoria Cross on the undermentioned Private Soldier, whose claim to the same has been submitted for Her Majesty's approval, for his gallant conduct at the Siege and Capture of Tubabecolong, Gambia River, as recorded against his name . . . Samuel Hodge, Private, 4th West India Regt. Date of Act of Bravery: 30 June 1866.

Hodge was presented with the Victoria Cross on 24 June 1867 while serving with his regiment in what was then called British Honduras, by which time he was a lance-corporal. Having been shot in four different places while winning the medal he was in less than perfect health at the time, and died a month later. It is much to be regretted that not only are the present whereabouts of his medal unknown, and that the position of his grave in the now disused Belize City military cemetery can no longer be identified, but that his name and deeds remain unrecognized in the island where he was born. As the first black soldier to be awarded the Victoria Cross he deserves to be better remembered.

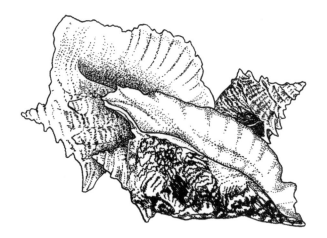

25 Anegada

'The drowned island'

Anegada . . . is the most northern of the cluster of islands and keys known by the name of the Virgin Islands, and is unhappily celebrated for the number of wrecks, in many cases accompanied with a heavy loss of life, which it has occasioned.

Of its history little is known; and there is no likelihood that it was settled early . . . the aborigines used it as an occasional rendezvous, where they procured great quantities of conchs (*Strombus gigas*); and large piles of these shells are still to be seen at the east end of the island, but nowhere else; which seems to prove decidedly that it was not permanently occupied, but merely resorted to from time to time . . .

At a later period the retired bays of the island served as a lurking place to the Buccaneers, Kirke and Bone being said to have especially frequented it; and the latter has bequeathed his name to a creek on the north side, which appears to have been his favourite resort. Ultimately, as the trade among the West India islands became more frequent, and repeated shipwrecks in this quarter held out hopes of advantage to those who might be in the neighbourhood to profit by them, settlers took up their permanent residence on the island, and were, at one time, more numerous even than they are now. They found that the loose ground which covered it was capable of bearing provision crops, and even cotton . . . The great object, however, always was, and still is, the wreck of vessels; and the indolence of the inhabitants is only thoroughly roused by the cry of – 'A vessel on the reef'. Then all are roused to activity; scarcely is the news announced, than boats of every description, shallops and sailing vessels, are pushed off with all haste towards the scene of action; arms which have been idle for weeks are brought into exercise; and both skill and intrepidity are tasked to the uttermost to get first on board. The scene, indeed, baffles description; and it is to be feared that few are attracted by motives of humanity, though some such do exist . . .

ROBERT HERMANN SCHOMBURGK, 1832

. . . Anegada, or the Drowned Island, thus called because it is water-logged with lagoons and is so low-lying as to be almost sea-swept in times of storm . . . It has been the scene of countless wrecks, since around it is the deadly and much-accursed Horse Shoe Reef.

SIR FREDERICK TREVES, 1908

The Anegada coast has always been known as a most dangerous spot for ships. In the days when St Thomas was one of the busiest ports of the West Indies, Anegada had more wrecks in two years than those two dreaded localities on the American coast, Cape Race and Sable Island, can now claim in thirty-six months. Tides and currents are nowhere in the West Indies as swift as they are here and in few spots in the Seven Seas are there so many reefs and hidden dangers. Occasionally mariners can hardly see the island owing to the mist caused by spray which forms when the great waves dash against the cliffs. This mist hangs over the island and often hides it completely. It is from this fact that Anegada derived its Spanish name, 'Drowned Island'.

There are no rivulets . . . Water is obtained from two curious water holes named 'The Wells' on the northeast coast . . . but the inhabitants prefer to drink the rainwater which they catch in their cisterns. They make use of the fresh water from The Wells for the cultivation of crops. These curious water holes have a mouth from ten to twenty-five feet in diameter, and a funnel-shaped formation. They are very deep, and the surface rises and falls with the tides. The water in them is not only fresh, but it is also colder than the sea water.

THEODOOR DE BOOY and JOHN T. FARIS, 1918

Even though Anegada had been inhabited, even if only by assorted pirates, wreckers and subsistence farmers, more or less continuously since it became a British possession in 1672, it was well into the nineteenth century before anyone other than its population took more than a passing interest in the island, and then it was by a man who was not even a British subject.

Robert Schomburgk, who carried out the first survey of the island, was born and educated in Germany where, undoubtedly inspired by the achievements of his countryman, the great traveller and naturalist Alexander von Humboldt, by the time he left university he had developed a passion for natural history equalled only by his urge to explore in the Americas. Leaving Germany in 1829 at the age of twenty-five, he was in St Thomas two years later when an American brig, the Lewis, *was reported wrecked on the south-east coast of Anegada. So little was then known of this island, other than of the number of wrecks it had claimed, that Schomburgk was inspired to go there and between August and October 1831, at his own expense, undertake the first proper survey of the entire island and the surrounding reefs. His chart, having been somewhat sniffily accepted by the Council and Assembly of the British Virgin Islands as 'a very accurate survey', was sent to the recently formed Royal Geographical Society in London. By itself, this probably would have been of only limited interest, but fortunately it was accompanied by a long report on Anegada, of which the following extract, together with that given above, provides some idea of the depth of knowledge and breadth of interest possessed by its author:*

The surrounding sea abounds in good fish, to which the ponds add likewise their number; without entering into details, I mention only one fact, which deserves a strict investigation. It is well known that the yellow-billed sprat . . . baracuta . . . the bottle-nosed Cavalla . . . rock-fish . . . and sometimes the king-fish . . . are occasionally poisonous, and are known to have caused immediate death. To what the poisonous quality of these fishes is to be attributed is very uncertain; it has been supposed that their feeding on copper-banks, of which there are some at St Eustatia, renders them poisonous; others deny this, and attribute it to their feeding on narcotic submarine plants. However, though frequently accidents happen in the neighbouring islands, not one instance of fish poison has been known in Anegada; and the yellow-billed sprat, the largest baracuta, and even the amber fish, are eaten with impunity. Who can solve this enigma? If we suppose that the feeding on copper-banks renders certain fishes poisonous, then the waters round Anegada must possess a powerful antidote, of which the neighbouring islands are deprived; or if the poisonous quality arise from the feeding on a narcotic submarine plant, then Anegada must not only be without it, but the dangerous quality of that plant must be instantaneous, and the fish must have been caught immediately after having fed upon it, because the distance between Anegada and Virgin Gorda being so trifling, one would suppose (even admitting that the seas near the first island are divested of it) that there would be, at least, one instance where the poisonous fish directed its course towards Anegada, and being caught there, proved injurious to those who ate of it. Mussels and crabs are likewise innocent. As there is almost no doubt left that these animals are rendered poisonous by living near manchineel trees ... and feeding upon their roots – and as Anegada possesses not a single tree of that kind – shall we therefore conclude, that not only mussels and crabs, but also the fishes mentioned before, are rendered poisonous by the roots of the manchineel, which are known to grow on the water's edge, and to send their roots to the same. I acknowledge myself negligent in not having investigated this point before, but I hope yet to add some further observations to the little knowledge we have of it. It is a blessing conferred alone on the inhabitants of Anegada, that they can enjoy any fish without being afraid.

This report, when published in the Society's Journal *in 1832, was to change the course of Schomburgk's life, and to link his name with three other parts of the Caribbean. His* Remarks on Anegada *attracted interest in just the right circles in London, and his name could not have been brought into prominence there at a more opportune moment, when British interest in exploring and mapping the lesser-known regions of the world was at its height. In 1835 he was asked by the Royal Geographical Society to undertake an expedition to British Guiana, in order to investigate the river system and to explore the interior. The astronomical observations he was required to make were to be extended in the north-west – no doubt to his great satisfaction – to connect with those obtained in the region of the upper Orinoco River by Humboldt some thirty-five years earlier.*

In the course of the next four years he literally put British Guiana on the map, filling in blank spaces and altering vague lines into authentic representations of the many tributaries of the three main rivers. To do so involved occupying some 174 survey stations, and making nearly 5000 astronomical observations, often under conditions where the 'purity of the air is so great ... that the planets Venus and Jupiter may be seen in the daytime'. He took an interest in everything – plants, animals, birds and geology, as well as the life of the Amerindian tribes he encountered. Among the numerous new plants he discovered was the magnificent water lily, Victoria Regia, *which has huge leaves often two metres in diameter, and which he described as 'the most beautiful specimen of flora of the western hemisphere'. His interest and enthusiasm were boundless, and after his return to London late in 1839 he not only organized a British Guiana Exhibition, but set about recording everything he had seen and done in* A Description of British Guiana, Geographical and Statistical Exhibiting its Resources and Capabilities, *together with the Present and Future Condition and Prospects of the Colony – a tome which was published the following year.*

In this book he drew attention to the fact that the colony's boundaries, other than that with Surinam in the east, were largely undefined, and that large areas of valuable land were in some danger of being seized by Brazil and Venezuela. As a result, and not surprisingly in view of the work he had already carried out, he was asked to return to British Guiana in charge of a commission appointed by the British Government to survey and mark the colony's boundaries with these two countries.

On his arrival in the colony in 1841 he was accompanied by his younger brother, Richard, a botanist who held an appointment in the gardens of the Prussian royal palace of Sans Souci near Potsdam, and who had been sent to make collections for the royal museum and botanical gardens in Berlin. Beginning in the north-west the boundary survey took three years to complete, being conducted at one stage from a base at Pirara, the village on the border with Brazil where for some weeks in 1842 the Schomburgks were caught up in the incident recounted earlier which involved a detachment of the 1st West India Regiment (see page 17).

The brothers' three years together produced two results. In 1847 Richard published in Germany his account of their adventures in Reisen in Britisch-Guiana, *only two out of the three volumes of which have ever been translated into English, and those not until 1922. It took almost as long for Robert's boundary survey – the second result – to be accepted by both Brazil and Venezuela, particularly by the latter after gold had been discovered in the border region. In the end it was only after the disputes had been made the subjects of international arbitration around the turn of the century that the 'Schomburgk Line', with slight modifications here and there, was recognized by all concerned as the true delineation of the colony's western and southern borders.*

The Schomburgks left British Guiana in May 1844; Richard for Germany with his collection, and to begin writing his opus, and Robert to London with his survey results and to receive the knighthood with which he was rewarded at the end of the year. It is highly likely that they never met again. Robert spent the next two or three years in Barbados and devoted himself to gathering material for his majestic History of Barbados, *a work still regarded as 'an indispensable guide to the history of the island up to and just after the time of emancipation'. This was published in 1848, very near the time when Richard, having fallen foul of the authorities in Germany during the revolutionary activities which took place that year, emigrated to Australia.*

In May 1848 Robert was appointed the British consul in Santo Domingo, the capital of the newly independent Republic of Dominica, a post he held until 1857 when he left the Caribbean for the last time in order to take up a similar appointment in what was then called Siam. He retired from public service seven years later and died early in 1865, the same year that his brother, who outlived him by a quarter of a century, became the director of the botanic gardens in Adelaide.

26 St Thomas

'This little Western Tyre'

. . . even in St Thomas there are more than a few persons, who think and feel seriously on matters of the highest importance. But we greatly fear that among the traffickers of many nations, and the confusion of many tongues in this little Western Tyre, the pursuits of religion are generally forgotten. Merchandise by day, and gaiety by night, seemed chiefly to engross the attention of the residents.

JOSEPH JOHN GURNEY, 1840

India goods, tea, spices, Canton crape, Madras coifs, nankeens, etc.; wines, spirits, and preserved fruits from France; dried meats, medicinal waters, linen, etc., from Germany; lumber, shingles, maize, salt fish, etc., from the States; the coffee, cotton and rum of the Antilles; these with articles of European manufacture, whether for use or luxury, from a toy to a steam boat, may find purchasers at St Thomas.

JOHN VAN VOORST, 1843

I shall probably have a word or two to say about St Thomas; but not now. It is a Niggery-Hispano-Dano-Yankee-Doodle place; in which, perhaps, the Yankee-Doodle element, declaring itself in nasal twang and sherry cobblers, seems to be of the strongest flavour . . .

The place belongs to the Danes, who possess also the larger and much more valuable island of Santa Cruz, as they do also the small island of St Martin [*sic*] . . . As St Thomas at present exists, it is of considerable importance. It is an emporium, not only for many of the islands, but for many also of the places on the coast of South and Central America, Guiana, Venezuela, and New Granada, deal there largely. It is a depot for cigars, light dresses, brandy, boots, and Eau de Cologne. Many men therefore of many nations go thither to make money, and they do make it . . . Things ought not, if possible, to be all bad with any man; and I cannot imagine what good can accrue to a man at St Thomas if it be not the good of amassing money. It is one of the hottest and one of the most unhealthy spots among all these hot and unhealthy regions. I do not know whether I should not be justified in saying that of all such spots it is the most hot and the most unhealthy.

ANTHONY TROLLOPE, 1859

At length, in the afternoon, we neared the last point, and turning inside an isolated and crumbling hummock, the Dutchman's Cap, saw before us, at the head of a little narrow harbour, the scarlet and purple roofs of St Thomas's, piled up among orange-trees, at the foot of a green corrie, or rather couple of corries, some eight hundred feet high. There it was, as veritable as a Dutch-oven for cooking fever in, with as veritable a dripping-pan for the poison when concocted in the tideless basin below the town, as ever men invented.

CHARLES KINGSLEY, 1871

St Thomas is a Danish island that has seen better days. It is one of the Virgin Group, a cluster of some hundred islands, rocks and cays . . .

Charlotte Amalia, the capital . . . is without any question the most picturesque town in the whole sweep of the Windward Islands. Placed within a magnificent harbour, and at the foot of a circle of green hills, Charlotte Amalia makes there a bravery of colour . . .

The island itself – as surveyed from the summit of the hill above the town – is a little desolate. The country appears to be uninhabited, given up to loneliness and allowed to grow wild. It is covered everywhere with low bushes, as if the land had relapsed again into savagery . . .

St Thomas once had an evil reputation for unhealthiness. The cemetery in the town testifies that this was not unmerited, and that there were some grounds for Kingsley's description of the place as 'a Dutch oven for cooking fever in'. Now, thanks to enlightened sanitary measures, it can claim to be a quite wholesome settlement.

SIR FREDERICK TREVES, 1908

To learn thoroughly the island of St Thomas one must either be a good pedestrian or obtain a sure-footed pony. There are practically no carriage roads. The only roads which allow a fairly long drive lead from Charlotte-Amalia to Brewer's Bay, about three miles west of the town, or from Charlotte-Amalia to Water Bay, about five miles east. This latter road, however, is none too good, and it has some stiff hills which make a strong horse a necessity. But what St Thomas lacks in carriage roads it makes up in attractive mountain trails and bridle paths.

THEODOOR DE BOOY and JOHN T. FARIS, 1918

Seen from any of its three hills, Charlotte Amalie looks more like a stage setting than a real town. Its sheet-iron roofs, many of them painted red, seem to be cut out of cardboard, and the steepness of the slopes on which the majority of its houses are built suggests the fantasy of the scene-painter rather than cold practicability. A single long, level street, still known, on its placards at least, as Kronprindsens Gade, runs the length of the town and contains nearly all its commerce. The rest start bravely up the steep hills, but soon tire, like the inhabitants, and leave their task incompleted . . .

HARRY A. FRANCK, 1920

A bad bargain?

After a number of trading voyages to the Caribbean in the early part of the seventeenth century, during which efforts were made to found a colony, the Danes eventually succeeded in 1672 with a settlement on St Thomas. Once this was well established attempts were made to colonize St John, the island immediately to the east, but these met with little success before 1718. Fifteen years later the much larger and more distant island of St Croix was bought from France, on the condition that it could not then be re-sold without French consent.

From then on St John and St Croix were developed as plantation islands, in the manner of the British and French sugar colonies to the east, while St Thomas, with its large sheltered harbour in front of Charlotte Amalie, was made a free port in the style of the Dutch island of St Eustatius. Although this encouraged a great deal of smuggling and privateering during the war years, it also enabled St Thomas to develop into a trade emporium of such repute that it can easily appear that this was all any visitor ever commented upon for the next 100 years or more. In 1819, after Road Town in Tortola had been destroyed by a hurricane, the island became a packet station, the rendezvous port for shipping from Europe and North America and a distribution point for cargo, passengers and mail to the West Indies and Central America.

In spite of the revenue this generated, by the middle of the nineteenth century the overall economy of all three islands was in serious decline, and for the Danish Government they had become, like St Barthélemy for the Swedes (see page 174), a liability. Negotiations with the United States about their sale which began in 1865 led to a treaty being signed two years later, which provided for American acquisition of St Thomas and St John for the sum of seven and a half million dollars. Because of possible French objection no mention was made of the sale of St Croix. This was followed by the publication in Denmark of a royal proclamation; the highfalutin content of which cannot, particularly in the final paragraph, disguise a strong whiff of hypocrisy:

We, Christian the Ninth, by the Grace of God, King of Denmark, the Vandals and the Goths, Duke of Sleswig, Holstein, Stornmarn, Ditmarsh, Lauenborg and Oldenborg. Send to Our beloved and faithful Subjects in the Islands of St Thomas and St John our Royal Greeting.

We have resolved to cede Our Islands of St Thomas and St John to the United States of America, and We have to that end ... concluded a convention with the President of the United States. We have, by embodying in that convention explicit and precise provisions, done Our utmost to secure to You protection in Your liberty, Your religion, Your property and private rights, and You shall be free to remain where you now reside, or to remain, retaining the property You possess in the said Islands or disposing thereof and removing the proceeds wherever You please, without You being subjected on this account to any contribution, charge, or tax whatever.

Those who shall prefer to remain in the Islands, may either retain the title and the rights of their natural allegiance or acquire those of Citizens of the United States . . .

As We, however, will not exercise any constraint over Our faithful subjects, We will give You the opportunity of freely and extensively expressing your wishes in regard to this cession . . .

With sincere sorrow do we look forward to the severing of those ties which for many years have united You to Us, and never forgetting those many demonstrations of loyalty and affection We have received from You, We trust that nothing has been neglected on Our side to severe the future welfare of Our beloved and faithful subjects, and that a mighty impulse, both moral and material, will be given to the happy development of the Islands, under the new Sovereignty. Commending you to God! Given at Our Palace of Amalienborg, the 25th October 1867, Under Our Royal Hand and Seal. Christian R.

The plebiscite it promised was held in January 1868, among the less than one-tenth of the total population of the two islands who were eligible to take part, and resulted in an overwhelming vote in favour of the transfer. The Danish Parliament, the Rigsdag, ratified the treaty later the same month. All then looked rosy until March 1870 when in Washington the Senate, now more concerned with reconstruction after the Civil War and the development of the American West, rather than the acquisition of overseas territories, refused its ratification.

Forty-seven years later, in 1917, when it seemed that Denmark might possibly be overrun and occupied by Germany, in which case the Danish colonies would become German possessions, the Senate was only too keen to take over the islands, and to pay twenty-five million dollars for all three (France now being just as anxious not to see St Croix fall into enemy hands).

In the half century which had elapsed since King Christian IX had sent them his 'Royal Greeting', his 'beloved and faithful Subjects' had been almost totally neglected, and the economy of the colony had suffered an almost continuous decline. When the islands were taken over they were found to be in such a poor state that one American visitor at least could not hide his disgust. 'I have yet to find any one who knows just why we bought the Virgin Islands, still less why we paid twenty-five millions for them' he recorded, before going on to moan:

Even had the purchase price of almost three hundred dollars an acre included everything of monetary value on the islands, from the wardrobes of the inhabitants to the last peasant's hut, we should have made a bad bargain. But about all we got for our twenty-five millions is the right to fly our flag over the islands, and half a dozen old forts and government buildings entirely stripped of their furniture. The Danish Government has the reputation of being conservative and economical. It surely is, in more senses than one. By the terms of the treaty 'the movables, especially the silver plate and the pictures, remain the property of the Danish Government and shall, as soon as circumstances permit, be removed by it'. By virtue of that clause they sold at auction every stick of furniture in the public buildings; they tore the mirrors off the walls; they removed the gilt moldings from them; they tried to tear off the embossed leathery wall-paper, and left the rooms looking as if a party of yeggmen had gutted them; they took down and carried away the rope on the government flagpole! Economy is a splendid trait, but they might have left us a chair in which to mourn the loss of our twenty-five – and more – millions.

HARRY A. FRANCK, 1920

27 St Croix

'Far more of a real country'

The appearance of Santa Cruz, as you approach it from the North, is picturesque and pleasing . . . a succession of rounded or conical hills and mountains, cultivated to their very tops; partly red (being the color of the soil) where the hoe had been at work; and partly bright green, were already covered with the sugar-cane – neat planting settlements visible in various spots; severally consisting of a mansion, a boiling house, a number of negro huts, and a windmill on some neighbouring elevation, for grinding the sugar – the green wooded dells between the hills – and the cocoa-nut trees, with their tall stems, and strange looking but elegant, deciduous branches, scattered over the whole scene.

JOSEPH JOHN GURNEY, 1840

Viewed from the bay, under the green shadow of the hill overlooking it, Frederiksted has the appearance of a beautiful Spanish town, with its Romanesque piazzas, churches, many arched buildings peeping through breaks in a line of mahogany, bread-fruit, mango, tamarind, and palm trees – an irregular mass of at least fifty different tints, from a fairy emerald to a sombre bluish-green. But on entering the streets the illusion of beauty passes: you find yourself in a crumbling, decaying town, with buildings only two stories high. The lower part, of arched Spanish design, is usually of lava rock or of brick, painted a light, warm yellow; the upper stories are most commonly left unpainted, and are rudely constructed of light timber. There are many arcades and courts opening on the streets with large archways. Lava blocks have been used in paving as well as in building; and more than one of the narrow streets, as it slopes up the hill through the great light, is seen to cut its way through craggy masses of volcanic stone.

But all the buildings look dilapidated; the stucco and paint is falling or peeling everywhere; there are fissures in the walls, crumbling facades, tumbling roofs. The first stories, built with solidity worthy of an earthquake region, seem extravagantly heavy by contrast with the frail wooden superstructures . . .

LAFCADIO HEARN, 1890

St Croix is far more of a real country than all the other islands of the group put together. Not only is it larger ... but is much more extensively cultivated. Three splendid roads run nearly the length of the island, with numerous cross roads in good condition. Only the rocky eastern end is a wilderness ... such ... that hunters rarely succeed in stalking the wary animals in the dense undergrowth. There are far more signs of industry in St Croix than in St Thomas; its estate-owners are on the whole an intelligent, progressive class, with a social life quite different from that on the more primitive islands. When one has seen St Croix, the twenty-five million [dollars] does not seem quite so complete and irreparable a loss.

HARRY A. FRANCK, 1920

The bastard son of a Scottish pedlar

Although in the West Indies the name of the American statesman Alexander Hamilton is usually associated with Nevis, the island where, according to John Adams the second president of the United States, he was born the 'bastard son of a Scottish pedlar', it has an equally relevant association with St Croix. This was the island on which he spent his formative years before going to the United States, and also the place where his mother, Rachel Faucett, had been married in 1745, at the age of sixteen, to a Danish planter named John Lavien.

In spite of a lavish ceremony and a honeymoon spent in Denmark the marriage was not a success. Lavien was much older than his bride and after two years, during which she gave birth to a son, Rachel left him to return to her parents in Nevis. Some years later, unable to obtain a divorce, she set up house with James Hamilton, the younger son of a Scottish landed family who had been sent out to the West Indies to make his fortune. As a result of this liaison Rachel gave birth to two more sons, the second of whom was born in 1755 and named Alexander.

In 1765 James Hamilton moved his family to St Croix, having been given a commission to oversee a court case involving the collection of a debt owed to a friend, and where he obtained work on a plantation owned by Rachel's brother-in-law. After a few months, perhaps in answering a call to the trade Adams was to single out for him many years later, he left the island and was never seen again by his common-law wife or either of his two sons. In order not to starve as a result of this desertion, Rachel was obliged to open a small shop in Christiansted, the island's second town, and both boys were sent out to work. Alexander, who while in Nevis had been well-schooled and had shown himself to be abnormally intelligent, at the age of eleven got himself a job in the office of Nicholas Cruger, the head of a firm of merchants and shippers with wide interests in St Croix and several other islands. Once he had found his feet Hamilton proved so adept at keeping accounts, and so quick at mastering other aspects of the firm's activities, that by the time he was sixteen he was being trusted by Cruger to deal with much of the day-to-day running of the business.

In the evenings he continued to educate himself. This was done under the informal tutelage of a local pastor, and it was this man, the Reverend Hugh Knox, who was to set him on the road to the university education which in turn paved the way for his subsequent career. This was achieved when Knox arranged for the publication in the island's leading newspaper of the text of a letter Hamilton had written to his father – with whom he had kept in touch after his abrupt departure – concerning a severe hurricane the island had experienced in August 1772:

St Croix, Sept. 6, 1772

Honored Sir,

I take up my pen, just to give you an imperfect account of one of the most dreadful hurricanes that memory or any records whatever can trace, which happened here on the 31st ultimo at night.

It began about dusk, at north, and raged very violently till ten o'clock. Then ensued a sudden and unexpected interval which lasted about an hour. Meanwhile the wind was shifting round to the south west point, from whence it returned with redoubled fury and continued till nearly three in the morning. Good God! what horror and destruction – it's impossible for me to describe – or you to form any idea of it. It seemed as if a total dissolution of nature was taking place. The roaring of the sea and wind – fiery meteors flying about in the air – the prodigious glare of almost perpetual lightning – the crash of falling houses – and the ear-piercing shrieks of the distressed were sufficient to strike astonishment into Angels. A great part of the buildings throughout the island are leveled to the ground – almost all the rest very much shattered – several persons killed and numbers utterly ruined – whole families wandering about the streets, unknowing where to find a place of shelter – the sick exposed to the keenness of water and air – without a bed to lie upon – or a dry covering to their bodies – and our harbors entirely bare. In a word, misery, in its most hideous shapes, spread over the whole face of the country. A strong smell of gunpowder added somewhat to the terrors of the night; and it was observed that the rain was exceedingly salt. Indeed the water is so brackish and full of sulphur that there is hardly any drinking it . . .

On publication of this, the perception and intellectual promise shown by its author made as great an impression on Nicholas Cruger and several other leading citizens as it had on Hugh Knox. So much so, that with their help within a few months Hamilton had foresaken his office stool and was on his way to North America, where he was to achieve far greater fame as one of the main participants in the events surrounding the birth of the United States, and as one of the premier statesmen of the new republic.

28 Turks & Caicos Islands

'Islands of the greatest consequence'?

The salt on these Islands is deemed equal, if not superior, to any in the world for curing fish and salting meat . . . since my arrival I have employed myself principally in examining the soil and find it very proper for raising of cotton . . .

The Islands called the Caicos which lie about two leagues to the Westward are from every advice I can learn, of the greatest consequence and I have the strongest reasons to believe (Jamaica excepted) the finest Islands belonging to His Majesty. The lands are level, well watered, rich and capable of producing sugar, indigo and every commodity in common with the other West Indian islands.

ANDREW SYMMER, AGENT FOR THE BAHAMAS.
In: *Letter to the Governor of the Bahamas*, 1767

Turks Islands derive their name from a beautiful scarlet cactus, in shape like a fez or tarbouch, which covered the islands in profusion when they were first discovered. Many whales used to be found here; and some of the cays are still called 'ambergris-cays', from the large quantity of that precious but very nasty-looking and horrid-smelling substance that used to be deposited upon them. Ambergris is something like coke, or perhaps more like black amber, in appearance, and is equally light . . . The product is the result of some internal disease from which the whale occasionally suffers – a sort of ulcer or cancer, in fact, which is formed in the stomach of the leviathan of the deep when the climate disagrees with him, and which ailment a change of air and water is supposed always to cure. It is not a very agreeable idea to entertain, that a substance of such unpleasant provenance should be the foundation of almost all the scents which we use . . .

LADY BRASSEY, 1885

Grand Turk Island is one of the most bleak and barren places imaginable, its desolation being only exceeded, if that be possible, by its neighbour, Salt Cay. These form part of a group known as Turks and Caicos Islands [which] derive their name from the indigenous Turk's Head Cactus, a globular, hairy, green plant, surmounted by a scarlet top, closely resembling the now obsolete Turkish fez. Patches of typical Bahamian dwarf-scrub thrive, if one can use that expression for such a meagre display, whilst the few trees lean steeply to westwards, bent thus by the constant and strong Trade Winds. At one time the northern part of the island was planted with sisal but slight vestiges of this one-time industry now remain, the inhabitants relying for their precarious livelihood on salt-raking and fishing.

COMMANDER R. LANGTON-JONES, 1944

There are no hotels or boarding-houses in the islands. Visitors should therefore furnish themselves with suitable introductions and make arrangements for board and lodging in advance . . .

A visitor to Turks and Caicos Islands can best spend his time in studying the life and character of the inhabitants and the manner in which their industries are carried on . . .

SIR ALGERNON ASPINALL, 1954

A bleak and barren place

Quite what a visitor to Grand Turk, the main island of the group and the only one with a town of any size, might have been expected to gain by observing the life and work of its inhabitants in the 1950s – or indeed during any other period in its history – is far from obvious. They still enjoyed nothing better than the ability to make a 'precarious livelihood' from 'salt-raking and fishing', just as they had before the Second World War and for two and a half centuries before that, and nothing was going to change very much for at least another decade and a half. Other than for the amount of salt which has been obtained from them throughout their recorded history the Turks Islands have never had any other value. Even though Europeans first came across them in about 1516 no attempt at a settlement was made before the last quarter of the seventeenth century, and then by people who saw them merely as an adjunct, useful for one reason only, to an existing colony.

These first settlers came in 1678, not from one of the large European possessions reasonably close at hand such as the Bahamas, Cuba or Hispaniola, but from Bermuda, a group of tiny islands over 700 nautical miles to the north which had become a British colony some fifty years or so earlier. The effect of the arrival of these Bermudians was to turn the Turks Islands into a dependency of a colony; and not just any colony, but the smallest and most insignificant of all that England then possessed.

Of course, once these settlers had established themselves, developed a lucrative trade in salt with all the North American colonies from South Carolina to Newfoundland, and begun to use both the Turks and the Caicos islands as bases for wrecking and piratical activities, others began to take notice. The Spanish attacked and occupied the Turks in 1706 and remained for the next four years. The value that came to be placed on the islands during their occupation is perhaps best illustrated by the fact that it took no more than the crew of a single small Bermudian privateer to eject whatever garrison remained there in 1710, and that Spain, other than in trying to prevent their use by pirates, took no further interest in their settlement.

The Governor of the Bahamas was the next to decide the islands were too valuable to be left in the hands of the Bermudians, and applied to London in 1736 to have them incorporated into his colony. Although this particular request was turned down, it was followed by so much argy-bargy between the Bahamian legislature and whatever passed for authority in the Turks Island that, in 1764, the decision was reversed. This only served to increase the ill-feeling and no formal incorporation took place for another thirty-five years.

During this period, presumably reckoning there had to be more to the islands than the Spanish had managed to discover during their occupation, the French made no less than three attempts to seize them, beginning in 1753. The men in command of that attempt and of another which followed eleven years later, having seen what was on offer ashore, both considered it was not worth having and departed – on each occasion taking away only a number of merchant vessels as prizes. The commander of the third attack in 1783 must have been rather more impressed by what he saw, or under stricter orders, because as he departed with yet more prizes he left behind an occupation force on Grand Turk.

When news of this eventually reached the outside world no one was greatly interested, except the 25-year-old captain of the 28-gun frigate HMS Albemarle who, after some frustrating, prizeless months in the Caribbean, was desperate for some action and a chance to bring his name, Horatio Nelson, to the attention of his superiors. Within a week, having collected together a scratch squadron of smaller ships, he was off Grand Turk. After anchoring his ships close inshore in order to make the greatest impression, an officer under a flag of truce was sent to invite the French to surrender. He returned with the news that the French commander not only rejected the offer, but was prepared to oppose any attempt at a landing with all the means at his disposal.

The following morning, as they might have expected had they known anything of the man they were up against, the French were alarmed to see a British landing party being rowed ashore. They may have been equally disconcerted when, after a brief exchange of fire on the beach and a few salvoes from the ships offshore, the attackers broke off the action, re-embarked, and the squadron then sailed away. Nelson afterwards explained away his abrupt withdrawal by making out that the island had been held in much greater strength than he had first thought, and that the French batteries had been too well sited.

Such excuses appear very lame, and their use does not fit in at all with what is known of Nelson's temperament, his ability as a leader of fighting men, his love of action, and his strong desire to make a name for himself. I for one find it much easier to believe once he had launched the attack, and then in the morning light had time to observe through a telescope (he then still had the use of both eyes and both arms) just what it was he had sent men ashore to fight for, he decided that Grand Turk was not worth even a single British life, and that the French were already being punished enough by having to remain in such abysmal surroundings.

29 The Bahamas

'Isles of Summer'

They are the most healthful of our Settlements; and though the ground be very rocky, it will produce whatever is put into it, the best of Cotton in all the Indies, Sugar-Cane, Inico, Dying wood, and great quantities of Salt made by Sun out of the Sea, Tortoise Shell, Oyl of Whale, Seal and Nourse and Spermeceti-Whale sometimes. Amber-Greece is often washed up on the bays.

·John Graves,
Memorial to the Proprietors and the Commissioners of Customs, 1708

As for Wrecks the People of Providence, Harbour-Island and Eleuthera, dealt in them as it is said the good Men of Sussex do: All that come ashore was Prize, and if a Sailor had, by better Luck than the rest, got ashore as well as his Wreck, he was not sure of getting off again as well. This perhaps is scandal, but it is most notorious, that the Inhabitants looked upon every thing they could get out of a Cast-away Ship as their own, and were not at any Trouble to enquire after the owners.

John Oldmixon, 1708

The Bahama islands enjoy the most serene and the most temperate air in all America, the heat of the sun being greatly allayed by refreshing breezes from the east; and the earth and sea are cooled by constant dews which fall in the night, and by gentle showers which fall in their proper seasons; so that as they are free from the sultry heats of our other settlements; they are as little affected with frost, snow, hail, or the north-west winds, which prove so fatal both to men and plants in our other colonies; it is therefore no wonder the sick and afflicted inhabitants of those climates fly hither for relief, being sure to find a cure here . . .

The Bahama islands, in general, are more conveniently situated for annoying the Spaniards in time of war than any of our other settlements, especially two of them. The first is Salvador . . . the eastermost of the whole . . . conveniently situated for intercepting the outward-bound trade of Old Spain . . .

The next is the Biminis . . . by which it has the full command of the gulph, through which all the homeward-bound trade of the Spanish West Indies must pass . . .

PETER HENRY BRUCE, 1782

Nassau is an exceedingly pretty town, the roads in it are excellent, and cleanly kept; its drainage is good; the houses of the white people are handsome, well-built, airy, and elegant; while those of the negroes are usually neat and suitable to their condition . . . the great support of the place is the wrecking business. Scarcely a week passes without one or more valuable cargoes being brought into Nassau for sale, from wrecks on some of the numerous shoals and reefs, which endanger the traffic carried on by the United States with Cuba and Central America. Sometimes these wrecks are suspected of being purposely effected, to the damage of the owners and underwriters, but to the gain of the captain and his crew, through collusion with the wreckers. The boats employed in this profitable but gambling traffic, are small schooners . . . manned almost entirely by black men, who, by long habit, have become daring and skilful sailors. But all classes participate in their gains; and from this source is derived the chief portion of the revenue, and the wealth which is very observable in Nassau . . . but so attractive is it, that nearly all other employments are neglected, and the development of the agricultural resources of the islands is to a great extent impeded.

EDWARD BEAN UNDERHILL, 1862

The modern West Indian 'wrecker' may be considered as a dim survival of the pirates and buccaneers of the past; just as . . . an extortionate London cabman [is] a survival of Dick Turpin. These wreckers are equally prepared to pilot or to wreck a vessel, as suits their purpose best. In the 'good old days', if the fishermen of the Bahamas saved life, they lost all claim for salvage on the vessel from which the rescue had been effected. Consequently it was by no means to their interest that any human being should be found alive upon a stranded ship. What this meant is obvious. The neighbouring coasts are desolate; the fishermen were both rapacious and lawless; and, as a matter of fact, the number of shipwrecked men brought to Nassau, in proportion to the cargoes recovered, was exceedingly small. This state of things, however, is now happily obsolete; and if local knowledge and skill can avail the perplexed skipper in the time of difficulty he will find both among the long-shore denizens of the Bahamas . . .

LADY BRASSEY, 1885

The geographical position of the Bahama Islands is such as to give to them many of the essential features of an ideal winter resort. The latitude of the group . . . insures a moderately high temperature throughout the year, with an average for the winter months very close to that which physicians regard as a most healthful temperature . . .

The Islands are apparently healthful and remarkably free from the diseases generally associated with warm climates. In addition to the favourable climatic condition of the Islands, they afford a pleasing, though somewhat limited, variety of tropical vegetation, marvelous beauty of the surrounding waters, and abundant opportunity for sailing and fishing, all of which combine to offer a constant temptation to the visitor to lead an outdoor life.

While the Islands admirably meet the requirements of those who desire to spend a few restful months in quiet and congenial surroundings, or of the invalid in search of health, the atmosphere lacks the tonic effect so characteristic of our northern climates, which make great exertion possible in all affairs of life.

OLIVER L. FASSIG, *The Bahama Islands,* 1905

In the Bahama Islands is color of a magnificence unequalled elsewhere. The St Lawrence river is mighty with its autumn-clad banks; Egypt is roofed with mother-of-pearl, and the Mediterranean is blue. But all these tones and tints are to be found in the Bahamas and a thousand more! Color in these islands never ceases its outpourings. Sky, flower, sea and fish are now flaming, now delicate, now bold, now soft in coloring. Even the houses are washed in salmons, grays, creams and pinks. The roads are white.

At dawn, color in the Bahamas is a symphony; and at midday, when the sunshine filters through jade waters, it is a rhapsody. The orchestration in the heavens at sunset is Wagnerian in its grandeur. Moonlight kissing the upturned red hibiscus petals introduces a lullaby. Stravinsky could compose nothing more modern than a poinciana tree in blossom, scarlet above a yellow wall, scarlet against a distant ocean background of lapis lazuli.

ROBERT A CURRY, 1928

The power of the merchant controls and exploits the Bahamas for the merchants' own good. There are two families which have three members each in the House of Assembly and every single member of the House can be found on or around Bay Street, which is the Bahamian shopping centre. When it is considered that the Bahamas consist of a vast quantity of islands extending over some ten degrees of latitude, whereas all the Members of the House of Assembly come from one island and one street in that island, it will be realised that the failure of elected representatives to give the people a square deal may be partially due to ignorance of conditions existing over so wide an area. There is no income tax in the Bahamas. There is no land tax. All taxation is indirect and thus falls too much 'on the shoulders of the poor'.

ROY LINDO, *Daily Gleaner* (of Jamaica), 1943

All the islands of the Bahamas have the same general appearance. They are long low coral banks, thick in bush, rising to between two and three hundred feet on San Salvador and Eleuthera, where there are also delightful lakes coloured clear brown or blue or lilac-grey under rolling hills, so that looking away from the sea and its ruffled palmettoes, the land is soft and gentle, very like Ireland or the Western isles of Scotland. There are no minerals and no industries.

ROSITA FORBES, 1949

Harmony in the government service

The Bahamas consist of something like 700 islands and islets, with around an-other 2000 cays and rocks, spread over an area which stretches almost from

Florida to Hispaniola. As such it is hardly surprising that in colonial times many of the inhabitants of what were then termed the 'Out Islands' were able to make a living from activities such as wrecking and worse, or that the merchants of Nassau were able to indulge so freely in all the shenanigans which led to their well-earned vilification as the 'Bay Street Boys'. What does appear strange is that so little effort seems ever to have been made by Britain to provide the sort of active and forceful administration such a sprawling and disjointed colony obviously needed (a failure exemplified, surely, by the appointment of an orna-mental and otherwise unemployable ex-monarch as governor during the Sec-ond World War). But even on the odd occasion when a governor with genuine administrative ability and the welfare of all Bahamians at heart was ap-pointed, he more often than not found his plans for the development of the colony thwarted or circumscribed by vested interests or the lack of money. Such a man could also be brought down, as George B. Matthew who became gover-nor in 1844 learnt to his cost, by the machinations of an ecclesiastical humbug:

Governor Matthew was not allowed to go through his whole administration in quiet. His private character was irreproachable, but it was on this side that he was attacked. Archdeacon Trew of the Bahamas was his chief assailant. Angered by a fancied personal slight, he set to work to secure the downfall of the Governor. He complained to the Colonial Department in London, published a letter in the London *Times* falsely representing the Governor's position, and was joined by unprincipled persons in spreading infamous reports connecting the Governor with a fallen woman. A plot was formed, and the Receiver-General's office became the meeting-place of the parties, where invectives were loudly declaimed against Governor Matthew. Petitions were sent to London and to the bishop of Jamaica praying for his recall. The archdeacon called a meeting of the local clergy, and rushed through it without discussion a set of previously prepared resolutions denouncing this alleged misconduct of the head of the government. Accusations were kept up until the autumn of 1848. But the evidence in the affair was not all against the Governor. The bishop, the local clergy, both Anglican and sectarian, the members of the two legislative bodies, and the general public, refused to believe in the accusations. The bishop reprimanded the archdeacon, and refused to admit him to holy orders. Finally the haughty ecclesiastic was humbled. He could gain no general credence for his accusations. He repented of his unprovoked course, but blundered again in attempting to make denials of his own misconduct to the bishop. It was too late to retract. His desire to get revenge had brought him only disrepute. To some of his accomplices, participation in this affair was only an added set of baseness. Such were the associates in iniquity of one who should have been an example to the people of the Colony.

This affair caused the removal of George B. Matthew from the government of the Bahamas. The Colonial Department in London acquitted him of the charges but would no longer intrust to him the administration of the government. Earl Grey, the Secretary of State for the colonies, had evidently thought that the woman, with whom he was accused, had some claims on him, for he had used his patronage to help her husband. On the discovery of this fact Earl Grey decided to recall him. On November 16, 1848, he wrote: 'The confidence of Her Majesty in the administration of your patronage would be absolutely destroyed by the discovery that you are using it to provide for an unworthy woman. Nor would it be possible after it became known, for you to enjoy the respect of the colonists necessary to your due influence in the government for a proper exercise of the duties of your office.' He was further informed that his successor would be sent out as soon as possible, and that he might retire from the Colony as soon as he desired. Governor Matthew left the Bahamas in February, 1849.

This administration marked an advance in the progress of the Colony. In many lines there had been an improvement. The Governor's solicitude for the welfare of the community became the subject of remark in the address of the Executive Council, which was nearest to him in the government. The House address was eloquent in praise of his efforts for the good of the Colony. It acknowledged the business ability of his administration, his accessibility to all classes, and expressed its appreciation of his efforts 'to carry out every measure calculated for the advantage of the Colony and the community'. His success therein was manifest on every side, in every department of the public service, and in every establishment at Nassau. The people acknowledged the advances made in the educational establishment. On his assumption of the government, wrote the Governor, 'the statute book was suited to the eighteenth century; a poll-tax on strangers impeded trade, the poorhouse at Nassau was the sole public institution and the militia was but a name'. In spite of the famine and depression in trade during his administration of four years the colonial debt had been reduced and a surplus revenue secured; the poor establishment was enlarged and a hospital and dispensary established; a public library was added to the equipment for education; the militia was placed on a substantial basis; the civil list was adjusted to the existing needs of the Colony and the efficiency of the officials was increased; salt ponds were everywhere worked, fruit growing extended and the tariff schedules readjusted; in every department the colonial service experienced the touch of an administrator. It was a hard fate that this man who had done so much for the Colony, the first Governor in the nineteenth century who had been able to secure harmony in the government service, should have become the mark of all the calumnies that were heaped upon George B. Matthew. 'A prophet is not without honour save in his own country.'

JAMES M. WRIGHT, 1905

The unfortunate governor may have been dismissed from his post in this unbecoming manner, but his name is still recalled in the Bahamas today – something which cannot be said of that of the Pecksniff who engineered his downfall. The one and only town on Inagua, the remotest and least developed of the Bahamas, was founded during his administration when, at his instigation, the island's salt-producing potential began to be exploited. What better name could then have been given to the island's first permanent settlement than that of Matthew Town?

Seven years after Matthew had left the Bahamas, Queen Victoria approved a new style of full dress uniform to be worn by the soldiers of the three West India regiments which were in existence at the time. As it was based very much on the design of the uniform worn by a colonial corps of the French Army recruited from among a North African tribe called Zouaves, it naturally enough was soon known as the Zouave uniform. It was very colourful and distinctly oriental in appearance, consisting of an elaborately braided, scarlet, sleeveless jacket worn over a long-sleeved white waistcoat with a braided front and twenty brass buttons; together with voluminous dark blue breeches piped with two yellow stripes on the front and rear of each leg, worn with white gaiters and black boots; and topped off by a red fez wound round with a white turban. When introduced in 1858 the Zouave uniform was issued only to the non-commissioned officers and men of each regiment. Their officers were specifically excluded from the change, an earlier suggestion that they too should adopt it having met with the Queen's strong disapproval. Regardless of this ban the commanding officer of the 2nd West India Regiment, then stationed in Nassau, chose to make up his own mind on the subject, as another of the regiment's officers recalled many years later:

Colonel H.D. O'Halloran, though somewhat eccentric, was a most kindly disposed man, besides being a most popular and able Commanding Officer. This Colonel is memorable for his habit of wearing a Zouave Uniform on special occasions: he appears to have been the only officer of a West India

Regiment who is known to have done so. On ordinary occasions, his appearance was sufficiently striking – very tall and thin, with piercing eyes set in an unusually small head, covered with a profuse growth of hair and flowing beard . . .

When mounted on field days, he made a most picturesque Commanding Officer: it was on these occasions that he wore his Zouave uniform, with hunting boots, Mameluke spurs and stirrups.

The Regiment would be drawn up in line, awaiting him on the town square at Nassau, when he would suddenly appear at a gallop to receive the salute – bearing a strong resemblance to 'Don Quixote' charging the windmills; and if by chance he spotted a soldier presenting arms incorrectly, he would jump off his horse and, taking the delinquent's rifle, would proceed to show the man his mistake.

His enforced retirement, in 1860, on full pay, was much deplored by us all, and came as a surprise to everybody. At his farewell tea-party, he expressed sorrow at his recall, and said that he had never treated any one unfairly, during his long period of service, and I don't believe he did.

Major William J. Ross,
The Zouave: Regimental Journal of the Second Battalion,
West India Regiment, 1911

Who it was among the many busybodies to be found in the Bahamian soci-ety of the day who considered O'Halloran's unorthodox behaviour was just as worthy of condemnation as that of George B. Matthew had been, and similarly required to be drawn to the attention of his superiors in London, is unknown. One might have thought that in a place like Nassau, which by this time had al-ready begun to attract winter visitors from North America, his bravura displays would have been welcomed as an early form of tourist attraction. The increase in revenue which would have followed a rise in the number of visitors attracted to the colony as a result of the colonel's parade ground antics would, in a differ-ent era, easily have outweighed any criticism of them. But in the Bahamas in 1860 this was not to be. There were too many straight-laced individuals around who were only too keen to criticize anything seen as a departure from the norm, to condemn any sign of eccentricity, or to deplore anything which smacked of impropriety, and as a result the dashing Don Quixote lookalike had to go.

That such attitudes if anything hardened in the Bahamas as the Victorian age progressed, but perhaps were not so entrenched everywhere else among the British West Indian colonies, is evident from incidents recorded by someone who served as a colonial official in Nassau during the 1890s:

I sometimes think that a good deal of the work of the Magistrates' Courts in these islands could quite well be performed by unpaid Justices of the Peace. It seems absurd that much of the time of a highly qualified stipendiary magistrate, frequently an English barrister, should be taken up in dealing with trumpery cases of abusive language, nuisances or petty assaults. A local JP could deal with such matters perfectly well and even with cases of more importance.

One would, of course, have to be careful in the selection of persons who would be authorized to hold Courts. I was told, when I was in the Bahamas, of a case where a 'Resident Justice' in one of the out-islands accepted and forwarded to headquarters the following verdict of a jury at an inquest on the body of a woman who had been drowned when bathing: 'Accidental death by drowning and a just visitation by Almighty God for the crime of Sabbath-breaking.'

I remember also hearing of a case where a magistrate in British Honduras officially reported to the Governor that a woman in his district had given birth to a frog. The Governor referred the report to the Principal Medical Officer who returned the paper with a minute to the effect that 'This case is evidently an instance of the lamentable indiscretion of some frog who would a-wooing go.'

SIR HESKETH BELL, 1903 (*see* HESKETH BELL, 1946)

30 Navassa

'The great petrified sponge'

The US lighthouse tender which was sunk by the German submarine U161 in the Caribbean entrance to the Mona Passage in 1942 (see page 63) was returning to Puerto Rico after having completed a regular visit to service an automatic light situated on a small island in the Jamaica Channel – the ocean passage between the island of that name and the south-western end of Haiti. The island from which the light was displayed, called Navassa, is barren, waterless, uninhabited, barely five square kilometres in area and, except by means of a small inlet on the south-western side, virtually inaccessible. It is of coral limestone formation, and consists of nothing other than an undulating plateau, from 40 to 70 metres in height, 'completely riddled with holes and pockets, some of great depth and having no visible bottom', rimmed all around by an abrupt escarpment and cliffs. It was well described in the 1920s as having 'the appearance of a great petrified sponge' and, as such, 'one of the strangest pieces of territory owned by the United States'.

The island had been claimed under the provisions of the 1856 Guano Act (see page 188), after a sea captain named Peter Duncan had forwarded a memorial to the State Department stating 'that on the first day of July, in the year of 1857, he did discover a deposit of guano on an island or key in the Caribbean Sea not occupied by the citizens of any other government, and that he did take peace-

able possession of and occupy said island or key of Navassa in the name of the United States'. Duncan transferred his discoverer's rights to an American guano trader based in Jamaica, who then sold them to a firm in Baltimore which immediately set up a subsidiary called the Navassa Phosphate Company.

Mining began soon afterwards, but as it then had to be suspended at the outbreak of the Civil War, did not really get underway until 1865. By then the company had invested heavily in the island, building warehouses, workshops and barracks for 140 workers, as well as a number of houses for the supervisory staff and a church. The guano was dug out with pick and shovel, using dynamite as necessary, and hauled in trucks on a light railway to the landing place, given the name Lulu Bay, where it was then sacked and stored to await shipment. Shipping was an equally laborious operation, involving loading boats by means of a crane and transferring their loads in a ceaseless cycle to a ship moored offshore. It goes without saying that, as in the British islands of Redonda and Sombrero where similar mining operations took place, all this was undertaken by an entirely black workforce under totally white supervision. What was different about the situation on Navassa was that both workers and supervisors were from the United States.

In the aftermath of the Civil War relations between blacks and whites from a state like Maryland, where all were recruited, were hardly likely to be anything but fraught. The work was gruelling enough on an island where everything including fresh water had to be imported, without it having to take place under a harsh and degrading set of rules enforced by a set of uncouth, bullying and abusive overseers. It can only be to the credit of successive droves of workers that they put up with such conditions for so long before rebelling. In 1889, finally driven to despair by their treatment, the workforce of the day of about 150 men did just that, instigating a riot during which the superintendent and four of his assistants were killed.

Word of this eventually reached the outside world and a frigate, the USS Kearsarge, was sent to restore order. Eighteen of the rioters were arrested and returned to Baltimore to face charges of murder. Their story of the regime on Navassa created a sensation. Black Americans in Maryland and elsewhere rallied to their cause and money for their defence was raised through a fraternal society called the Order of the Galilean Fisherman. In the end, having taken the cases as far as the Supreme Court, three of the defendants only were found guilty and sentenced to death. This inspired a further response and black churches throughout the United States subscribed, along with some of the white jurors from the trials, to a petition for clemency. This eventually reached President Benjamin Harrison in 1891 and the sentences were commuted to imprisonment.

The whole sorry episode marked the beginning of the end for the Navassa Phosphate Company. Mining resumed at a greatly reduced level and continued for another few years, but the start of the Spanish–American War of 1898 brought operations to an end and forced the company into bankruptcy. The workings were abandoned in 1901.

No further interest was taken in the island until the opening of the Panama Canal in 1914. It was then realized that, as the main route for shipping between the eastern seaboard of the United States and the canal was via the Windward Passage between Cuba and Haiti, and then through the Jamaica Channel, Navassa – which had always been a hazard to navigation – now lay in the middle of a major shipping lane.

In order to render it less of a hazard in 1916 the US Lighthouse Service began building a substantial reinforced concrete lighthouse on the highest part of the island. As with the previous century's mine workings everything, including the sand and water needed in the construction, had to be brought from elsewhere, either from Guantanamo Bay in Cuba or from Jamaica. In addition to the 46-metre tower, a substantial 'Spanish-style' dwelling, consisting of quarters for three keepers and their families grouped around a central courtyard, was built immediately adjacent. All the labourers employed by the American engineers were hired either in Jamaica or Cuba. When completed in October 1917 the tower displayed a powerful light at a height of over 120 metres above sea level which could be seen, in normal visibility at a range of nearly thirty nautical miles.

The lighthouse was manned, and Navassa inhabited, until 1929 when an automatic beacon was installed which only needed to be serviced twice a year. Except during the Second World War, when an observation post was maintained there, the island has remained uninhabited ever since. In 1996 the US Coast Guard, which had absorbed the Lighthouse Service in 1939, dismantled the light and removed the automatic equipment, the widespread use of the Global Positioning Satellites system of navigation has rendered their continued maintenance unnecessary. Attempts since to give Navassa the status of a protected conservation area have met with opposition from Haiti, the country which has always disputed the American claim to the island.

31 Jamaica

'A marveilous fertil Isle'

This Isle is a marveilous fertil Isle, & is as a garden or store house for divers parts of the maine. It is full of plaine champion ground, which in the rest of the Indies we have not seene: it aboundeth with beeves and Cassavi, besides most pleasant fruits of divers sorts. We have not found in the Indies a more pleasant and holsome place.

SIR ANTHONY SHERLEY, 1597

The Iland as it is natuorallie the Best in all the Indges: it hath a great deale of Leuill ground, and many braue Sauanas full of Cattell, and abundant of braue Horses, But thay are all wild: and many wild hoges: and wild foull an abundant: a many parrates: and Muckeas: and plentie of fich: heare are abundant of Alliegators and many larg snakes. This ground will bare anything that they can plant one it: the spaniyard doth say that it will bare all sorts of spices, and Shugor, and Indico, and Cottaine, and tobaco, and very good grapes . . . This Illand is Brauelie watered with fresh riufers: and hath 3 braue harbors in the South side, and one in the North side: But the midellmust in the South Side is one of the Best in the Wordell . . . This is all I can say of this Iland, for at present it is pore, But it may be made one of the riches spotes in the wordell; the Spaniard doth call it the Garden of the Indges, But this I will say, the Gardeners haue bin very bad, for heare is very litell more than that which groweth naterallie.

HENRY WHISTLER, 1655

An immense amphitheatre of mountains, irregular in their shape and various in their verdures; some steep and rugged, others sloping gently, and presenting the thickest foliage and the most varied tints of green, interspersed with the gardens of little settlements, some of which are tottering on the very brinks of precipices, others just peep out from the midst of coconut trees and bamboos, the latter looking really like large plumes of green feathers. The buildings are like little Chinese pavilions, and have a most picturesque effect. In front is a view of the sea, and the harbours of Kingston, Port Royal, Port Henderson, etc., full of ships of war and vessels great and small; the whole affording an exceedingly busy and interesting scene. The plain, from the Liguanea mountains, covered with sugar estates, penns, negro settlements, etc., and then the city of Kingston, the town of Port Royal, all so mixed with trees of different sorts and all so new to a European eye, that it seemed like a Paradise; and Clifton, where I stood, the centre of a blissful garden.

MARIA NUGENT (in 1802) Lady Nugent's Journal, 1839

Were it arranged by Fate that my future residence should be in Jamaica, I should certainly prefer the life of a country mouse. The town mice, in my mind, have but a bad time of it. Of all towns that I ever saw, Kingston is perhaps, on the whole, the least alluring, and is the more absolutely without any point of attraction for the stranger than any other . . .

I have spoken in disparaging terms of the chief town in Jamaica, but I can atone for this by speaking in very high terms of the country. In that island one would certainly prefer the life of the country mouse. There is scenery in Jamaica which almost equals that of Switzerland and the Tyrol; and there is also, which is more essential, a temperature among the mountains in which a European can live comfortably.

ANTHONY TROLLOPE, 1859

Our first view of Jamaica impressed us greatly; and no wonder; for we were gazing on the celebrated Blue Mountains, which deserve all the epithets of admiration that have ever been bestowed on them. Rising from a richly-cultivated plain, principally of sugar-cane, we could revel in the light and shade and colour of their sides and low peaks, intersected by fertile valleys; while their summits, between 7000 and 8000 feet high, were hidden in masses of floating clouds and wreaths of driving mists . . . Never were mountains so appropriately named as these; for not only their summits but their valleys were tinged and filled with every imaginable shade of azure.

LADY BRASSEY, 1885

Jamaica, as the world well knows, is a gracious and beautiful island, of whose delights many appreciative accounts are to be found in the literature of the West Indies. Possessed of an infinitely picturesque coast line, of glorious valleys and romantic glades, of such heights as the Blue Mountains, of such rivers as the Roaring River and the Rio Cobre, Jamaica may claim to be, as John Sparke (the record-keeper of John Hawkins's expeditions) would express it, 'a country marvellously sweet'.

SIR FREDERICK TREVES, 1908

The first view of Jamaica and of its capital is pleasing. A mountainous mass, gradually developing on the horizon, grows into a series of ranges which promise to rival the beauty of Porto Rico. Beyond a long, low, narrow, sand-reef lies an immense harbor, on the further shore of which Kingston is suspected, rather than seen, only a few wharves and one domed building rising above the wooded plain on which the low city stands. The hills behind it tumble into a disordered heap culminating in the cloud-swathed peak of what are most fittingly called the Blue Mountains . . .

One's first impression of the Jamaicans, as they lounge about the wharf eyeing each trunk or bundle several minutes before summoning up the energy to tackle it, is that they are far less courageous in the face of work than their cousins, the Barbadians. This is closely followed by the discovery that Kingston is the most disappointing town in the West Indies. With the exception of a few bright yellow public buildings and a scattered block or two of new business houses, it is a negro slum, spreading for miles over a dusty plain. Scarcely a street has even the pretense of a pavement; the few sidewalks that exist are blocked by stairways, posts, and the trash of a disorderly population, or degenerate every few yards into stretches of loose stones and earth. The only building worth crossing the street to see is that domed structure sighted from the bay, the Catholic Cathedral. To be sure, the earthquake wrought great havoc, but that was thirteen years ago, time enough, surely, in which to have made a much farther advance toward recovery.

HARRY A. FRANCK, 1920

The abiding impression of Jamaica ... may be compared to the effect produced on the mind by the lifting of a stage curtain and the revelation of a beautiful, golden, sunlit scene – a dream picture of exotic-looking vegetation, of bright flowers and charming waters, complete with a magnificent background of mountains. This, perhaps, is the simplest way in which to describe Jamaica. The features of an ideal stage setting may be found in the Isle of Springs, but not a make-believe – to be obliterated when the play is over . . . In Jamaica all the ingredients of the pretty stage-scene are there and it is not merely a warm and sunny vision enjoyed for a brief hour – the Jamaica counterpart is real, live and throbbing – a thing to be revelled in day after day, in a land of eternal summer . . .

PHILIP P. OLLEY, 1937

A catastrophe in Kingston

A large part of the city about which both Trollope in the nineteenth century, and Franck early in the twentieth century, felt they could be so rude was burnt to the ground three times between 1780 and 1882. On each occasion, although not too many people were killed, the fire brought about an enormous loss of mostly uninsured property, particularly among the business community. On the afternoon of 14 January 1907 yet another fire began to rage, started by a maid overturning a bunsen burner in a doctor's surgery, but whether this would have had equally disastrous consequences to Kingston will never be known, as within less than an hour of it breaking out the city was hit by a devastating earthquake.

The shock was felt throughout the island. It caused damage to buildings in all the eastern parishes but at the epicentre, under Kingston itself, it was immensely destructive. In ten seconds or less the city was completely wrecked and well over 1000 people had been killed outright or buried alive. 'Details of the catastrophe, gained from various sources', wrote one observer, 'help to complete the picture of what happened in this fateful fraction of a minute':

An officer on a steamer by the quay heard the weird wind, felt the ship shaken as by an explosion, and then, looking ashore, saw the long wharf rock up and down as thin ice rocks over a wave, saw people thrown to the ground and others in strange attitudes trying to keep their balance, leaning forwards as men caught in a hurricane, leaning back as men in peril on a slope, standing with legs wide apart or clinging to posts and bollards. The great buildings swayed to and fro. Then came the din of falling walls, with the rattle of an acre of corrugated iron tumbling from roofs – whereupon the scene was immediately blotted out by dust . . .

In the streets, filled as they were with a yellow fog of dust, the scene was paralysing and uninterpretable. On all sides was the cannonading of crumbling houses: bricks came down like rain; walls were rent as if made of paper; the great timbers of a floor snapped like a bundle of sticks; telegraph poles swayed as reeds in a wind . . .

Within twenty minutes, as the fire which had begun shortly before the shock had been allowed to spread unchecked, and many others had resulted from the earthquake, the city was ablaze.

The fire raged for four days, hampering rescue work and destroying most of what had been left undamaged or only partially damaged by the earthquake, as well as any moveable property not already taken by looters. Untold numbers of the dead were effectively cremated, while many of the bodies which were recovered had to be hastily buried in mass graves. The Governor, Sir Alexander Swettenham, authorized the patrolling of what was left of the city by armed soldiers in order to prevent further looting, and to control the numerous homeless people camping out in the parks and open spaces.

On 17 January a squadron of three American warships under the flag of Admiral C.H. Davis arrived with doctors and much-needed medical supplies from the United States Naval Base at Guatanamo Bay in Cuba. This was the first part of a relief effort initiated by the US Government, and a fourth vessel loaded with 2000 tons of foodstuffs was expected within another day or so. It was a genuine humanitarian gesture, but one which, because of Governor Swettenham's stiff-necked inability to abandon fixed ideas about protocol in the midst of a crisis, and Admiral Davis's over-sensitive ego, achieved nothing but the creation of a minor diplomatic incident.

The squadron arrived before order among the ruins had been completely restored and, as armed guards had been posted on what was left of some of the more important buildings, Davis had no hesitation in conceding to the American Vice-Consul's request for guards to be provided for his damaged consulate.

Unfortunately the admiral did not first clear this with the governor who, when informed of the presence of armed US marines in the city, insisted they be withdrawn. This so offended Davis that once the marines had been re-embarked he immediately ordered his ships to sea. He headed back to Cuba, having not only provided no worthwhile assistance to the stricken city, but also having left instructions with the Vice-Consul that none of the imminently expected 2000 tons of relief supplies were to be landed. Both Swettenham and Davis showed considerable contempt for the sufferings of a great many people in their response to a matter which, it is very difficult not to believe, could have been resolved with the exercise of a grain of tact on one side, and the acceptance of just a little loss of face on the other.

As soon as details had been passed to London, and in order to avoid any further escalation of the incident, Swettenham was instructed to offer Davis an apology. This he did, but with no good grace, before immediately resigning as governor. The relief work then had to proceed without the aid of either man, using the island's own material resources, appeal funds raised in Britain, and a substantial loan from the British Government.

But while the homeless were being provided with shelter and the necessities of life, to a visitor who arrived in Jamaica in the middle of February it appeared that Kingston no longer existed:

The roads had been cleared, but no attempt of any kind had been made at even a casual restoration. Almost as strange as the silence was the greyness of the scene, the absence of all colour, the sense of a desert of pale stone. With it too was the unwonted light, for as all the roofs and upper stories had vanished, and as many of the houses were left no higher than a garden wall, the city seemed bared to the heavens, bared to its very bones and whitened ribs . . . There hung above the town at the time a mist of dust, horrible to breathe, and with it drifted, now and then, a loathsome smell which was not merely that of smouldering debris.

The rebuilding work was delayed for the best part of two years, as the insurance on property did not cover damage from fire when the fire was caused by an earthquake, and it took this length of time and a long court battle to establish beyond question that part of the city had been ablaze – due to the accident in the doctor's surgery – well before the earthquake had struck. Restoration work began in 1909 after the insurers had paid 85 per cent on the face value of the policies, but had still not been completed – as Franck was only too quick to point out – even eleven years later.

A military Paradise

Of almost as much interest to nineteenth- and early twentieth-century visitors to Jamaica as the Blue Mountains, on the undoubted beauty of which most of them had to exalt, was the army camp contained within the mountains about fifteen kilometres to the north of Kingston. It was built in 1841, to house the white troops of the garrison under more salubrious conditions than were found in the barracks in Kingston. From shortly after it was opened it became very much a place that any visitor with pretensions to a social standing felt he, or she, had to visit:

One would almost enlist as a full private in one of her Majesty's regiments of the line if one were sure of being quartered for ever at Newcastle – at Newcastle, Jamaica, I mean. Other Newcastles of which I wot have by no means equal attraction. This place also is accessible only by foot or on horseback; and is therefore singularly situated for a barrack. But yet it consists now of a goodly village, in which live colonels, and majors, and chaplains and surgeons, and purveyors, all in a state of bliss – as it were in a second Eden. It is a military paradise, in which war is spoken of, and dinners and dancing abound. If good air and fine scenery be dear to the heart of the British soldier, he ought to be happy at Newcastle.

ANTHONY TROLLOPE, 1859

The mountain road to Newcastle is very good – as, indeed, it ought to be, for all the military and other stores are conveyed over it to the camp on the backs of mules. It looked so smooth and wide that I was surprised when the sergeant who led the way warned us to be careful, as a lady had fallen backwards over the precipice into the river a few weeks ago, and several horses and mules had met with similar accidents at various times . . .

The camp at Newcastle is the station of the white troops in Jamaica, who consist generally of a battalion of a regiment and part of a battery of artillery. It is situated about 4000 feet from the level of the sea. We were much amused by the inscriptions over the officers' quarters, which are all distinguished by sign-boards suspended from adjacent trees, and bearing such names as 'Poverty Flat', 'Jumbo's Lair', 'The Penitentiary', and 'The Ark'; the latter standing on the highest point of what is officially designated Mount Ararat . . . There is a common saying among military men to the effect that 'the first year you are quartered in Jamaica you admire the scenery; the second year you collect ferns; the third year you go mad'.

LADY BRASSEY, 1885

Having ceased to quarter our regiments in mangrove swamps, we now build a camp for them among the clouds . . . Captain C——— had undertaken that I should see Newcastle . . . The track was so rough and narrow that we could only ride in single file, and was often no better than a watercourse; yet by this and no other way every article had to be carried on donkeys' backs or human heads which was required for the consumption of 300 infantry and 100 artillerymen . . . They are there for health's sake only, and to be fit for work if wanted below. An hour's ride brought us to the lowest range of houses, which were 4000 feet above the sea. From thence they rose, tier above tier, for 500 feet more . . . The hillside was bare, and the slope so steep that there was no standing on it, save where it had been flattened by the spade; and here in this extraordinary place were 400 young Englishmen of the common type of which soldiers are made, with nothing to do and nothing to enjoy – remaining, unless they desert or die of ennui, for one, two, or three years, as their chance may be . . . The officers come down now and then on furlough or on duty; the men rarely and hardly at all, and soldiers . . . cannot always be made happy by the picturesque. They are not educated enough to find employment for their minds, and of amusement there is none.

JAMES ANTHONY FROUDE, 1888

If I were a soldier I should pray all day long that I might never see the military station at Newcastle. Imagine a small parade-ground, levelled by spade work; a straggling collection of huts, built on never-ending steps; a few cottages for the officers; a very obvious burial-ground, well stocked with tombstones streaked with names, planted among the huts just outside the reading-room, and you have the contonments of Newcastle. On the parade-ground, half a yard from the face of a step of rock thirty feet high, a couple of posts and a tape enable the sporting *Tommy* to practise goal shooting from dawn till sunset. Failing this he has half-a-dozen six-week-old English newspapers in the reading-room, and a magnificent view of Kingston always to be seen through the mists and rain which seem for ever to bedim this eerie camp. The officers, I believe, have a tennis-court; but for Tommy it is shooting goal, the newspapers, or the view, if he wishes to avoid the cells. Otherwise . . .

I heard the story from Tommy himself. He showed us the camp; first the burial-ground, and then – 'Well, there ain't much more to see 'ere. That's the parade-ground, and that's the sergeants' mess. We sleeps over there, and bein' Sunday, the canteen don't open to-day till six. We usually shoots the goal, and smokes, and sometimes we rags the blacks. See that nigger 'ut? Well, we goes there sometimes – of course, it's out 'er bounds – and takes the beer and rags the blacks. Once we chucked three or four of 'em over the gully because they set on one of ours. There's one or two in cells now for molestin' the natives. Then some of us deserts, you know. Goes off down to the coast, ships as firemen and gets to the States' . . . I gathered that in spite of the parade-ground and kicking goal; in spite of the reading-room, with its platform and soldier-painted scenery; in spite even of the tiny billiard-table and the picturesque cemetery, the life of Tommy in garrison at Newcastle is not a jolly one. Tired of doing the things he is allowed to do, and without the means to appreciate expensive joys of the canteen, the youthful, full-blooded soldier sallies forth on mischief bent. Then he experiences a salutary change of scenery in the confines of the cells. Sometimes, as our friend remarked, he deserts.

JOHN HENDERSON, 1906

'High, high, high up in the hills' behind the capital, appearing as white specks on the mountainside, are the military cantonments of Newcastle, hanging in terraces like a monastery in Tibet. Formerly one had to drive up the valley of the Hope River to Gordon Town and then take to the saddle or 'Shank's pony' to reach that elevated base; but now one can ride all the way in a motor-car . . . Perched at a height of four thousand feet above the level of the sea . . . In this eyrie the remnant of the white garrison must find time hang rather heavily on its hands, since there are no shops, and no petticoats for miles, and few of the amenities that make garrison life what it is; but to compensate for these shortcomings there is the fresh mountain air and exquisite scenery . . .

SIR ALGERNON ASPINALL, 1927

An honourable gentleman

As is well known Jamaica is by far the largest of the English-speaking West Indian islands. What is perhaps not so well known is that it is not only one of the very few of the old British West Indies on which Columbus ever set foot, but it is also the only Caribbean island other than Hispaniola on which the explorer ever lived for any length of time.

This occurred during his fourth and final voyage of discovery when, over a year after leaving Spain and after having sailed along much of the coast of

Central America, he was making his way back via the south coast of Cuba to the main Spanish settlement in Hispaniola. By this time he had only two ships left of the four with which he had set out, both badly worm-eaten and barely able to be kept afloat. Neither was in any condition to complete the last leg of the voyage, which was against both wind and current.

While off the north coast of Jamaica on 25 June 1503, all efforts to prevent them from foundering came to an end when Columbus, realizing he had no option if he and his men were not all to drown, began to search for somewhere to beach the ships. The place he chose, and named Puerto Santa Gloria, is just to the west of the modern port of Ocho Rios in a small harbour now known as St Ann's Bay. Having run their ships ashore, although none of them had any way of of knowing it, Columbus and his crews were to remain marooned in Jamaica for the next twelve months.

The story connected with Columbus's enforced residence on the island which is most often re-told is that to do with his knowledge of a predicted total lunar eclipse, and the use he made of this (in a way that was a godsend to writers of boys' adventure stories ever after) to intimidate the local Amerindians, called Tainos, into continuing to provide him and his men with food. Not nearly so well known, although equally worthy of Boys' Own Paper treatment, are details of the way in which the rescue of Columbus and the hundred-odd men he had with him was accomplished.

Neither ship was seaworthy, all their boats had been lost or destroyed earlier in the voyage, and there were not enough tools nor sufficient expertise among the crews to enable any other sort of craft to be constructed. Fortunately, Columbus had with him a man who throughout the voyage had proved to be a loyal and helpful ally, and someone who was always willing to do things that others either could not or would not do. Captain Diego Méndez de Salcedo had joined the expedition as a gentleman volunteer, and it was he who now, as always, realized what had to be done and was prepared to take the lead in doing it. Within a matter of days he had bartered a brass helmet and some articles of clothing for a sizeable canoe from the local Taino tribe. After raising its freeboard and fitting it out with a mast, sail and a false keel he set off in it for Hispaniola on 8 July, accompanied by one other Spaniard and six Indians hired as paddlers.

The distance from Puerto Santa Gloria to Santo Domingo, their destination in Hispaniola, is about 440 nautical miles, with every mile having to be made against a westward-flowing current and in the face of the prevailing easterly wind. Long before reaching the open water of the 100-mile-wide channel between Jamaica and Cap Tiburon, the south-western tip of Hispaniola, it was clear to Méndez that it would be foolish to attempt the crossing with only six working members of his crew. After going ashore briefly somewhere in the vicinity of the present Port Antonio he turned the canoe around and returned to Puerto Santa Gloria. A week or so later he set off again. This time he took with him five other Spaniards and ten paddlers, and was accompanied by a second similarly-manned canoe.

It took almost four days of non-stop paddling to cross the Jamaica Channel to the only place where they could find some rest – the rockbound, waterless and uninhabited island of Navassa about thirty miles off Cap Tiburon. By then one of the Indian paddlers had already died, and all the rest of the voyagers, Spanish and Taino alike, were suffering from the combined effects of exposure to the tropical sun and a severe shortage of fresh water. The water they managed to find in pools among the rocks on Navassa proved a mixed blessing, as several of the Indians drank so much they subsequently collapsed and died. The remainder, together with the Spaniards under the direction of Méndez, managed to sate their thirst with more caution and by the evening were all ready to re-embark in order to complete the crossing by night. The canoes were beached on Cap Tiburon the following morning.

After resting for two days, Méndez acquired six new paddlers from among the Indian tribe who inhabited the Tiburon peninsula to make up for those from Jamaica who had expired, and resumed his journey. As far as he was concerned the worst part was over, and even though he still had over 200 miles to go this could be completed in easy stages through relatively sheltered coastal waters. In fact his major problems had yet to begin, and he was not to reach Santo Domingo, the only place where he could hope to find a vessel he could charter to send to Jamaica, for another seven months.

He could do nothing without first obtaining the permission of Don Nicolás de Ovando, who had been appointed Governor of Hispaniola in succession to Columbus, after the explorer's third voyage had ended with his return to Spain in chains. Under such circumstances it was not surprising that Ovando had been alarmed when Columbus had reappeared in the Caribbean in 1502 on yet another voyage of discovery. As he had then refused even to let the explorer's ships use Santo Domingo harbour, his reception of the news of Columbus's present plight was likely to be mixed to say the least.

When Méndez reached the settlement of Azua, some seventy miles short of Santo Domingo, he was told that the Governor was busy 'pacifying' some of the interior Indian tribes. Reckoning time was of the essence he abandoned his canoe and trekked inland to report to Ovando in his field headquarters, where he arrived in the middle of August. If he had believed before his arrival that the plight of Columbus and his men would make any difference to Ovando's attitude, he was soon to discover his error. The Governor was only too pleased to *learn that the man he considered a dangerous rival was in serious trouble, and he kept Méndez hanging about his encampment until the following March before allowing him to make his way to Santo Domingo. Once there Méndez was refused the use of the single vessel he found in the harbour, and was forced to wait another two months for others to arrive from Spain before being able to charter one of them to send to Puerto Santa Gloria.*

By the time this vessel arrived there towards the end of June 1504 Columbus was already a sick man. As well as having had long confrontations with the Tainos and a serious mutiny among his own men to deal with, some months before he had had the mortification of seeing a ship, which had been sent by Ovando merely to spy on the marooned men, approach the port and then sail away again. It is little wonder that within six months of his return to Spain in November, and at the age of only fifty-four, he was dead.

It is not known whether he and Méndez, who had returned to Spain earlier, ever met again, or when the latter returned to the West Indies. What is known however, is that details of his epic rescue mission retained a particular importance for him throughout the rest of his life; so much so that in his will he asked that his tombstone should read:

Here lies the Honourable Gentleman Diego Méndez, who greatly served the Royal Crown of Spain in the Discovery and Conquest of the Indies with the Admiral Don Cristóbal Colón of Glorious Memory, who discovered them, and afterwards with his own Ships and at his own Cost. He died —. He begs for Charity's sake a Pater Noster and an Ave Maria.

In the middle of the said stone let there be carved a canoe, which is a dug-out tree in which the Indians navigate, for in such a one I navigated three hundred leagues; and above it let them set the letters that say CANOA.

A rarity and present

The 'Alliegators' said by Henry Whistler in the middle of the seventeenth century to be 'abundant' in Jamaica were in fact crocodiles. Although the representation of one still occupies a prominent place on the island's coat of arms the reptile itself – which is always called an alligator by Jamaicans – is now so uncommon as to be in danger of extinction.

Today the disappearance of any species of wildlife is almost universally deprecated, and it is now considered that crocodiles are just as entitled to their place in the scheme of things as the world's more gentle and less unattractive creatures – a view subscribed to, presumabably, by Jamaicans as much as by anyone else.

That this was not an opinion which the inhabitants of the island in the days when 'allagators' were thick on the ground would have found easy to share was made obvious to one visitor at the beginning of the eighteenth century:

They are very common on the Coasts and deep Rivers of Jamaica, one of nineteen Feet in Length, I was told was taken by a Dog, which was made use of as a Bait, with a piece of Wood ty'd to a Cord, the farther End of which was fastened to a Bed Post. The crocodile coming round as usual every Night, seiz'd the Dog, was taken by the Piece of Wood made fast to the Cord, drew the Bed to the Window and wak'd the People, who kill'd the Allagator which had done them much Mischief. The Skin was stuffed and offer'd to me as a Rarity and Present, but I could not accept it because of its Largeness, wanting Room to stow it.

SIR HANS SLOANE, 1707

32 Cayman Islands

'Certaine Islands of sand'

The fifth of July we had sight of certaine Islands of sand, called the Tortugas (which is lowe land) where the captaine went in with his pinnesse, and found such a number of birds, that in halfe an houre he had laded her with them; and if they had been ten boats more, they might have done the like. These Islands beare the name Tortoises, because of the number of them, which there do breed, whose nature is to live both in the water and upon land also, but breed onely upon the shore; in making a great pit wherein they lay egges, to the number of three or foure hundred, and covering them with sand, they are hatched by the heat of the Sunne; and by this meanes commeth the great increase. Of these we tooke very great ones, which have both backe and belly all of bone, of the thickness of an inch: the fish whereof we proved, eating much like veale; and finding a number of egges in them, tasted also of them, but they did eat very sweetly. Heere wee ankered six houres, and then a faire gale of winde springing, we weyed anker, and made saile toward Cuba . . .

SIR JOHN HAWKINS. In: *Hakluyt's Principall Navigations of the English Nation*, 1564

The Grand Cayman . . . is a small, low-lying, tree-covered island belonging to Great Britain. It does a trade in turtles and cocoanuts, rears cattle, and boasts of a prison and other evidences of civilisation. It is a colony perched on the pinnacle of an isolated submarine mountain whose northern slope is 10,662 feet high, while on the south the depth from the streets of its little town to the solid earth is 20,568 feet, or nearly four miles. If the sea were to drain away, as did the snow from around Baron Munchausen's church steeple, then would George Town, the capital of the Grand Cayman, appear on the very apex of a mountain which (viewed from its southern valley) would be nearly a mile higher than Mont Blanc.

SIR FREDERICK TREVES, 1908

This dependency consists of Grand Cayman . . . Little Cayman, and Cayman Brac . . . The islands are governed by a Commissioner assisted by a Vestry, the Commissioner being appointed by the Jamaica Government. The chief industry is that of the Turtle fisheries. Sailing vessels are built . . . Many of the inhabitants bear the names of British seamen wrecked either on the islands or on the neighbouring coast of Cuba.

PHILIP P. OLLEY, 1937

Grand Cayman, on maps, is hard to find unless the atlas is large and your patience long – one speck of British pink on the broad blue Caribbean. It arches its seventeen-mile back just a few feet above the sea there south of Cuba; an isle of glossy and shimmering green leaves, ringed about with the white of surf or whiter sands . . .

By agreement between Nicaragua and the British Crown, only these islanders have the right to net turtles on the Mosquito Bank. Such is the present form of monopoly they established for themselves when the catch in home waters dwindled, and maintained a great many years thereafter by dint of hardihood, looking sharp, and not being afraid to dare . . .

In the long pursuit of this one business the islanders have learned a great deal about it. The management of their sloops and schooners, whose sails continually brighten the western Caribbean, in two hundred years has made them that sea's most respected sailors. No yacht cruises the West Indies, people say, without at least one Caymanian aboard . . .

GLANVILLE SMITH, 1942

Turtles and swans

The turtles after which the islands had been named by Columbus were already scarce in Cayman Island waters well before the end of the eighteenth century, and the islanders were forced to fish for them further and further afield. By the early years of the next century their schooners were to be found all over the western Caribbean during the turtling seasons, which lasted from January to March and from July to September. As time went by, in order to be closer to the turtle cays on the Mosquito Bank, the vast expanse of shallow water off the eastern coasts of Nicaragua and Honduras, a number of fishermen and their families moved to live on some small islands off the north coast of Honduras. This group, the Bay Islands, had long been considered a British possession, connected with the colony of British Honduras. Once these were established other Caymanians decided to settle on two very small and lonely islands about halfway between Grand Cayman and Roatán, the largest of the Bay Islands.

The Swan Islands, which were probably named by or after Captain Swan, a buccaneer who operated in these waters in the seventeenth century, are a pair of coral limestone islets separated by a shallow passage about two cables wide. They are both less than three kilometres long and no more than twenty metres in height. The smaller eastern island, which is covered in bush, has no easy access nor any source of fresh water and is uninhabitable. West Swan on the other hand, with its one or two sandy bays and a good supply of water, is far more appealing, and this became the home of the first settlers. As well as fishing for turtles they also established a coconut plantation which before the end of the nineteenth century had been expanded to cover over half the island.

A dispute with Britain over ownership of the Swan and the Bay Islands began soon after Honduras became a separate republic, following the collapse of the Central American Federation, in 1838. The Honduran claim to the Bay Islands, as they were not only much bigger but much closer to the mainland, was made with some resolve and eventually settled in the republic's favour. That to the Swan Islands, being more tenuous was made with less conviction and, as the islands were of little value to anyone other than the two dozen or so Cayman islanders living there, with no great vigour. As a result the question of ownership remained unresolved until well into the twentieth century.

The United States also began to show an interest in the middle of the nineteenth century, as the search for Caribbean guano deposits took place and in 1863 an American managed to obtain a lease to the islands from the Honduran Government. Although this proved to be worthless, and no phosphate workings were ever established, enough American interest was shown over the next couple of decades to persuade the inhabitants in 1888 to petition Queen Victoria to formally annex the islands to the British Crown.

Even though this plea was dismissed the British Government still continued to prevaricate over the sovereignty of the islands, and the dispute with Honduras – now a subject to be dealt with at a slightly higher bureaucratic level because of perceived American interference – was allowed to linger on. Even as late as 1937 a light cruiser, HMS Dragon, was sent to the islands in order to demonstrate continued British interest in their ownership. The ship anchored off the south-western end of West Swan to find, as one of her officers wrote later, 'a stone jetty with a flagstaff, from which – lo and behold! – flew the Stars and Stripes'. On going ashore he met 'one or two of the inhabitants, who had no idea what power, if any, claimed the islands, and who told me that the only reason they flew the American flag was that it was the only flag they had! (This was soon rectified: with our gift of a large Union Jack flying from their flagstaff, our captain was able to report "Mission Accomplished".)'

This visit followed the establishment by the United Fruit Company of a wireless relay station on the island to act as a link between the company's headquarters in New Orleans and its extensive holdings in Central America. The station staff presumababbly had been responsible for providing the offending 'Stars and Stripes', a flag which may well have flown again during the Second World War when the islands were taken over by the US Government and this installation became a weather reporting station. American use of the islands continued until 1971, when, at long last and without any objection from any other government, the islands became the undisputed property of the Republic of Honduras.

33 Belize

'The first place settled after the deluge'

Although no other Advantages have hitherto been in Question, except that of cutting wood for Dyeing, yet His Catholick Majesty, as a greater Proof of his Disposition to oblige the King of Great Britain, will grant to the English the Liberty of cutting all other Wood, without even excepting Mahogany, as well as gathering all the Fruits, or Produce of the Earth, purely natural and uncultivated, which may besides, being carried away in their natural State, become an Object of Utility or of Commerce, whether for Food or for Manufactures: But it is expressly agreed, that this Stipulation is never to be used as a Pretext for establishing in that Country any Plantation of Sugar, Coffee, Cacao, or other like Articles, or any Fabrick or Manufacture, by Means of Mills or other Machines whatsoever (this Restriction however does not regard the Use of Saw Mills for cutting or otherwise preparing the Wood) since all the Lands in Question being indisputably acknowledged to belong of Right to the Crown of Spain, no Settlements of that Kind, or the Population which would follow, could be allowed.

*Article III of the Convention agreed between Spain and
Britain over rights in the Honduras Settlement 1786*

Christmas ... is the season that in this country brings all ranks together – the bond and the free; and the hilarity which prevails among the former order cannot possibly be more largely partaken of by any beings in the world ... The morning of Christmas-day is invariably ushered in by the discharging of small-arms in every direction; and the master's house (where the festivity commences), and whatever it contains, is now open to all ...

The endurance of the negroes during the period of their holidays, which usually last a week, is incredible. Few of them are known to take any portion of rest for the whole time; and for the same space they seldom know an interval of sobriety ...

The people of colour and free-blacks ... all possess some property; a few are rich, and are alike distinguishable for the feature which so strongly characterizes the same race throughout the West Indies, an expansive gratification of their appetites, and an extravagant passion for dress.

CAPTAIN GEORGE HENDERSON, 1809

... the first place settled after the deluge; every other that I have seen in the course of my Military Peregrinations is an improvement on it.

MAJOR GEORGE ARTHUR, 1814

Belize! Oh sweet Belize! I smell thy swamps once more.

JAMES WILSON, 1829

... before I had been an hour in Balize I learned that the great work of practical amalgamation, the subject of so much angry controversy at home [the USA], had been going on quietly for generations; that colour was considered mere matter of taste; and that some of the most respectable inhabitants had black wives and mongrel children, whom they educated with as much care, and made money for with as much zeal, as if their skins were perfectly white.

I hardly knew whether to be shocked or amused at this condition of society ...

JOHN L. STEPHENS, 1841

Belize, the capital of British Honduras, is situated on one of the mouths of the Old River, near Fort George, and occupies a position on both sides of it.

The name of Belize is supposed to be a Spanish corruption of Wallace, the name of a Scotchman, a noted pirate. Or, possibly, it may be derived from the French *balise*, a beacon, which might have been erected to warn mariners of the abode of pirates. The town is practically cut off from the interior by numerous lagoons, one of which, however, is now bridged. The site of the town is somewhat facetiously described as composed of mahogany chips, and sand dredged out of the harbour. Be that as it may, the town is one of the brightest and cleanest in the West Indies, and although small, is the seat of an extensive trade, not only with the settlements in the colony itself, but with all the neighbouring Republics.

D. MORRIS, 1883

The irreverent have said that the best view of Belize, its capital, is obtained from the stern of a departing steamer; but the implication contained in this statement is grossly unfair. As a matter of fact the appearance of the town as you approach it from the sea by a tortuous channel through a maze of coral islets or cays, many of them wooded with coco-nut palms, is singularly attractive and pleasing.

The first object to strike the eye after you have successfully negotiated the cays is a substantial building like one of those huge seaside hotels on the sea front at Atlantic City. New-comers are disappointed when they learn that Belize has no such luxury, and that this edifice of promising appearance is St John's College, a Roman Catholic institution conducted by American Jesuits . . .

SIR ALGERNON ASPINALL, 1927

British Honduras has recently had a considerable windfall, in the form of a legacy, amounting to approximately a million and a half dollars, bequeathed it by the late Baron Bliss.

This would not bulk as a very large sum in England, but when judged by small colony standards it represents a vast fortune, for it exceeds the total revenue of the Colony for an entire year; it would easily pay off all its indebtness, and, if applied in that comfortable way, would support in idleness and moderate comfort the entire population of ten thousand families, more or less, for nearly a year – for neither their wages nor their standard of living are, from an English point of view, very high.

Why should they be, indeed, in a climate where Nature undertakes to dry-nurse all her children, where a comfortable house can be put up by half a dozen men in a couple of days, from material provided by her, practically at the back door; where the fertile soil only needs scratching with a machete to yield abundant crops of yam, plantain, bananas, oranges, mangoes, and a hundred other fruits and vegetables; where the delightful climate renders clothes rather a question of decency than protection against the weather; where one has only to throw a hook into the river, or cast a net into the sea, to get as many fine fish as one needs, and, when a fish diet begins to pall, take an early morning stroll into the bush and bring in a peccary, an antelope, a gibnut, a few brace of pigeons or parrots, or whatever else the gods may see fit to send for the pot.

THOMAS GANN, 1928

Have you ever been to Belize? It is the capital and port of that little-known Crown Colony, British Honduras, sandwiched between Yucatan and Guatemala and bordered by the Caribbean Sea. If you haven't, don't go, unless you have a stomach of cast iron and no sense of smell. It is incredible that in this age the capital of a British colony, with some thousands of inhabitants, ranging from white through every subfusc shade to black, should still remain in the condition in which the traveller will find it to-day . . .

Once in Belize, there is no escape until a boat arrives, for the reason that there are no roads leading anywhere out of the town, which is hemmed in on every side except towards the coast by thick bush and jungle. It is historical that Belize was built on a swamp filled in with mahogany chips and empty gin bottles. I often wonder why it was built at all. Go where you will, you will find no capital like it . . .

British Honduras has ever been a land of mystery. With hardly a break a sinister and impenetrable jungle covers nine thousand odd square miles. Fifty-five miles south of Belize . . . the Cockscomb Mountains rise in three ranges, one behind the other, and here are fastnesses which up to the present no white foot has ever trodden . . .

From twelve to fifty miles offshore along the entire coast . . . innumerable tiny islands and coral reefs rise from the hot tropic waters, and no pen can describe the Elysian beauty of the scenery. The lazy rollers curl and break on these reefs leaving a white line of surf, and in the lee of the barriers rise the emerald-green, palm-clad islands with their blinding white coral-sand beaches. The translucent water surrounding them is ever changing – rose-pink at sunrise, tawny orange deepening to scarlet as the rim of the setting sun touches the horizon and sinks in a sea of blood; while at noon every shade is reflected from vivid jade green to the deepest of purple and sapphire blue . . .

F.A. MITCHELL-HEDGES, 1931

The defence of Orange Walk

For three years in the middle of the nineteenth century the Yucatan peninsula, of which the country of Belize forms one small part, was the scene of a bitter war – now known as the War of the Castes – fought between the indigenous Mayan Indians and Mexican government forces. Because what was then the colony of British Honduras had an undefended border with Mexico, and a sizeable Mayan population of its own, it soon became caught up in the conflict, and was then plagued by the skirmishes that continued to take place within its northern and north-western borders long after the war in Mexico had ended in 1850. Refugees who had fled from the Yucatan into the relative safety of British territory invited incursions by Mexican troops, until detachments from the garrison were posted along the border to deter them. This move was later followed by a series of cross-border attacks by disaffected Indians, principally members of the Ycaiche tribe led by a man named Marcus Canul. These began in earnest in 1866, and only came to an end as the result of events which took place in a small town about ten miles inside the colony's northern border six years later.

The defence of the outpost at Orange Walk, which was attacked in September 1872, while not conducted on the same scale as that of Rorke's Drift on a different continent nearly seven years later, involved a similar degree of heroism among all those who took part, and deserves to be far better remembered. Unfortunately, it took place in a colony which, as must be readily apparent from the views given above, was hardly on a par with Natal in anyone's affections. Also, and even more to the point, the defenders were officers and men of a regiment which, because its troops were black, had no standing in the British Army in any way comparable with that held by the South Wales Borderers. Today the defence of Orange Walk, like the regiment involved, is almost totally forgotten. The nearest to a first-hand account of the action was written by the then commanding officer of the regiment thirteen years after it had taken place:

On the 1st of September, 1872, a most determined attack was made by the Ycaiche Indians on the outpost of Orange Walk . . . which was garrisoned by thirty-eight men of the 1st West India Regiment, under Lieutenant Joseph Graham Smith.

Orange Walk is situated on a deep and sluggish stream in the northern district . . . and, in 1872, contained a population of about 1200 souls, the majority of whom were either Indians or Hispano-Indians, and indifferent to British rule. The business portion of the town, and most of the shops or stores, were on hilly ground, considerably above the river-bed, and built here and there, without an attempt at order or regularity. About midway between the river and this upper portion of the town was the barrack, consisting of one large room, sixty feet by thirty feet, the two ends of which were partitioned off, leaving the central part for the men's quarters. The partitioned portion at the south end was used as a guard-room. The walls of the building were constructed of *pimentos*, or round straight sticks, varying from half-an-inch to three inches in diameter, driven firmly into the ground, in an upright position, as close together as possible, and held in their place by pine-wood battens. The roof was composed of palm-leaves, or 'fan-thatch'. The floor was boarded.

On the south-eastern side of the barrack, the ground fell towards the river, which was about fifty yards distant. About ten yards from the water's edge was a large quantity of logwood, packed in piles four feet high, and some little distance from each other. Across the road, on the southern side, were several native houses; to the east, and about forty yards distant, was a group of four small buildings consisting of commissariat stores and the officers' quarters; whilst the nearest building on the north was the Roman Catholic Church, about eighty yards off.

How or when the invaders crossed the Rio Hondo, the northern boundary of the colony, has not been ascertained; but it is a significant fact, suggestive of strong suspicions against the loyalty of the Indian and mixed Spanish–Indian population, whose small settlements were dotted here and there on the line of march of the invaders, that no information was conveyed, either to the district magistrate at Orange Walk, or to the officer commanding the small detachment, that an enemy was at hand, prepared, as the settlers must have known, to attack and plunder the town.

The Indians, consisting of about 180 braves, or fighting men, and 100 camp followers, led by Marcus Canul . . . approached the town about 8 a.m. on Sunday, 1st September. They were divided into three sections, each of 60 men, and they entered the town at three different points; one attacking the upper portion, and pillaging and setting fire to the houses and stores, the other two marching directly upon the barracks, but from opposite sides. Of these latter two, one took up position behind the stacks of logwood, thus commanding one side and one end of the barrack; and the other established itself close to the officers' quarters, under cover of a stone building, which commanded the other side of the barrack and the end already commanded from the stacks of logwood.

So sudden and unexpected was the attack, that Lieutenant Graham Smith and Staff-Assistant-Surgeon Edge, who were both at the time having their morning baths, barely had time to escape to the barracks; Lieutenant Smith, with nothing on but his trousers, and Dr Edge in a state of nudity; while the first notice the men in the barrack had of the approach of the enemy, was the shower of lead which rattled on the building . . .

Before Lieutenant Graham Smith had reached the barracks, the two divisions of the enemy had taken up their respective positions, and were pouring in unceasing discharges of ball, which penetrated the pimento sticks and raked the building from end to end. The guards, the only men who had ammunition in their possession, returned the fire, and at this moment Lieutenant Smith arrived with Dr Edge.

Sergeant Belizario, coming forward and asking for ammunition to serve out, reminded Lieutenant Smith that he had left the key of the portable magazine, in which the ammunition was kept, in his quarters. The open space between his quarters and the barrack-room was swept with an unceasing shower of lead; but there was no help for it, and the key had to be fetched. Accompanied by Sergeant Belizario, Lieutenant Smith ran over to his house, seized the key, and ran back. Most marvellously both escaped injury, though the ground all around them was cut up by bullets. The portable magazine was kept in the partitioned end that served as a guard-room, and there was no door of communication between the central portion, where the men lived, and this room. Sergeant Belizario therefore ran out of the barrack-room, along the side of the building, into the guard-room, and endeavoured to drag the portable magazine back with him. He succeeded in moving it outside the guard-room and a little way along the wall, but further he could not drag it. All this time he was exposed to a heavy fire, and every musket-barrel from the stone building on the eastern side of the barrack was pointed at his body. Finding that all his efforts to move the magazine were fruitless, Sergeant Belizario unlocked it, and, taking out the ammunition, passed packet after packet to the men inside, through the opening under the eaves left for ventilation . . . till the magazine was emptied. This done, he returned to the barrack-room. He seemed to have borne a charmed life, for he was untouched, while the portable magazine was starred with the white splashes of leaden bullets.

A hot fire was now opened by the soldiers, and Lieutenant Graham Smith, taking a rifle, placed himself at the west door of the barracks to try to pick off some of the most daring of the Indians. Whilst there he was struck in the left side, and, at the same instant, Private Robert Lynch, who was standing next him, fell dead, pierced by two shots.

Notwithstanding his wound, which was very severe, the ball penetrating the left breast a little above the heart, and passing nearly through him, finally lodging under the left shoulder-blade, Lieutenant Smith continued directing and encouraging his men; and finding that the whole interior was swept by the missiles of the enemy, against which the frail pimento-sticks were no protection, he ordered the men to turn down their cots, and, lying on their beds, to fire over the iron heads of the cots. In this position they were tolerably well sheltered, though the Indians were so close that several of the iron heads were shot through.

In this place it will be proper to refer to a soldier who, all this time, was outside the barrack. This was Private Bidwell, who, when the Indians arrived, had just been posted sentry on a commissariat store close to the officers' quarters. The occupation of one of this group of buildings cut him off from the barrack-room; so, after bayoneting one Indian, he ran over to an enclosure belonging to Don Escalente, situated to the north of the store. From the shelter of the fence of this enclosure he fired into the Indians in the stone building till his ten rounds of ammunition were exhausted. He then said to Don Escalente, 'I am going over to the barracks for more cartridges', and, before he could be dissuaded, ran out from the shelter and endeavoured to cross the open space to the barrack. On the way he received a mortal wound, but succeeded in joining his comrades.

The Indians, impatient at the delay caused by the obstinate resistance of the soldiers, now vacated the houses on the further side of the road, opposite the southern end of the barracks, and set fire to the thatched roofs, hoping to involve the barracks in a general conflagration. The houses burned fiercely, and the flames spreading across the road, caught a small kitchen situated not ten yards from the barracks. The Indians raised yells of triumph, for they considered it certain that their foes would now be driven from their shelter and then easily overpowered by force of numbers. Indeed, it is difficult to understand how the dry palm-thatch of the barracks did fail to ignite, but it did so fail, and the kitchen, after blazing up violently for a few minutes, fell in and burned itself out harmlessly.

By the destruction of these buildings the position of the soldiers was improved, the Indians now having no cover immediately opposite the south end of the barrack, and being compelled consequently to concentrate behind the stacks of logwood. A party, however, of them made a circuit and appeared on the north-west corner of the barrack, from whence they commanded the road bounding the north side of the building.

After the firing had continued for an hour and a half, Mr Price, and another American gentleman from Tower Hill Rancho, about four miles from the barracks, having heard what was taking place, mounted and rode towards the scene of conflict. Creeping up the river bank unperceived through the thick woods, they suddenly rode into and fired upon the Indians who were in rear of the stacks of logwood. The latter, taken by surprise, and not knowing by what unexpected force they were attacked, left their cover for a moment and appeared on the side nearest to the barracks. The soldiers perceiving this movement, and thinking that the Indians were going to attempt to rush the building, fixed bayonets, and some ran to the doors to defend the entrances. Mr Price and his companion, taking advantage of this and the momentary surprise of the Indians, rushed forward and threw themselves into the barracks.

The enemy's fire redoubled after this, and it was hotly kept up until about half-past 1 o'clock; it then began to slacken, and by 2 o'clock had ceased altogether. For some time no one stirred, it being suspected that the cessation of the attack was only an Indian ruse; but after a quarter of an hour had elapsed, Sergeant Belizario was sent out with a party to reconnoitre. He reported that the enemy was in full retreat, and was sent to follow them up and watch their movements. No pursuit could be attempted. Lieutenant Graham Smith was, by this time, incapable of further action, and out of the detachment of thirty-eight men, two had been killed and fourteen severely wounded.

The attack lasted altogether six hours. The Indian loss was about fifty killed; the number of their wounded could not, of course, be ascertained, but among them was Marcus Canul himself, who was mortally wounded, and died before recrossing the Hondo. Of the civilians, the son of Don Escalente, a boy fourteen years of age, was killed, and seventeen wounded . . . Over 300 bullet-holes were counted in the walls of the barrack-room, and in many places the palmettos were shot away in patches . . .

Recognition of the defenders' courageous stand came in the middle of November, and in various forms. Lieutenant Smith was given immediate promotion to the rank of captain; Sergeant Belizario was awarded the Distinguished Conduct Medal with an annuity of £10; Lance-Corporals Spencer and Stirling were also each awarded the DCM, but with no annuity; Doctor Edge was informed he would be promoted to the rank of Surgeon 'as soon as he qualified for the higher position'; and six other men who were commended had to be content with their commanding officer being 're-quested to record their claims, and give such recognition of them regimentally as may be possible from time to time'.

A considerable windfall

The large legacy left to British Honduras, about which in 1928 the archaeologist Thomas Gunn felt the need to be so supercilious, had been given to the colony two years earlier under the most unusual circumstances by an English country gentleman named Henry Bliss who, from out of an equally strange set of circumstances had acquired – and always used – the non-English title of Baron Bliss.

His father, who entered the world as Henry Aldridge in 1818, was born bearing in his mouth the largest possible silver spoon. At the age of twenty-seven, under the proviso that he changed his name to that of his benefactor, he inherited the Suffolk mansion and entire estate of an uncle of 'immense wealth' named Edward Bliss. Ten years later, now as Henry Bliss, he was informed that he had succeeded to the estates and title of a Portuguese cousin, the Barão de Alreyjo. In order to acquire the title as well as the property that went with it without breaking the terms of his uncle's will, under which he was strictly forbidden to use any other surname but Bliss, he obtained letters patent from the King Regent of Portugal which allowed him to succeed as the third baron with the title of Barão de Bliss. In 1867 another Portuguese relative, Colonel Carlo Antonio Barreto, died leaving the baron yet more property, this time in Spain. The conditions of the Colonel's will obviously demanded a change of name as, in 1869 and ignoring the stricture contained in his uncle's will, he obtained Portuguese royal consent to style himself the Barão de Barreto. His son, Henry Edward Ernest Victor D'Alreyjo de Barreto, who was to become the benefactor of British Honduras, was born the same year.

Henry Edward, or Victor as he preferred to be known, retained his de Barreto surname until he succeeded his father as the fourth baron in 1890, when it became expedient for him to resume the name of Bliss. For the remainder of his life, in spite of his title being rendered worthless when Portugal became a republic in 1910, he preferred to be addressed as Baron Bliss. Although he inherited his father's wealth he did not share the same good fortune. In 1911 he was afflicted with poliomyelitis which left him partly paralysed; an extremely cruel blow for a man keenly interested in field sports and other outdoor activities, particularly sailing and deep-sea fishing. After the First World War the prospect of spending the rest of his life in a wheelchair in England proved too much for him, and in 1920, parting amicably from his wife, he left for Nassau to live on board the luxurious motor yacht Sea King, *which he had had built and sent ahead of him across the Atlantic.*

He remained in the Bahamas for the next five years, acquiring property on one or two of the islands, but spending most of his time on board his yacht and indulging his passion for fishing. In time he grew to dislike the exclusivity and pretentiousness of Bahamian society, and in 1925 decided to try life elsewhere in the West Indies. After a brief foray to Trinidad, where a bout of food poisoning and the poor prospects for fishing in the Gulf of Paria soon brought his stay to an end, he ordered course to be set for the opposite end of the Caribbean. Having been told by a friend, Willoughby Bullock, of the excellent fishing to be had off the barrier reef and around the cays of British Honduras, he arrived off Belize City in the middle of January 1926.

As Bullock just happened to be the colony's Attorney-General the Baron was particularly well received, and for the next few weeks enjoyed not only some splendid fishing, but also a cordial relationship with the Governor and other colonial officials. In addition, and just as importantly in view of what was soon to transpire, he enjoyed the friendly and helpful attention of many of the local fishermen who ferried him out to the cays from the Sea King. Regrettably, the strain on his physique imposed by his incapacity, and the lasting effects of the illness he had suffered in Trinidad, combined to ruin his health just as he seemed to have found his Shangri-La. On 10 February he was confined to his bed on board the yacht and a week later, aware that it was unlikely he would ever leave it alive, he executed and signed a new will.

In this document, which must be unique in the annals of the British Empire, having made suitable provision for his wife and various relatives and friends, he appointed the holders of the positions of Governor, Colonial Secretary and Attorney-General of British Honduras as the executors of the residue of his estate, which was left to the colony in the form of the 'Baron Bliss Trust'. The will specified that the trustees could use the income derived from the Trust 'for the benefit or development of the Colony of British Honduras' in any form of public works except churches, chapels, dancing halls, or schools other than those needed for agricultural or vocational training. All he requested in return for his generosity was that he might be buried at a spot overlooking Belize Harbour, in a grave of his own design, and close to an obelisk from which a harbour navigation light could be displayed.

Baron Bliss died on 9 March and was buried a week later in a temporary grave while the tomb and lighthouse he had asked for were being built. Such was the amount of capital available to the Trust once all the other bequests had been met, and even after the British Government – quite shamelessly – had taken its share in the form of death duties, that Belize has benefited from it ever since. His singular generosity has been, and continues to be, of great help to the country and his name remains just as honoured among Belizeans today as it was in colonial times.

In his will the Baron stated that his life had been 'a very happy one', and that 'having never experienced an unhappy day I hope to die happy'. There can be little doubt that he did, and even less that his shade has not remained at peace ever since.

Epilogue

One of the earliest books about the West Indies, the Caribbean, the Spanish Main – call the lands which Columbus found where the sea had an ending what you will – was published towards the end of the sixteenth century. It was written by a Spanish Jesuit who, after spending over a quarter of a century in the New World, returned to Europe only a year or two before his death in 1600. Although, as is only to be expected, his Historía natural y moral de las Indias, *published in Madrid in 1590, contained a sophistical defence of Spanish colonial policies, it was more concerned with the flora, fauna and human inhabitants of the region, and as such excited a great deal of interest outside Spain. Within little more than a decade of its publication, it had been translated into Italian, French, Dutch, German, Latin and English. The English edition, at least, has been reprinted at intervals ever since, most recently in 1970 in New York.*

While it is doubtful if the author, José de Costa, ever lived on any Caribbean island other than Hispaniola, or saw more than even a handful of the rest, the words of his panegyric to the region in which they lie seem just as relevant today as when he wrote them over 400 years ago. I can do no better, using the translation found in a volume of Hakluytus Posthumus or Purchas his Pilgrimes, *than to use them to bring my own book to a close:*

Considering with my selfe, the pleasing temperature of many Countries at the Indies, where they know not what Winter is, which by his cold doth freeze them, nor Summer which doth trouble them with heat, but that with a Mat they preserve themselves from injuries of all weather, and where they scarce have any neede to change their garments throughout the yeere. I say, that often considering of this, I find that if men at this day would vanquish their passions, and free themselves from the snares of covetousnesse, leaving many fruitlesse and pernicious designes, without doubt they might live at the Indies very pleasantly and happily: for that which other Poets sing of the Elisean fields & of the famous Tempe, or that which Plato reports or feignes of his Atlantike Iland; men should find in these Lands, if with a generous spirit they would choose rather to command their silver and their desires, than to remayne to it slaves as they are . . .

Bibliography

Andrews, E.W. (ed.). *Journal of a Lady of Quality: Being the Narrative of a Journey from Scotland to the West Indies . . .* New Haven, 1921.

Aspinall, Algernon E. *The Pocket Guide to the West Indies.* London, 1954 (1st edn 1907).

Aspinall, Algernon E. *A Wayfarer in the West Indies.* London, 1927.

Atwood, Thomas. *The History of the Island of Dominica.* London, 1791.

Aytoun, James. *Redcoats in the Caribbean.* Blackburn, 1984.

Baird, R. *Impressions and Experiences of the West Indies and North America in 1849.* Philadelphia, 1850.

Banks, E.P. 'A Carib Village in Dominica'. *Social and Economic Studies*, 5, 1956.

Bell, Hesketh. *Glimpses of a Governor's Life.* London, 1946.

Brassey, Lady. *In the Trades, the Tropics, and the Roaring Forties.* London, 1885.

Breen, H.H. *St Lucia: Historical, Statistical and Descriptive.* London, 1844.

Browne, Thomas Henry. *see* Buckley, Roger Norman.

Bruce, Peter Henry. *Memoirs of Peter Henry Bruce Esq.* London, 1782.

Buckley, Roger Norman (ed.). *Napoleonic War Journal of Captain Thomas Henry Browne, 1807–1816.* London, 1987.

Bulkeley, O.T. *The Lesser Antilles: A Guide for Settlers in the British West Indies, and Tourists' Companion.* London, 1889.

Capadose, H. *Sixteen Years in the West Indies.* London, 1845.

Clifford, George. *see* Purchas, Samuel.

Coard, F.M. *Bittersweet and Spice.* Grenada, 1970.

Coleridge, Henry Nelson. *Six Months in the West Indies in 1825.* London, 1826.

Collymore, Frank A. *Notes for a Glossary of Words and Phrases of Barbadian Dialect.* Barbados, 1955.

—— *Rhymed Ruminations on the Fauna of Barbados.* Barbados, 1968.

Crocker, John. *The Centaur Guide to the Caribbean and El Dorado.* Fontwell, 1968.

Cundall, Frank (ed.). *Lady Nugent's Journal: Jamaica One Hundred Years Ago.* London, 1907.

Curry, Robert A. *Bahamian Lore.* Paris, 1928.

Day, C.W. *Five Years' Residence in the West Indies.* London, 1852.

De Booy, Theodoor and John T. Faris. *The Virgin Islands: Our New Possessions and the British Islands.* New York, 1918.

De Leeuw, Hendrik. *Crossroads of the Buccaneers.* London, 1957.

Edwards, Bryan. *The History, Civil and Commercial of the British Colonies in the West Indies*. London, 1793.

Ellis, A.B. *The History of the First West India Regiment*. London, 1885.

Eves, C. Washington. *The West Indies*. London, 1889.

Fassig, Oliver L. *see* Shattuck, George B.

Fergus, Howard A. *Montserrat: History of a Caribbean Colony*. London, 1994.

Firth, C.H. (ed.). *Narrative of General Venables: with an appendix of papers relating to the expedition to the West Indies . . .* London, 1900.

Fiske, Amos Kidder. *The West Indies: A History of the Islands of the West Indian Archipelago*. New York, 1899.

Forbes, Rosita. *Islands in the Sun*. London, 1949.

Forrest, A.S. and John Henderson. *Jamaica*. London, 1906.

Franck, Harry A. *Roaming through the West Indies*. New York, 1920.

Froude, James Anthony. *The English in the West Indies, or the Bow of Ulysses*. London, 1888.

Gann, Thomas. *Discoveries and Adventures in Central America*. London, 1928.

Gordon, Helen Cameron. *West Indian Scenes*. London, 1942.

Gurney, Joseph John. *A Winter in the West Indies: Described in Familiar Letters to Henry Clay, of Kentucky*. London, 1840.

Hakluyt, Richard. *The Principall Navigations, Voyages, Traffiques and Discoveries of the English Nation*. London, 1598–1600.

Harcourt, Robert. *A Relation of a Voyage to Guiana*. London, 1625.

Harding, Dorothy. 'On the Fringe of the Empire'. *East and West*. July, 1903.

Hawkins, John. *see* Hakluyt, Richard.

Hearn, Lafcadio. *Two Years in the French West Indies*. New York, 1890.

Henderson, George. *An Account of the British Settlement of Honduras*. London, 1809.

Henderson, John. *see* Forrest, A.S. and John Henderson.

Henderson, J.E. *A Visit to the West Indies*. London, 1939.

Hiss, Philip Hanson. *Netherlands America: The Dutch Territories in the West*. New York, 1943.

Honychurch, Lennox. *Dominica: Isle of Adventure*. London, 1998 (3rd edn).

Hughes, Griffith. *The Natural History of Barbados*. London, 1750.

Jones, S.B. *Annals of Anguilla 1650–1923*. Anguilla, 1936.

Joseph, E.L. *A History of Trinidad*. Trinidad, 1838.

Kingsley, Charles. *At Last: A Christmas in the West Indies*. London, 1871.

Kirke, Henry. *Twenty-five Years in British Guiana*. London, 1898.

Labat, Jean Baptiste. *Nouveau voyage aux isles de l'Amérique*. Paris, 1722.

Lanaghan, Mrs. *Antigua and the Antiguans*. London, 1844.

Langton-Jones, R. *Silent Sentinels*. London, 1944.

Laudonniere, René. *see* Hakluyt, Richard.

Leach, J. *Rough Sketches of the Life of an Old Soldier: During a Service in the West Indies . . .* London, 1831.

Lewis, Gordon K. *The Growth of the Modern West Indies.* London, 1968.

McCormick, Donald. *Islands for Sale.* London, 1950.

Mannington, George. *The West Indies.* London, 1925.

Messenger, John C. 'The Influence of the Irish in Montserrat'. *Caribbean Quarterly*, 13(2), June, 1967.

Mitchell-Hedges, F.A. *Land of Wonder and Fear.* London, 1931.

Morris, D. *The Colony of British Honduras: Its Resources and Prospects with Particular Reference to its Indigenous Plants and Economic Productions.* London, 1883.

Morris, James. *Farewell the Trumpets: An Imperial Retreat.* London, 1978.

Neillands, Robin. *Fighting Retreat: The British Empire 1947–1997.* London, 1996.

Nicholls, Henry A. *Dominica.* Dominica, c. 1875.

Norie, J.W. *West India Directory: Part I, The Caribbee Islands.* London, 1836.

Nugent, Lady Maria. *see* Cundall, Frank.

Oldmixon, John. *History of the British Empire in America.* London, 1708.

Olley, Philip P. *Guide to Jamaica.* Jamaica, 1937.

Palgrave, William Gifford. *Ulysses, or Scenes and Studies in Many Lands.* London, 1887.

Peters, F.E. *Montserrat: Her Disasters.* Montserrat, 1928.

Pinckard, George. *Notes on the West Indies: Written During the Expedition Under the Command of the Late General Sir Ralph Abercromby.* London, 1806.

Poyntz, J. *The Present Prospect of the Famous and Fertile Island of Tobago.* London, 1683.

Purchas, Samuel. *Hakluytus Posthumus or Purchas His Pilgrimes.* London, 1625.

Raleigh, Walter. *see* Hakluyt, Richard.

Rees, Abraham. *The Cyclopaedia: or Universal Dictionary of Arts, Sciences and Literature.* London, 1819.

Rutter, Owen. *A Traveller in the West Indies.* London, 1933.

St Clair, Thomas Staunton. *A Soldier's Sojourn in British Guiana.* London, 1834.

St-Johnston, Reginald. *From a Colonial Governor's Note-Book.* London, 1936.

Savage, Raymond. *Barbados, British West Indies.* London, 1936.

Schaw, Janet. *see* Andrews, E.W.

Schomburgk, Robert H. 'Remarks on Anegada'. *The Geographical Journal*, 2, 1832.

Shattuck, George B. (ed.). *The Bahama Islands.* New York, 1905.

Sherley, Anthony. *see* Hakluyt, Richard.

Sloane, Hans. *A Voyage to the Islands of Madeira, Barbados, Nieves, St Christopher and Jamaica.* London, 1707.

Smith, Glanville. *Many a Green Isle.* London, 1942.

Smith, John. *The True Travels, Adventures and Observations of Captain John Smith in Europe, Asia, Africa and America.* London, 1630.

Smith, William. *A Natural History of Nevis and the Rest of the English Leeward Caribbee Islands in America.* Cambridge, 1745.

Southey, Thomas. *A Chronological History of the West Indies.* London, 1827.

Stephens, John L. *Incidents of Travel in Central America, Chiapas, and Yucatan.* London, 1841.

Treves, Frederick. *The Cradle of the Deep: An Account of a Voyage to the West Indies.* London, 1908.

Trollope, Anthony. *The West Indies and the Spanish Main.* London, 1859.

Underhill, Edward Bean. *The West Indies: Their Social and Religious Condition.* London, 1862.

Van Dyke, John C. *In the West Indies.* London, 1932.

Van Voorst, John. *Letters from the Virgin Islands.* London, 1843.

Waller, J.A. *A Voyage in the West Indies, Containing Various Observations Made During a Residence in Barbados, and Several of the Leeward Islands.* London, 1820.

W.B.F. *In the West Indies.* London, 1905.

Wentworth, T. *The West India Sketch Book.* London, 1834.

Whistler, Henry. *see* Firth, C.H.

Williams, Eric. *History of the People of Trinidad and Tobago.* André Deutsch, 1964.

—— *Inward Hunger: The Education of a Prime Minister.* London, 1969.

Wilson, James. *A Brief Memoir of the Life of James Wilson.* London, 1829.

Wright, James M. *see* Shattuck, George B.

Young, Everild and K. Helweg-Larsen. *Caribbean Cocktail.* London, 1955.

Biographical Notes

ASPINALL, Algernon Edward (1871–1952). Secretary to the London-based West India Committee 1898–1938. Knighted 1928. Consultant to the Imperial College of Tropical Agriculture 1940–1949. Served on numerous committees to do with West Indian agricultural, shipping and currency matters. His very popular *Pocket Guide to the West Indies* went through ten editions between 1907 and 1954.

ATWOOD, Thomas (?–1793). West Indian lawyer who after some years as the senior judge of Dominica became Chief Justice of the Bahamas, where he wrote his *History of Dominica.*

BELL, Henry Hesketh (1864–1952). Colonial administrator who entered the Colonial Service in 1883. After holding various positions in the West Indies he became Administrator of Dominica from 1899 to 1905. Later Governor of Uganda, Nigeria, the Leeward Islands and Mauritius. Knighted 1907. Author of several books, including one on witchcraft in the West Indies.

BRASSEY, Anna (1839–1887). Traveller and wife of the Liberal MP, Thomas Brassey (created Baron Brassey in 1886). Wrote several books about long sea voyages taken in their yacht *Sunbeam.* Died, as she would have wished, at sea, while off the east coast of Australia.

BROWNE, Thomas Henry (1787–1855). Lieutenant-General. Born in Wales, he entered the army in 1805 and served with the 23rd Regiment of Foot (the Royal Welch Fusiliers) in the West Indies and North America, and in the Peninsular War. Knighted in 1818, and promoted to lieutenant-general in 1854 when he became Colonel of the 80th Regiment of Foot.

BRUCE, Peter Henry (1692–1757). Military engineer born in Germany of Scottish descent, who was employed in Prussia and Russia before settling in Scotland in 1724. He was in charge of the construction of fortifications in the Bahamas between 1740 and 1744.

CLIFFORD, George (1558–1605). Naval commander who succeeded as the third Earl of Cumberland in 1570. After a misspent youth, during which he gambled away his estates, he took up a career at sea. He was in command of one of the ships which engaged the Spanish Armada in 1588. He later fitted out ten privateering expeditions against Spain and her possessions in the New World. The four of these he led himself, including that of 1598, were no more successful than any of the others.

COLERIDGE, Henry Nelson (1798–1843). Barrister who was called to the Bar soon after returning from his six months in the West Indies. In 1829 he married his cousin Sara, the daughter of the poet, Samuel Taylor Coleridge. He wrote nothing else after *Six Months in the West Indies* except for some pamphlets, but after becoming S.T. Coleridge's literary executor in 1834 he brought out the poet's *Table Talk* and edited other of his writings.

EDWARDS, Bryan (1743–1800). London merchant with considerable business interests in Jamaica, where he lived for some thirty years. He was later an English member of Parliament, holding strong anti-abolitionist views. Besides his *History of the British Colonies in the West Indies*, he also wrote a similar book concerning the *French Colony in the Island of St Domingo*.

EVES, Charles Washington (1838–1899). Another London merchant with large business interests in Jamaica, who remained intensely interested in West Indian affairs throughout his life.

FORBES, Joan Rosita (1893–1967). English writer and traveller, who used her experiences to produce a long serious of unconventional travel books (of which *Islands in the Sun* was the last), several novels and three volumes of autobiography.

FRANCK, Harry A. (dates unknown). American writer and traveller. He spent part of his life as a policeman in the Panama Canal Zone in the early 1900s: an experience which did not endear him to the many West Indians who worked on the construction of the canal. This in turn led him to take a very jaundiced view of the inhabitants of the Caribbean islands he roamed among soon after the First World War.

FROUDE, James Anthony (1818–1894). English historian and man of letters who, among many other works, wrote a twelve-volume *History of England from the Fall of Wolsey to the Death of Elizabeth*. He was sent on a government mission to South Africa in 1874, and subsequently travelled in Australia and the West Indies before being appointed Regius Professor of Modern History at Oxford in 1892. Although it contains some excellent descriptive passages his *The English in the West Indies* suffers from an almost total absence of anything good to say about non-white West Indians, among whom it caused great offence. Accordingly both book and author have been held in some contempt in the Caribbean ever since.

GANN, Thomas William (1867–1938). British archaeologist who was a medical officer in British Honduras from 1894 to 1923. During this time he was responsible for the discovery and excavation of the remains of Maya civilization at several sites, and became an expert on Maya architecture. He later lectured on Central American archaeology at Liverpool University.

GURNEY, Joseph John (1788–1847). English banker, philanthropist and writer. After having become a Quaker minister in 1818 he devoted himself to such matters as prison reform, the abolition of capital punishment and slave emancipation. He travelled extensively in Europe, North America and the West Indies, and wrote mainly theological works.

HAKLUYT, Richard (*c*. 1552–1616). English cleric who ended up as archdeacon of Westminster in 1603, but who is better remembered as a geographer, publicist for exploration, and the man responsible for the introduction of globes into English schools. He published a number of books, of which by far the most influential was his *Principall Navigations . . . of the English Nation.* The Hakluyt Society, which was founded in 1846, still publishes scholarly editions of exploration narratives.

HARCOURT, Robert (*c*. 1574–1631). English traveller and colonist. He took possession of a tract of land on the north coast of South America in 1609, and later obtained letters patent for the first settlement of the colony which many years later would become British Guiana.

HAWKINS, John (1532–1595). Naval commander, and the first Englishman to traffic in slaves. He made several voyages to the West Indies, before taking a leading part in the fight with the Spanish Armada in 1588. He later sailed with Drake's expedition to the West Indies and died at sea off Puerto Rico.

HEARN, Lafcadio (1850–1904). American journalist and writer of Irish–Greek descent born in Greece. After publishing his *Two Years in the French West Indies* he went to Japan, became naturalized, and remained there for the rest of his life writing almost exclusively about Japanese life and customs.

HUGHES, Griffith (dates unknown). Anglican clergyman who was rector of St Lucy's parish in Barbados in the middle of the eighteenth century. His *History of Barbados* is his only known work.

JOSEPH, Edward L. (?–1840). English (?) newspaper editor and novelist. He lived in Trinidad from 1820 onwards, and published the first history of the island written in English two years before his death.

KINGSLEY, Charles (1819–1875). English clergyman, historian and prolific author. At various times during his not very long life, while remaining rector of a parish church in Hampshire, he was Professor of Modern History at Cambridge, a canon of Chester, a canon of Westminister and chaplain to the Queen. His numerous books include the historical novel *Westward Ho!* and the children's fantasy *The Water Babies*.

KIRKE, Henry (1842–1925). English lawyer who, during his twenty-five years in British Guiana, rose from being a magistrate to a judge of the Supreme Court. He afterwards became the Attorney-General of Jamaica.

LANGTON-JONES, Ronald (1884–1967). Naval officer. After having served in the Royal Navy from 1897, he retired as a Commander in 1928 to join the Imperial Lighthouse Service. He was then resident Inspector for this institution in the Bahamas until 1949.

MITCHELL-HEDGES, Frederick Albert (1882–1959). English explorer and writer. He led many expeditions to Central America in the first half of the twentieth century, and was responsible for the discovery of the important Maya ruins at Lubaantun in 1924. Also a keen fisherman, he acquired a number of world records for giant fish and contributed much to ichthyological science.

MORRIS, Daniel (1844–1933). British botanist and zoologist. He served in Jamaica and British Honduras from 1879 to 1886, before becoming the Assistant Director of the Royal Botanic Gardens at Kew. He was connected with the exploration of the agricultural potential of British Honduras, and later even more with the agricultural development of the whole of the West Indies.

NORIE, John William (1772–1843). Author and publisher. As well as writing his own books on navigation, he also published a whole range of other people's navigation textbooks and tables which, together with charts, he then sold from 'Navigation House', his business premises in London.

NUGENT, Maria (dates unknown). The wife of Lieutenant-General Sir George Nugent, who was lieutenant-governor of Jamaica from 1801 to 1806.

OLDMIXON, John (1673–1742). English historian, poet and playwright. The author of many dull, partisan history books, and several long-forgotten stage works. His *The British Empire in America* was the first history of that subject.

PALGRAVE, William Gifford (1826–1888). English diplomat. After a very brief taste of army life he became a Jesuit missionary in Arabia and Syria until 1864. Then, having lost his faith, he left the Jesuits to join the diplomatic service. He subsequently held consular posts in places as far apart as Abyssinia, the Philippines, the West Indies and Bulgaria. He was reconciled to the Church not long before his death, while British minister in Uruguay.

PINCKARD, George (1768–1835). A British physician. Soon after qualifying he was appointed a doctor to the forces which took part in an expedition to the West Indies, dispatched soon after the outbreak of the French Revolutionary War in 1793. He spent the last thirty years of his life under more congenial circumstances in London, as the physician of the Bloomsbury Dispensary.

POYNTZ, John (dates unknown). A naval commander who fought for Parliament during the British Civil Wars. After the restoration of the monarchy he found it expedient to depart for America and the West Indies, and eventually to publish his proposal for the colonization of Tobago.

PURCHAS, Samuel (1577–1626). English clergyman and compiler of travel books. He published a number of such works between 1613 and his death, the last of which, *Purchas his Pilgrimes*, was based on the unpublished manuscripts of Hakluyt (q.v.) and the archives of the East India Company.

RALEIGH, Walter (1552–1618). English military and naval commander and author. His exploration of the coasts of Trinidad and part of the Orinoco delta in 1595, in a quest for the fabled El Dorado, was only one episode in an incredibly adventurous life which ended with his being beheaded on a spurious charge of treason.

REES, Abraham (1743–1825). English rabbi and encyclopaedist. In addition to his rabbinical duties and the teaching of mathematics and Hebrew in independent London academies, he spent many years re-editing another man's encyclopaedia before embarking on his own. His *Cyclopaedia*, on which he worked for nearly twenty years, eventually appeared in forty-five volumes.

RUTTER, Owen (1889–1944). English traveller and author. He worked as a colonial civil servant for some years before becoming a full-time writer. As well as history and travel books, he also wrote novels, poetry and children's stories.

ST-JOHNSTON, Reginald (1881–1950). British colonial administrator. He qualified both as a barrister and as a physician before joining the Colonial Service in 1907. His association with the West Indies began after the First World War when he was appointed Colonial Secretary of the Leeward Islands, and continued until 1936 when he retired after six years as Governor of that colony.

SHERLEY, Anthony (1565–1635?). English adventurer and traveller. His expedition to the West Indies in 1596 was one of the more peaceful interludes in a life which took him, via escapades in Europe, Persia, Russia and North Africa, to a death in poverty in Spain.

SLOANE, Hans (1660–1753). British physician and botanist. As a young man he spent two years in Jamaica as physician to the governor, during which time he collected a herbarium of over 800 species. His later career in London involved becoming secretary and later president of the Royal Society, acquiring a baronetcy, and being made physician-general to the army. Later still he became president of the Royal College of Physicians and was appointed a royal physician.

STEPHENS, John Lloyd (1805–1852). American lawyer and traveller. With substantial private means, arising from his position as a shipping and railway executive, he was able to indulge in travel, 'for the sake of his health', in Europe, Russia and the Middle East before undertaking the journey which resulted in his *Incidents of Travel in Central America*. He took a leading part in the building of the Panama Railroad which began in 1850, but in so doing contracted the fatal disease which led to his early death.

TREVES, Frederick (1853–1923). British consultant surgeon. As well as becoming a professor at the Royal College of Surgeons, personal physician to Queen Victoria, and Sergeant Surgeon to her successor (on whom he operated in 1902) Treves was also a founding member of the British Red Cross. Once established at the peak of his profession, and suitably awarded with a baronetcy, he was able to indulge in a passion for travel which led to the publication of *The Cradle of the Deep* and a number of other books.

TROLLOPE, Anthony (1815–1882). English novelist, civil servant and traveller. While working as a Post Office official between 1834 and 1867, and in spite of being sent abroad on occasions, he found time to write many books, including all of the Barsetshire and Palliser novels. *The West Indies and the Spanish Main* resulted from his being sent to examine the postal services of the region, and was the first of his four travel books.

UNDERHILL, Edward Bean (1813–1901). English Baptist missionary advocate. After many years as a grocer he devoted himself to the missionary work of the Church by becoming joint-secretary from 1849, and sole secretary from 1869 to 1876, of the Baptist Missionary Society. It was while holding this office that he visited the West Indies and was able to observe for himself 'their social and religious condition'.